W9-BUT-256

March of America Facsimile Series

Number 38

A Natural
and Civil History of California
VOLUME II

Miguel Venegas

A Natural and Civil History of California

VOLUME II

by Miguel Venegas

ANN ARBOR

UNIVERSITY MICROFILMS, INC.

A Subsidiary of Xerox Corporation

XEROX

COPYRIGHT © BY UNIVERSITY MICROFILMS, INC., 1966

ALL RIGHTS RESERVED

LIBRARY OF CONGRESS CATALOG CARD NO. 66-26312

MANUFACTURED IN THE UNITED STATES OF AMERICA

979.401
V45n
1966
V, 2

A Natural
and Civil History of California
VOLUME II

74806

Sorcerers of California.

A NATURAL and CIVIL
H I S T O R Y
O F
CALIFORNIA:

C O N T A I N I N G

An accurate Defcription of that COUNTRY,

Its Soil, Mountains, Harbours, Lakes, Rivers,
and Seas; its Animals, Vegetables, Minerals,
and famous Fifhery for Pearls.

T H E

CUSTOMS of the INHABITANTS,

Their Religion, Government, and Manner of Living,
before their Converfion to the Chriftian Religion by
the miffionary Jefuits.

T O G E T H E R   W I T H

Accounts of the feveral Voyages and Attempts made for
fettling California, and taking actual Surveys of that
Country, its Gulf, and Coaft of the South-Sea.

I L L U S T R A T E D   W I T H

Copper Plates, and an accurate Map of the Country and
the adjacent Seas.

Tranflated from the original Spanifh of MIGUEL VENE-
GAS, a Mexican Jefuit, publifhed at Madrid 1758.

I N   T W O   V O L U M E S.

V O L II.

L O N D O N:

Printed for JAMES RIVINGTON and JAMES FLETCHER,
at the Oxford Theatre, in Pater-Nofter-Row. 1759.

CONTENTS

OF THE

SECOND VOLUME.

PART III.

SECT. XIII.

SECT. XIV.

SECT. XV.

C O N T E N T S.

CONTENTS.

SECT. XX.

SECT. XXI.

SECT. XXII.

C O N T E N T S.

P A R T   IV.

I N T R O D U C T I O N.

A P P E N D I X   I.

A P P E N D I X   II.

A P P E N D I X   III.

CONTENTS.

APPENDIX IV.

APPENDIX V.

A

A

NATURAL and CIVIL

HISTORY

O F

CALIFORNIA.

❋❋❋❋❋❋❋❋❋❋❋❋❋❋❋❋❋❋❋❋❋❋❋❋❋❋❋❋❋❋❋❋❋❋❋❋

PART III. SECT. XIII.

New forces sent from his majesty to CALIFORNIA; father Salva-Tierra dies in his way to Mexico; state of affairs in that country.

THE year 1717 began in the midst of the solicitudes and cares mentioned in the preceding volume. The indefatigable Salva-Tierra was now stooping beneath a weight of years and disorders; the stone, with which he had been long afflicted, became more violent; but his zeal would not allow him to remit his useful labours, except when he was not able to stand, and even then he took care to direct every particular with the greatest care and attention. It was however too soon conspicuous, that his labours drew near their period.

In the month of March father Nicholas Tamarral appointed for the proposed mission of La

Puriffima came to San Dionyfio or Loretto bay;
he brought letters with him from the provincial
father Gafpan Kodero, informing him that on
the 10th of Auguft the preceding year, the
new vice-roy Don Gafpar de Zuniga, Marquis de Valero, arrived at Mexico, and had
brought with him the moft pofitive and particular orders from the court relating to the reduction of California; and that he himfelf was
ftrongly inclined to put them in execution.
In order to this, his excellency was defirous of
conferring with the father; and therefore he
fhould without delay repair to Mexico; and
trufting in his immediate compliance he had
fent father Tamaral, at whofe return others
fhould accompany him, even though the province fhould want fubjects. Accordingly neither
difeafe, pain, age, folicitude, want, or danger,
could hinder the brave Salva-Tierra from embarking on the 31ft of the fame month for
Matanchel, accompanied by brother Jayme
Bravo, who refufed to leave him in his melancholy condition, while the care of every thing
was committed to father Ugarte. They had
an eafy paffage of nine days over the gulf;
but the motion of travelling by land to Tepique,
fo increafed the tortures of the aged father,
that he was not able to mount a horfe; and
to ftay at Tepique, neither his zeal for the

govern-

government, nor the occasion of his journey would permit; so that there was a necessity of carrying him to Guadalaxara on the shoulders of Indians: which also was attended with extreme pain. Here his tortures encreased to such a degree, that he lay two months in the greatest agony. When perceiving that his last hour was now arrived, he called brother Jayme, gave him instructions and powers for managing at Mexico the concerns of the mission, and contentedly resigned his breath. All the city and even the province were extremely troubled with the account of his danger. They had for several years loved him as their father, and respected him as a man of exemplary life, and remarkably zealous for the conversion of the Indians; but one circumstance greatly affected persons of all ranks, namely the extraordinary grief of the Californians whom he brought with him.

The whole city assisted at his interment, every place resounded with his praise, and his remains were deposited in the chapel he had erected to our lady of Loretto.

Father Bravo, having digested the several papers repaired to Mexico, where he found the viceroy perfectly disposed to promote the good of the missions, and the reduction of California. The order for the purpose signed by his majesty Philip V. on the 29th of January 1716,

after

after recapitulating all the former till the laft of the 26th of July 1708, concludes : " And as no account has been remitted to any council of the Indies of what has been executed purfuant to my laft exprefs order, nor of the prefent ftate of the converfion of the natives of California ; and confidering the great importance of encouraging and promoting religion there by all poffible means, I have thought proper to communicate to you thefe affairs, that, being informed of them, you may, as I hereby enjoin you, carefully and vigoroufly apply yourfelf to facilitate and forward the execution of the warrants dated the 26th of July 1708, attending particularly to the advancement of the conqueft, tranfmitting me an account of every particular that may happen in carrying this command into execution ; but without altering in the leaft, that form of government which has hitherto fubfifted in California, that after examining the reports you remit, proper meafures be taken : for fuch is my pleafure." This order entirely proceeded from the ftrong defire of reducing California, entertained by the Abbé Julio Alberoni, then at the head of publick affairs ; and whofe comprehenfive ideas not only imparted new life and vigour to the commerce and navigation of Spain in Europe, and the eaftern coaft of America ; but alfo extended to the coafts

of

of the S. Sea, which at that time the enemies privateers openly infulted with impunity. This fagacious and vigilant minifter, who was foon after promoted to the purple, having ordered all the affairs depending in the council of the Indies to be laid before him, found among them, buried in an oblivion of eight years, a plan of the conqueft of California which had been already attempted. His vaft genius immediately faw the advantageous confequences which muft attend the fuccefs of this enterprife; and without delay procured further informations concerning it. At this juncture a man of great wealth in New Spain, made an offer to the king in council of advancing 80000 dollars, in confideration of his being made governor of California, and chief alcaldi of Acaponetra and Santipac. This was a ftrong temptation to a minifter who was in want of money, and much more, when meditating the vaft and expenfive enterprifes which then engroffed his thoughts. But Alberoni never acted without a fyftem; nor was his attention limited to prefent exigencies. The petition therefore, when fully confidered, appeared to have dangerous confequences, as the projector would probably indemnify himfelf afterwards by ruining every thing in his power; and therefore this fmall fupply would draw after it the lofs of many

pro-

provinces, and especially destroy California;
wherein his majesty must either be at infinitely
greater expences, or that province still remaining entirely independent of his crown.   It was
also suspected, that the projector would oppress
to the utmost not only the Jesuits and Californian christians, but even the soldiers and mariners of California, together with the inhabitants and Indians on the opposite coast.   And
thus, for the insatiable avarice of one man,
thousands would wretchedly perish, and a vast
extent of country be lost to the crown.   The
king therefore returned him for answer, that
he should first produce certificates from the
bishops, who had the inspection over these countries, whether his proposal was detrimental or
not to the good of those christian settlements:
and if it appeared that it was not, it should be
taken into consideration.

This offer turned Alberoni's thoughts to the
north part of the South sea, where he formed
very grand designs.   Among several others was
that of settling new colonies on the North American coasts of the South sea, and at the same
time to extend the dominion of Spain on those
immense and unknown countries north of Sonora, from the rivers Gila and Colorado, that
they might find a market by sea for their products of these colonies, and receive in exchange

change other neceffaries.   He was alfo defirous
that the commerce and fubfiftence both of thefe
colonies and of the other new fettlements in the
inland provinces, fhould not depend entirely on
the goods and commerce of New Spain and
Europe: on the contrary his principal plan
was to extend the trade and navigation of the
Philippine iflands; defigning to make them
the center and ftaple of all the commerce of
China, and other parts of the Eaft; as being
very advantageoufly fituated for it.   From
thefe iflands a trade was to be carried on with
both fides of North and South America; and
New Spain was a fure channel for conveying all the merchandifes of the Eaft, to Old
Spain, and other parts of Europe; the
commerce of the latter with both Americas, and of thefe with the Eaft, being fo regulated, as not to break in upon, or diminifh
the neceffary and due dependence of the Weft
Indies with regard to Old Spain; but on the
contrary greatly increafe the advantage of both,
by decreafing, if not utterly deftroying, that dif-
advantageous commerce which has been long
carried on between Europe and America, the
greateft part of the goods being the property
of other nations: the labour and danger only
being the portion of Spain.

It would be foreign to our purpofe, to expatiate on the meafures projeded, and partly put in execution, for recruiting the navy, reftoring it to its ancient fplendor, and erecting manufactures and trades of all kinds; for promoting plenty and commerce between the provinces; for recruiting the exhaufted treafury without new impofitions, or rather by eafing the people; for abolifhing abufes in the foreign cuftoms, and fettling them in an uniform manner, that fhips might for the future go to the Indies from any parts of Spain, and return thither again without moleftation; for rendering the voyage from one part to another more fecure; for fuppreffing all illicit trade; for increafing the traffick between fubjects and fubjects to the general benefit and augmentation of the revenue, not by raifing the prices and duties on account of the fcarcity, but by multiplying fmall profits arifing from the plenty and facility of acquiring them: for roufing old Spain from its lethargy, that inftead of its trade in Europe, which is merely paffive, it may be its own agent for concentring the advantages of both Americas in itfelf, and by uniting ftocks render it the chief proprietor of the commerce even in the Eaft Indies, and all parts of the South fea: and laftly, for giving new fpirit and vigour to the whole nation.

Let

Let it fuffice to fay that for carrying this plan into execution for the mutual advantage of both New and Old Spain, meafures were to be taken for fupplying both Americas with goods at a much cheaper rate, that the fubjects there might reap the fruit of their labours; for afferting his majefty's dominion over the Atlantick and Pacifick oceans, and for difperfing thofe corfairs and privateers, who fcandaloufly defy our power. This would render the Spanifh nation the real proprietor of its own commerce in both feas, and thus, the nation would reap the profit of it: and the vaft advantages of both Americas and the Philippine iflands center in Old Spain; in the fame manner the French, Dutch, and Englifh reap the benefit of their fettlements in the Eaft Indies, and their colonies in America.

It is very eafy for a perfon to entertain his imagination with fuch magnificent ideas; but the execution depends on many heads and hands; the firft motives muft be formed and regulated by the general fyftem; but the execution is too often attended with infuperable difficulties. The minifter knew by experience, that there was nothing too arduous for the magnanimity of his prince to undertake, provided it tended to the glory of his crown: and therefore, in order to venture upon the execution of thofe

vaft

vaſt projeɕts as far as they related to California and the countries and ſeas contiguous to it, the new viceroy was ordered to encourage the Sonora miſſions, and proceed according to the above inſtruɕtions relating to California: the miniſter likewiſe verbally recommended to him the ſettlement of colonies and garriſons on the ſouth coaſts, and the further diſcovery of others yet unknown.

Accordingly the viceroy, purſuant to ſuch poſitive orders, conferred, ſoon after his arrival at Mexico, with the father provincial Gaſpar Rodero, on the moſt proper means of carrying them into execution; and direɕted him and father, Alexandro Romano, agent for California, to attend at a general council of the miniſters. Here the viceroy having ordered his inſtructions to be read, declared his intention of founding at leaſt one Spaniſh colony on the weſtern coaſt of California.   This was approved of by all the miniſters; but father Alexander being better acquainted with California, made a ſhort ſpeech, in which he obſerved, that the fathers had always this deſign at heart, as ſufficiently appeared from their many expenſive ſurveys and unſucceſsful attempts; but that the enterpriſe was attended with more difficulties than they were aware of, no convenient harbour, with water, wood, and arable land near it, having yet been
found

found all along the coaft; and if it were poffible to find a place with all thefe advantages,
his majefty muft for fome years be at the expence of fubfifting the colony; for the country
was fo very barren, as not to afford a fubfiftence for the miffionaries few foldiers now
there; much lefs that plenty and variety requifite for a colony. He then mentioned the
difficulties relating to the fhipping, the prefent
deplorable fituation of the fathers with only an
old bark, and the famines, hardfhips, and fhip-
wrecks to which they were expofed. This
fpeech induced the viceroy and council to fend
for father Salva-Tierra, that, by his advice, who
was of all men the beft acquainted with the
project under confideration, the moft proper
meafures might be taken. But the death of
that worthy man difconcerted this fcheme, and
rendered it neceffary for them to confult Jayme
Bravo. Accordingly the father provincial introduced him to the viceroy, who found him a
perfon of greater abilities than he had at firft
expected. He explained to him all the difficulties that attended a fettlement of this kind,
and prefented two papers to his excellency; one
giving an account of the country and the inhabitants of California, the coaft which had been
difcovered, and the foundation and prefent condition of the miffions; the other, meafures which

he

he thought moſt conducive for extending the
conqueſt, and accompliſhing his majeſty's
orders.   The viceroy therefore ordered theſe
papers to be referred to the great council which
he immediately aſſembled.

On the 25th of September, all the ſchedules,
with reports and orders relating to California,
from that iſſued on the 26th of September
1703, down to the two memorials delivered in
by brother Bravo, were read before the aſſembly.   All the articles contained in the laſt, relating to the execution of his majeſty's orders
were immediately diſcuſſed : after which the
ſolicitor delivered his opinion, which was confirmed by the votes of the whole aſſembly,
and the following reſolution was unanimouſly
agreed to.

" It is reſolved, purſuant to his majeſty's
orders, that the miſſions of California be ſupplied with every thing neceſſary for the payment of twenty-five ſoldiers, with a captain,
ſeamen, boys, and ſhipwrights, for a veſſel of a
conſtruction ſuitable to the uſe ſhe is intended
for, and alſo a ſmaller for conveying proviſions :
and that if the allowance of thirteen thouſand
dollars be not ſufficient to defray thoſe expences,
the deficiency be ſupplied from the treaſury ; and
that the additional charge may not retard the
execution, that all delay, as far as poſſible, is to
                                                              be

be avoided, to prevent the total lofs of all the
labour taken by jefuits, without any confiderable expence to the royal revenue, for this
work; the fums expended having been raifed
by contributions, tho' they amounted to above
five hundred thoufand dollars: it being his
majefty's pleafure expreffed in repeated orders,
that not only thofe miffions be maintained, but
as far as poffible extended; likewife that all
diligence be ufed for difcovering fome harbour
where a fortification may be erected, and a garrifon placed for the conveniency of the annual
fhip from the Philippine iflands; where fhe may
fafely put in, victual, refrefh her company,
leave her fick men, and be enabled to continue
her voyage to Acapulco, without any of the
dangers now attending this voyage, both from
the enemy, and the great numbers of men
which die at the fhip's firft arrival on this
coaft. And for obtaining this important end,
as foon as a proper veffel can be built, and
manned with a proper number of foldiers and
feamen, fhe fhall fail to California, that an
accurate furvey of the coaft may be made, according to the direction of the fathers, who,
being perfons acquainted with the country,
coafts, and feas, the entire conduct and direction of this affair is to be committed to their
difcretion; it being found, that after an immenfe

menfe charge to this revenue, all the perfons
employed, have been fo far from fucceeding,
that this country, of fo great importance, and
fo much defired to be known, remained in the
fame darknefs and obfcurity as at the beginning: and that by the charts, jointly with the
memorials and opinions of the faid fathers, the
pilot and the proper perfons, an harbour may
be chofen, and preparatives made for building
a fort and every other particular relating to
the accomplifhment of his majefty's order.
And, as to the appointments of the miffionaries in the miffions hereafter to be founded,
regard will be had to the great inconveniencies
and hardfhips attending the difcharge of their
office in the country, and the difficulty of
conveying provifions, apparel, and other neceffaries, efpecially as it is to be done by
fhipping, in this cafe differing from thofe
whofe miffions lay up the country. But with
regard to the falt pits, afked for the fanctuary
of Loretto, (they being a regality belonging to
his excellency) we leave it to his pleafure, that
he may beftow this favour for a limited time,
or for ever."

The firft article which father Bravo afked,
was pay for fifty foldiers, and another garrifon,
either at La Paz, or Cape San Lucas. This
was alfo granted; as was likewife a petition
for

for a feminary for educating the children of California. The falt pits are thofe in the ifland of Carmen, near Loretto. Father Salva-Tierra had often made intereft for them, but was difappointed ; neither have they fince been granted. Other articles requefted by father Bravo, as a reward for capt. Don Eftevan Rodrigues, the exemption of the two villages of Ahome, and Yaqui, from the Mita, and the works of his Indians were likewife referred to the viceroy. But the day following, the father met with a very unexpected mortification. The treafurer Mendoza, who had always zealoufly countenanced the concerns of the miffion, and even in an affair quite foreign to government, and who in the council had been approved of, and fupported the vote, afterwards recollected that, for fifty foldiers, building and manning veffels, difcoveries of coafts and harbours, maintaining garrifons at La Paz, and the fouth coaft, new miffionaries, feminaries, and other articles included in the votes, the thirteen thoufand dollars, allowed by the king, (tho' till then never paid) would be fo far from fufficing, that there would be a neceffity of tripling or quadrupling the fum. This filled him with apprehenfions that the court of Madrid would highly difapprove of fuch profufion, and the chief blame would fall upon him. It is not at

all

all ftrange, that this gentleman fhould be afraid of Madrid, as till the happy reign of Philip V. nothing was heard of from thence but difficulties, debts, deficiencies, and orders for the ftricteft favings in the royal revenue; the confequence of which was, that the nation in Europe and America, was like a body without a foul. The next day he communicated his thoughts and apprehenfions to the viceroy, and prevailed on him to order that the vote, having not yet paffed thro' all the forms fhould not be regiftered. He immediately fent for the fathers; and tho' thefe with the greateft folidity enlarged on the reafons, adduced in the council, the viceroy fluctuating betwixt the orders of their court, and the exaggerated apprehenfions of the treafurer, he reduced the number of the foldiers from fifty to twenty-five; refufed the fettlement of a garrifon of fifteen foldiers at La Paz or San Lucas, tho' evidently neceffary; would not admit the feminary, tho' before he thought one not fufficient, and denied the falt pits. In fhort, his ardor for every particular feemed quite cooled. This did not difcourage father Bravo from ftrenuoufly pufhing the affair, but the remembrance of Madrid checked his refolution to remove the difficulty for fettling the pay of twenty-five foldiers, and the feamen on the footing of thofe of Cinaloa, New Bifcay,

Biscay, and the South sea; but this amounting
to a sum of near nineteen thousand dollars, he
thought it too great; and altered the establishment to that of the guard of the palace of
Mexico, and the garrison of Vera Cruz, and
the Leeward islands. Thus the sum was reduced to ten thousand dollars. This seemed
too little to father Bravo, who, finding his re-
presentations of little consequence, required a
certificate of all that had passed, in order to ap-
peal to his majesty. This the viceroy was unwilling to give, tho' he allowed that the orders to him from his majesty and the mini-
ster, were very short and positive, that the enterprize should be attempted at any expence.
At last, after several delays, the treasurer and
viceroy flattering themselves with the hopes
that, in case of complaint, they should excuse
themselves from the absolute resolutions of
the council, where every thing that had been
asked was readily granted, the first vote was
signed and registered; but with these restrictions,
that the soldiers were reduced to half the number, the seminary, the garrison at La Paz, and
the other articles in it, totally omitted: but
this vote was not added to the acts of the council, among which only were entered brigadier
Jayme's memorials; and three years after, together with all the papers relating to the coun-

cil, were left in the house of a private person. Eighteen thousand two hundred and seventy-five dollars and four reals were allowed for the pay of the soldiers and sailors, being on the same footing with those of New Biscay, and the South sea.   Three thousand and twenty-threedollars were allowed for discharging the debts left at the death of father Salva-Tierra. Four thousand dollars were issued out of the treasury as the purchase-money of a vessel for the service of California; but after all this expence, she was lost the very next year in Matanchel harbour, through a fault in her keel. Every other particular which had been ordered, terminated only in the good inclination of the viceroy, who was entirely for reducing and peopling California, and making settlements along the coasts; but was unwilling to advance the necessary sums for executing that advantageous project.

But the king and ministry of Spain were very far from that sordid parsimony as the council in America apprehended. At the same time, namely, towards the end of the year 1717, father Piccolo wrote a familiar letter to father Brassal Jua, then rector of the college of Guadiana, in which he gave him an account of his discoveries in the north of California, and his successful progress; the good dispositions of the

the inhabitants of the fouth and oppofite coaft for receiving the faith, if they had inftructors, and laftly of the poverty, danger, and melancholy condition in which they all lived for want of barks, provifions, clothing and ftock. This letter came to the hands of Don Pedro Tapiz, bifhop of Durango, to which diocefe California belongs ; and who was fo extremely moved with this account, that he defired the original letter might be left with him, and he would tranfmit it to his majefty, together with a memorial from himfelf. Accordingly, on the 18th of February, 1718, he inclofed father Piccolo's letter in one which he wrote to his majefty, wherein, after a pathetick reprefentation of the affairs of California, intermixed with political arguments, he begged the king to encourage thefe new chriftian fettlements, and augment the miffionaries, that they might convert fuch multitudes of people to the chriftian faith. Thefe letters were received at Madrid in the year 1719, and his majefty ordered them to be laid before the fupreme council of the Indies ; and with their advice, fupported by the influence of cardinal Alberoni, he figned, on the 19th of January 1719, a new fchedule, directed to the viceroy, in which, after inferting what was given him at his departure for Mexico, " he again charged him in the ftrong-

eft

eft expreffions to perform and execute what he had been ordered, as hitherto his majefty had received no advice concerning it ; and fpeedily fend him an account of the progrefs made therein."

On receiving this fchedule, the viceroy had the mortification to find, that the acts of the council had not been tranfmitted to court, and that no account could be given of the papers relating to it. At laft, they were found in a private houfe, as I have before mentioned : and tho' it is believed, that the viceroy had in his letters given his majefty an account of the pub-lick tranfactions ; yet it does not appear by the offices, that the acts of the council were fent to court.

In the fame year 1719, cardinal Alberoni left Spain, and at the fame time his vaft projects relating to America, the Philippine iflands, and the South fea, together with thofe concerning Europe, which are known to all the world, fell to the ground.

S E C T.

SECT. XIV.

Progress of the miffions under father Siftiaga and Tamaral. The miffion La
Puriffima founded. A veffel built in
CALIFORNIA, by the diligence of father
Ugarte. Father Bravo, obtains another
at Mexico; and founds the miffion de
la Paz. At the fame time father Helen
founds that of Guadalupe.

After father Jayme Bravo had difpatched
the affairs of the miffion at Mexico, and paid
his compliments of thanks to the viceroy and
other minifters, his firft care was to purchafe
the provifions and goods fo greatly wanted;
after which he arrived together with father Sebaftian de Siftiaga at Loretto, in July 1718,
in the Peruvian veffel, purchafed by the viceroy.

In autumn 1717, a moft terrible hurricane
arofe, which extended all over California and
its gulf, accompanied with fuch violent rains
as fwept every thing away before it. The
church and father Ugarte's houfe were laid
level with the ground, and he himfelf faved his
life under a rock, where he ftood expofed to
all the feverity of the weather for twenty-four
hours. The channel for conveying the water
away was choked up, the fluice at San Xavier

carried

carried away, and the land which had been sown both there and at Mulege was utterly destroyed, and covered with stones. Such was the force of the blasts, that at Loretto, a Spanish boy, called Matheo, was taken up by one of its gyrations, and never seen more, tho' the strictest search was made after him. Several barks belonging to the divers, on the coast of California, were also lost; and two belonging to Compostella, in which four persons perished; but the rest saved themselves in two large bilanders, which happened to lie near them, and were strongly moored under the shelter of a rock. In these the unhappy persons were carried to Loretto, where father Ugarte received them with the most liberal affection, till they had an opportunity of returning to New Galicia in the viceroy's vessel; and she also was soon after lost. The fathers had seen many hurricanes and heavy rains here, but none equal to this for violence or continuance. If in former ages these hurricanes were frequent in California, it is not surprising that all its mould should have been swept away, its bare rocks alone remaining, and its plains and vallies covered with heaps of stones.

Now father Tamaral, with better hopes, went to the village of San Miguel, whither, as the first fruits of his mission, came two rancherias of Gentile Indians requesting to be baptized, which,

which he accordingly performed. After which, with extreme difficulty, he made his way through the Sierra mountains to the rancherias of Cadigomo, which some years before had been visited by father Piccolo. Here he was met by the rancherias of La Puriffima Conception. He hoped at La Puriffima to find greater conveniencies both for corn and pasture than at Cadigomo, where, tho' he afterwards made a fluice or ditch for collecting water, it proved lost labour, thro' the torrents and carelessness of the Indians. At La Puriffima he found the foil washed away by the late rains ; but at last, after the toils of some years, he built a church and a house ; and had several fields of maize in different parts for himself and his Indians. Another work of great difficulty was to make a way practicable for beasts to the mission of Santa Rosalia, being the nearest, in order to procure provisions ; the villages of San Miguel and San Xavier lay out of the way, besides the danger and cragginess of the road. He presided over this new mission several years, and as a proof of his zeal and fervour, it is sufficient to say, that under a very weak constitution and frequent illness, he extended it above 30 leagues in a mountainous, rocky country, and inhabited by above forty rancherias, which were continually shifting from place to place ; thirty three of them he civilized and instructed ;

and the number of fouls baptized by him a-
mounted to near two thoufand. Thus he
modelled thofe wretched favages into one of the
moft numerous and beft governed miffions in
thofe parts of the world.

Animated by the good difpofition of Madrid
and Mexico, father Ugarte determined to attempt the execution of enterprizes which he
alone was able to bring to an iffue. He was
very folicitous for an exact furvey of both
coafts of the gulf of California, and to determine beyond all doubt whether it was joined or
not to the continent of New Spain; which
many, notwithftanding father Kino's difcoveries very much doubted; apprehending, that
betwixt Loretto and the river Colorado, there
might be fome channel or ftreight, thro' which
the gulf iffued into the South fea, and had
been the paffage for thofe veffels which were
faid formerly to have failed quite round California. He was no lefs defirous of reconnoit-
ring by fea the fouth coaft, in queft of an harbour for the Philippine fhips; not only as
fuch a defign had been on foot from the very
beginning of the undertaking, but as it was now
ftrongly recommended by the fuperiors, in the
name of the viceroy, as an article of his majefty's orders. For fuch expeditions, it was
neceffary to be provided with a large, ftrong,
and fecure veffel; but fuch could not be procured

cured in all thofe feas. The old San Xavier was not at all fit for the purpofe; and that given by the viceroy was very little better. If they attempted to purchafe another veffel on the coaft of Acapulco, they were fure of being cheated as before; for the Peruvians are not very exact as to the ftrength of fuch veffels, knowing the voyage is on a fea which, except certain periodical gales, is truly pacifick. To build a new veffel on the coafts of New Spain, might be faid to throw both men and money into the fea, on account of the former fpecimens of the ignorance, fraud, and wickednefs of the builders and workmen there in the feveral barks called the San Fermen, San Jofeph, and Rofaria.

The Philippine iflands, tho' the diftance of them would neceffarily occafion a long delay, might have afforded a veffel fufficiently large, as at prefent they build there veffels of all kinds. But the fyftem of the commerce of Spain and Mexico made the Philippine iflands an afylum, or refuge, which was not then thought of, notwithftanding the lights afforded in the orders of king Philip * III. The only refource was to build a complete veffel, and in poor barren California, where there was neither planks, fails, rigging, tar, or any other neceffaries

* See this prince's fchedule of the 19th of Auguft 1706, part 2, fect. iv.

for fuch a work: they had neither builder, fhipwright, fawyers, or other naval artificers; nor even fo much as fubfiftence for fuch a number of men.

Thefe difficulties appeared unfurmountable, efpecially as the miffion, even with the new allowances, laboured under great difficulties, the garrifon and the expences having increafed more than in proportion; yet no other way was left for executing the king's orders, with which the advancement of religion was connected. Father Ugarte therefore undertook, and happily finifhed, this difficult tafk: he brought a builder and artificers to Loretto, with a defign to fetch the timbers from the other fhore, as he had done with regard to thofe for his churches. For none of the parts, hitherto difcovered in California, afforded any of this kind. But being informed by the Indians, that 70 leagues north of Loretto there were large trees, he went in September 1719, with the builder, two foldiers, and fome Indians to Mulege. From thence, in company with father Siftiago, he paffed thofe craggy mountains which at prefent join to the miffion of Guadalupe; and after inexpreffible difficulties and toils, he found at length 30 leagues from Mulege a confiderable number of guarivos; but ftanding in fuch bottoms and

floughs,

floughs, that the builder thought it impoffible, confidering the difficulty of the road, even to bring them to the fea fhore. The father however made no anfwer to the builder, but returned to Loretto, where the whole enterprize, and particularly this journey, had been the jeft of the people. The father was not however intimidated; he again returned to the mountains, and in four months not only felled the timber, but cleared a road of 30 leagues, and brought the planks to the fhore of Santa Rofa-lia Mulege, by the oxen and mules belonging to the miffion. Three artificers only of the other coaft offering their fervice to fell the timber, all the other being chriftians of California, or Gentiles of the neighbouring rancherias; and the carriage of which was performed by the favages of the mountains, whom at the fame time he took an opportunity of civilizing and inftructing in the principles of virtue and religion. Thus, at length, under this father's conduct, a veffel was built, which, for beauty, largenefs, ftrength, and contrivance was much fuperior, in the judgment of the American and Philippine artifts, to any which had ever been feen on thofe coafts; and in fo fhort a time, that the fame father launched her in September, 1709, and called her the Triumph of the Crofs. The building of this fhip had exhaufted the

whole

whole remainder of the provisions and money of the mission, tho' the Indians always took proper care to receive their allowance. He even did not spare the presents sent to him from his friends at Mexico for his private use. Yet in examining the account, the cost of the vessel appeared to be less than if she had been built in New Spain.

Whilst this vessel, the only one till then of its kind, was building in California, the mission received another new vessel, and a new agent in their temporal concerns. The Peru bark, given by the viceroy having been lost in August 1719, and California being very much streightened by the ordinary and extraordinary expence of the new soldiers and artificers at Mulege, brother Jayme Bravo, as purveyor, or agent, went from the mission to the coast of Cinaloa, to procure goods and provisions. There he found letters from father Alexandro Romano, now provincial, in which, by order of the father Tamburini, the general, he was directed to come to Guadalaxara, and there to be ordained priest, that he might be qualified to be a missionary for California. The brother was greatly surprised at such an order, but there was no declining it; and going to Guadalaxara, he in three successive days, according to the privileges of
the

the fociety, was invefted with the proper orders by Don Manuel de Membela, who received
him with all the effufions of paternal affection.
From hence, by order of the fame provincial,
he went to Mexico, to give an account of the
miffion. The greateft want at that time was
fhipping; for tho' the bilander was fuccefsfully
completed, fhe was rather fit for making difcoveries than for carrying goods and provifions. This induced him in a kind of petition-
ary memorial to apply to the marquis de Valero, as viceroy, who referred the cafe to the
treafurer, as he did to the chamber of accounts;
and the chamber to the council; and the difcuf-
fion and decifion of the affairs of California
have ever been lodged in it. The council, on
the 15th of March 1720, ordered to be delivered to father Jayme, a bark for Peru, which
the viceroy had mentioned with the arms and
ftores he had defired. The bark was not at
Acapulco, but Guatulco, and from whence fhe
did not return till June. In the mean time,
the marquis de Villa Puente, from his great
fenfe of the neceffity that the Guaycuros fhould
be civilized and reduced, advanced the ufual
fund for erecting a new miffion at La Paz,
defiring at the fame time that father Bravo
would be the founder. The father the more
readily accepted of the offer, as the enterprife
in

in all appearance was not without imminent danger; and in July he set sail for Acapulco, in his new bark, having on board clothing, utensils, &c. for the garrison and'mission. He touched at Matanchel for taking in provisions, and in August, to the great joy of all, he entered the bay of San Dionysio, where he found the new Californian bilander.

The same year, 1720, was remarkable for the foundation of two new missions, one south, and the other north, of Loretto, by which, besides securing the conquest, christianity became considerably promoted. The first and the most necessary was that in La Paz bay, 80 leagues from Loretto, among the Guaycuros, tho' this is not the proper name of the people of those countries, but Periques. The name of Guaycuros was given them in some former expeditions, when the soldiers heard the Indians often call to one another Guaxoro, Guaxoro, which, in their language, signifies friend; and from that time they were called Guaxoros, and since Guaycuros. Ever since the expedition of admiral Otondo, these Indians have been very suspicious of the Spaniards, and at continual war with the divers, who visit their coasts. Generally both sides were sufferers, several being killed and taken prisoners in these rencounters; and it was to be feared, that some time

or

or other, the Guaycuros would raise a rebellion, even among the converted nations. This induced father Salva-Tierra to pay them that unsuccessful visit, which we have already related. It was necessary to enter the country, both by sea and land, at the same time; by land, in order to open a way for an intercourse with Loretto, and to civilize the intermediate nations; and by sea, for the more ready conveyance of men, provisions, and other necessaries in so dangerous an enterprise. The expedition by land was committed to father Clemente Guillen for his mission of San Juan Baptista Ligui; that of the sea, father Ugarte took upon himself, and made the first trial of the Californian bilander, called the Triumph of the Cross. He embarked with father Bravo, who was extremely desirous of entering on his mission on the 1st of November 1721; and being happily arrived at La Paz, the people were landed with all the care and regularity necessary in an enemy's country. But it soon appeared, that the danger was not so great as had been imagined, for tho' some Guaycuros at a distance appeared in arms, as soon as they saw the fathers, who advanced towards them with only an Indian interpreter, they sat themselves down on the ground, as a sign of their friendly dispositions. The fathers with many affectionate

gestures

gestures distributed among them some pieces of
sackcloth, knives, razors, and other utensils,
and also some toys; which they received with
great joy as highly valuing them, and by means
of the Indians they were given to understand,
that the fathers came to be their friends and to
bring about a reconciliation between them, and
the inhabitants of the islands of San Joseph,
and Spiritu Santo, and other neighbouring
people, who were inveterate enemies to the
Guaycuros, and had committed several massa-
cres on them.   They expressed a great deal of
joy; but for several days were something shy
of the soldiers.   At length they gradually came
even from distant rancherias, being principally
encouraged by the three prisoners left by father Salva-Tierra, who had given them a full
account of their kind entertainment at Loretto;
which, with the singular talent of father Ur-
garte to procure respect, and even the love of
the savages, gave so happy a turn to affairs,
that arbours and huts were erected for all the
people, and a piece of ground was cleared for
the church and a village.   The provisions and
beasts were brought ashore from the bilander,
and to the great surprize and delight of the
Guaycuros, the new mission was founded.

But what occasioned no little disquietude,
was, that no account came of father Guillen's
                                        company.

company. He had undertaken the journey with some soldiers and Indians; but such were the difficulties occasioned by the mountains, woods, and bogs, that they travelled above 100 leagues before they came in sight of the bay; where they saw the bilander, which they saluted with their musquetry. Boats were immediately sent to bring them to the huts, where they landed with reciprocal joy, and without meeting with any opposition, or even signs of apprehension in the Guaycuros. Father Ugarte continued three months at La Paz, and gained in a surprising degree the affection of these savages. He also negociated a peace between them and the islanders, whom, by the irresistible sweetness of his temper, he persuaded to land upon the continent, where both parties shewed all the marks of a sincere reconciliation. They were also very urgent with him to deliver them from the tyranny of the divers. Accordingly he left father Bravo, and some soldiers for their security; and toward the end of January 1721, embarked for Loretto, and the Ligui returned by the new roads made thro' these inhospitable deserts; father Bravo only remaining with some soldiers. The father here, as in every new mission, first applied himself to learn the language; after which he built a church, parsonage, and huts, and applied him-

self with the greatest assiduity to conciliate their
affections, civilize, instruct, assist, and relieve
them in every thing within his power. These
true christian offices he continued till the year
1728, when he returned to Loretto to assist
father Piccolo, who, besides his advanced age,
was in a bad state of health. In these six
years he baptized above six hundred children
and adults; increased the mission to eight hundred adults, whom he assembled in three villages, Nuestra Sennora del Pilar de la Paz,
Todos Santos, and Angel de la Guarda. He
prevailed on several savages to live in friendship; and discovered some tracts 20 leagues from
La Paz, proper for planting maize, which he
accordingly caused to be cultivated.

During the stay of the three fathers at La
Paz, the north mission, under the patronage
of Nuestra Sennora de Guadalupe was founded.
Father Ugarte, while he continued amongst
the mountains, felling timber for the bilander,
had inspired all the Cochimies of those parts
with such a love for christianity, that messengers were sent daily to him with requests that
he would again visit them. The father readily
complied, and was accompanied by father
Everard Helen, a new missionary, who had
been sent to California in April 1719. On
his re-imbarking for La Paz, he left directions
for

for commencing that foundation; and foon after fent father Helen thither, who had already learned fomething of the language, under the difagreeable inftruction of an Indian. He was accompanied by the captain and fome fol-diers; and on the 26th of December 1720, arrived at Huafinapi, 60 leagues north of Loretto.

This country lies in 27 deg. N. latitude in the centre of the Sierra, 27 leagues N. W. of San Ignacio, and 30 from Concepcion; the climate cold and unhealthy. Hither the Indians re-paired from all the rancherias of the coun-try, expreffing the greateft fatisfaction and joy that the father was come to live among them. Immediately a church was begun, and dedi-cated to Nueftra Sennora de Guadalupe, a houfe for the father, and likewife cottages and huts for the Indians; and what was very ex-traordinary, the captain and foldiers, laying afide their ufual difguft and floth, readily af-fifted in all thefe works. In the midft of this fuccefs, he alfo received feveral meffages, de-firing he would vifit the moft diftant rancherias, to inftruct the fick and aged, who were un-able to come to the miffion.

In the mean time the captain and his men diligently forwarded the little buildings of the miffion; and at the end of fix weeks, every

thing

thing being in a good condition, the captain departed, leaving four foldiers as guards, which, from the diftance of the country, and the little reliance that can be placed on the Indians, he thought the more neceffary. The fervour of the Indians continued in its full force, fo that father Helen was enabled to celebrate the firft baptifm of adults on Eafter-eve 1721. This awakened impatient defires in the other diftant rancherias, which were very urgent for baptifm; but the father gave them to underftand, that this was not to be expected till they were inftructed to his fatisfaction, and brought to him the little pieces of wood, hair, cloaks, deers feet, a kind of periwigs, and other trumpery ufed in their preftiges and impoftures, as they had done who were baptized. This was a difficult point to gain, the more artful among them practifing thefe tricks to infpire others with veneration, and draw from them every thing they wanted. The father, however, did not find among them any formal idolatry, or real forcery, or that they had any compact with evil fpirits or any thing of that nature. But on the contrary, was convinced, from repeated inftances, that thofe called forcerers, were mere cheats by profeffion, who pretended to be invefted with a fecret power from heaven, for doing good or harm; and that this trade was

gene-

generally followed by perfons advanced in years, in order, by thefe delufions, to acquire a plentiful and eafy fubfiftence, when they were no longer able to feek it among the mountains and forefts. They alfo fet up for phyficians and to undertake to teach children ufeful and aftonifhing myfteries; but the whole was entirely founded on falfhood and deceit; and their intention nothing more than to fubfift by the labours of others. * This was however the greateft impediment to the propagation of chriftian religion. And therefore father Helen, in imitation of the other miffionaries, infifted on their bringing to him all the inftruments of their fuperftition, and this the Indians at laft complied with, and a great quantity of them being brought from all the rancherias, the father publickly burnt them.

The following years 1722, and 1723, were very calamitous to all California, and particularly to the new miffion of Guadalupe. In the year 1722, the whole peninfula was invaded by fuch multitudes of locufts, that fometimes like thick clouds they intercepted the rays of the fun in their flight. The pitahayas and other fruits, on which the Indians chiefly fubfift, were confumed by thefe infects, and had not the fathers diftributed

* See part. I. fect. VII.

maize

maize at the miffions, great numbers of the Indians muſt abſolutely have periſhed. But as there
was not a ſufficiency to ſupport all of them,
eſpecially in Guadalupe, the Indians endeavoured to deſtroy the inſects in order to prevent the
ſame plague the enſuing year, and uſe them for
food in their preſent diſtreſs. But the conſe-
quence of feeding on theſe creatures, was a
general epidemia accompanied with malignant
ulcers, which carried off great numbers. It is
impoſſible to expreſs the fatigue of father Helen
on this occaſion, for the relief of his Californian
children. He was continually going from one
rancheria to another, among thoſe craggy mountains, in the ſeveral capacities of phyſician, con-
feſſor, prieſt, nurſe, and father. The height of
ſuch a complication of diſtreſſes pierced his
heart : but much more when he heard of the
monſtrous inhumanity of ſome rancherias,
where, when any one was ſeized with the diſtemper, and had any food remaining, they buried
him alive, or covered him with boughs, and ſo
left him to periſh.

Scarce was this epidemia over, when in the
following year 1723, a dyſentery raged with
ſtill greater havock. The father continued during this ſecond viſitation, the ſame devout and
charitable offices with ſo little regard to his own
health, that he contracted a dangerous hernia,

and

and an inceffant defluxion of the eyes, attended with fuch extreme pain, that he was obliged to retire to Loretto for fome months, another father being fent to fupply his place. But as foon as he was able he returned to his miffion, where he was received with all the marks of efteem and veneration by his afflicted Indians, who had been witneffes of his conftant attendance on 228 adult chriftians of feveral rancherias who died at that time: befides a great number who, under God, entirely owed their lives to his affiftance. The father availed himfelf of this love of the grateful Californians for promoting the chriftian religion, fo that father Juan de Gandulain in his vifitation in the year 1726, found no lefs than 32 rancherias converted; containing 1707 chriftians of all ages. Some of thefe were incorporated into the miffion of Santa Rofalia Mulege; and others to that of San Ignacio fince founded, as more conveniently fituated for their benefit. Twenty rancherias difperfed among the mountains as the conveniency of water would admit, remained to the care of the miffion of Guadalupe. Thefe the father gathered together in five villages, each with a chapel; and here the Indians live in the moft pleafing order and devotion, according to the general method already defcribed. The fowing of any grain has been found impracticable all

over

over the Sierra. But the father had procured
some cattle which he distributed among them;
and these, with the maize given them, made a
great part of their subsistence. They have
besides their native fruits and vegetables, which
they go in search of in small bodies. As nature
must necessarily in process of time sink under
violent and continual labours, so father Helen's
former disorder returned upon him, complicated
with others : yet, in this melancholy condition,
he was for dying among his Indians. But his
superiors consulting his relief more than he himself did, ordered him to a more easy function
in New Spain. And thus at the end of the
year 1735, to their reciprocal grief, he left his
Guadalupe Indians.

S E C T. XV.

Father Guillen undertakes to survey the
    western coast ; and father Ugarte that
    of the gulf of CALIFORNIA to the river
    Colorado : three harbours discovered on
    the coast of the South sea.

The long desire of finding, on the western
coast of California, a convenient harbour for the
Philippine ships was revived by the strict injunc-
tion of his excellency the marquis de Valero
                                            the

the viceroy, who, purſuant to the orders ſent
him from Madrid, was concerting meaſures
for eſtabliſhing colonies and garriſons on the
coaſt. In order to accompliſh this deſign, three
operations were more particularly neceſſary. The
firſt was to take a punctual ſurvey by ſea of
the whole ſouth coaſt from cape San Lucas
northward, as before had been done in the preceding century by captain Viſcaino. But this
was now impoſſible to be executed by the jeſuits, though father Ugarte was confident of
ſucceſs; for if, with many and large ſhips well
manned and provided with neceſſaries, and the
treaſury open to anſwer any expence, that officer's voyage was attended with ſuch danger,
delays, and diſappointments, how ſhould the Californian miſſion of itſelf attempt ſuch an enterpriſe with only its veſſels, ſtock of proviſions, and
people, all which were far from being ſufficient for
taking a ſurvey adequate to the purpoſe? The
ſecond operation was to go in queſt of ſuch an
harbour by land. This had been attempted ſeveral times at a great expence and to no purpoſe: for after carefully viewing by land, ſeveral parts of the oppoſite coaſts, no harbour
ſufficient to anſwer the intention could be found;
nor was the land fit for making ſuch ſettlement,
neither freſh water, wood, paſtures, nor arable lands being known on the whole coaſt:
and

and there was little hopes of meeting with a more favourable country, as the coast did not extend itself farther to the northward than some of the missions already established. However, to remove all complaint of a want of care and diligence, father Clemente Guillen was charged to make a new attempt. The third operation relative to the same design of both the northern coasts, was to take a survey of the gulf of California: and to ascertain whether California was joined to the continent of New Spain as father Kino affirmed; or whether, on the contrary, it was an island; and that the gulf issued through some unknown passage into the South sea, either on this or the other side of the mouth of the river Colorado, according to the opinion that then prevailed in Mexico; where some did not scruple to treat the discoveries of father Kino as chimeras, notwithstanding the applause they met with in Europe. If California was connected with the continent, the noble plans of the fathers Kino and Salva-Tierra, for extending their respective missions northward, remain in full force, though at that time unsuccessful: Kino's plan related to those of Pimeria, and Salva-Tierra's to those of California: and these were to be extended till they met on the banks of the Colorado in 33 or 34 degrees latitude. And from thence with united

endea-

endeavours, and reciprocal affiftance, as fuccours might be then eafily conveyed to them by
land, their refpective territories were to be continually enlarged thro' countries, which from information and appearances had fo good a foil
as to make ample returns for any culture, till
they reached the coaft of the famous Puerto de
Monte Rey, and Cape Mendozino in 37 and 40
degrees, being the moft proper fituation for
a port for the Philippine fhips. This furvey of
the gulf, being an enterprife of the greateft
difficulty and danger, father Ugarte undertook ;
and whilft he was making the neceffary difpofitions for it, he defired father Guillen to execute the expedition with which he was charged.

It was known by the narrative of captain
Vifcaino, that in the latitude of 24 or 25 degrees, he had difcovered in the South coaft a
fpacious bay, where fhips might be fecure from
the violence of the winds and fea, and had
called it La Magdalena. Hither, as to a place
already difcovered by fea, and lefs difficult to
be furveyed by land, father Clemente Guillen
directed his courfe in the year 1719, accompanied by captain don Eftevan Rodrigues Lorenzo, a party of foldiers, and three bodies of
Californians armed in their manner. They travelled twenty five days amidft all the hard-

fhips and fatigues naturally to be expected in
fuch a craggy and barren country : and the Indians every where taking the alarm at feeing
fuch a number of ftrange people in their country, rendered it neceffary to obferve the greateft
order and circumfpection in the march. At
laft they came to Magdalena bay, which lies
in the diftrict of the miffion of St. Luis Gonzaga
fince founded. It was every where fheltered
from the winds by lofty mountains, and about
half a league in breadth, running up the country
towards cape San Lucas. Near this arm they
difcovered a rancheria of Indians, with whom,
by means of little prefents, they entered into
terms of peace and amity. On enquiring of
the Indians after water, they were informed,
and their own fearches confirmed their report,
that the only frefh water thereabouts was in
a well dug in the fand, and which the Indians made ufe of. They added that a neighbouring ifland called Santa Rofa which they
frequently vifited, afforded a fufficiency of water : but they were without any means of crof-
fing the channel to it; neither did they find in
the bay thofe azure fhells, or appearance of the
rich pearl beds with which this coaft was faid
to abound. It being known that the bay had
two entrances, the captain fent fome of his
men to reconnoitre that on the fouth fide, and
by

by following the course of a brook observe whether the other arm of the bay, which forms the harbour called del Marques, afforded a watering place. In this survey they observed at a distance the second mouth or arm; but found that the brook long before its joining the sea, ran thro' some ponds of brackish water, so that there was no possibility for the ships to water here. This discovery induced them to attempt a survey of the whole tract: but in some parts the inaccessible rocks, and in others impassable marshes obliged them to make a circuit to the rancheria called San Benito de Aruy, four leagues from the sea, where the Indians gave them the same discouraging account of the want of water on the coast. Here all the people met, and father Guillen used his utmost endeavours for inducing them to undertake a survey of the remaining part of the coast, or at least as far as possible towards the south. But the captain and soldiers were not to be prevailed upon: and the Indians after such discouraging circumstances insisted on returning to Loretto. Thus father Guillen was obliged to renounce his scheme, and prepare for a return, taking with him for guides some Indians of that coast with whom he had contracted a friendship; and by their direction avoided so many circuits and difficult passes, that in fifteen days they reached
ed

ed Loretto, after travelling about seventy leagues.

The enterprise which father Ugarte had taken on himself proved more fortunate, tho' the fatigues and dangers were incomparably greater. On the 15th of May 1721, he sailed from the bay of San Dionysio de Loretto in the bilander built here, and called the Triumph of the Cross, carrying with him a boat also built here, and called the Santa Barbara, six feet broad, eleven in the keel, and without a deck: the use of it was to found and survey those parts the bilander could not approach. On board the bilander were twenty persons, six of whom were Europeans; and of these two had passed the streights of Magellan; another, besides being acquainted with the Atlantick ocean, had made a voyage to the Philippine islands, and been carried prisoner to Batavia, when the Philippine ship was taken off cape San Lucas, and another had made several voyages to Newfoundland: the rest were Indians of the country. The pilot called Guilermo Estrafort was a man of learning and experience: in the pinnace or boat were eight persons, two Chinese or Philippines, which, in the common language of New Spain, is synonymous, a Yuaqui Indian and five Californians; making in all twenty eight persons. The stock of provisions which they

took

took on board was but very small for so uncertain a voyage, expecting agreeable to a promise made the year before by a missionary of Pimeria, to meet with a plentiful supply on the opposite coast of the Seris. They sailed up the gulf with a fair wind to Conception bay and the river Mulege, where father Ugarte visited the mission of Santa Rosalia and its missionary father Sistiaga. Thence they proceeded to take draughts of the coast of California as far as the neighbourhood of the islands of Sal-si-puedas: and then across the gulf to the harbour of Santa Sabina, and the bay of San Juan Baptista, both lying near those islands on the coast of the Tepoquis and Seris. They reached the harbour in five days: but on landing met with no Indian on the shore; tho' before they came from the ship, they saw an Indian, who, after fixing a cross in the sand, retired. our men immediately made up to the cross, approaching it with all the gestures of reverence. At this the Indian gave a shout, and immediately his companions, who lay concealed, and had likewise observed that the bilander had a cross on her bowsprit, made their appearance with all the signs of peace and friendship. Father Salva-Tierra had informed them of these signs, and recommended to them a hospitable behaviour towards the companies of all such ships as

I   carried

carried a crofs, it being a fure fign that they belonged to the fathers of California.

The Indians were fo impatient of feeing the father, that inftead of waiting till he came afhore, feveral of them threw themfelves into the fea and fwam on board the fhip, embraced his feet, kiffed his hands and face, with other tokens of rapture and affection. The father, who was not wanting in fuitable returns, entertained them, as he did thofe on the land. Two of them he charged with a letter to the father miffionary of San Ignacio, who had made an offer of provifions; and thefe he before had rewarded with a canvafs frock and fome toys. Immediately all the empty cafks were carried afhore for taking in water: and the fight of them feemed to raife a difpute among the Indians. Soon after they all went away intimating by figns that they would return the next day. Our men were not without apprehenfions: and it growing late, for their greater fecurity they returned on board; early the next day the Indians appeared in troops, and all with water veffels; the men each with two in nets hanging from a pole acrofs their fhoulders, and the women with one. This kindnefs the father returned, and they earneftly requefted him to vifit the Indians in the neighbouring iflands as being their kinfmen. He complied with their defires, and that very
- evening

evening setting out with two Indians of the coast, they found themselves very early in the morning in a narrow channel, which they imagined to run betwixt the island and the continent, and were therefore for examining it. In order to which the canoe and the pinnace went further up, but soon found themselves in a place from whence they could hardly return. The channel, besides being narrow and crooked, was so full of shoals, that tho' the pilot went before in the boat as a guide, the bilander stuck, and was in danger of being lost: but was at last got off with great difficulty. Another accident which increased their concern was, the canoe and pinnace being carried away by the current to such a distance as not to be seen. The bilander was now under a necessity of going further up the channel, notwithstanding the many dangers visible on every side.

At last after three days of continual danger, they reached the mouth of the channel, where they found the boat and pinnace: but instead of running into the gulf, as they had imagined, it opened into a large and spacious bay, whence having a clear view of the island they were going to, they steered for it, without any difficulty or danger. The pinnace led, and at about the distance of a musket-shot, observed that the people on it were armed in their manner

with

with bows and arrows, and a kind of helmet
of feathers, making the shores ring with their
shouts, intending to intimidate the people in the
pinnace: but the Indians, their countrymen,
having swam ashore and informed them that
the father was come in that ship to visit them,
laid down their arms, received our people
with all the marks of pleasure, and directed
them to the harbour where they found both good
water and a safe anchoring-place. Accordingly
the bilander went thither and came to an anchor:
but father Ugarte was seized with such violent pains from his waist downwards, that he
found it impossible to go ashore. This distemper he had contracted in the harbour of
the Seris, where he was thoroughly wet by the
sea at landing, but laboured as much as any
of the sailors in taking in water. The islanders seeing that the father did not come ashore,
made thirteen balsillas or small floats on which
fifty Indians went on board the bilander, requesting him that he would come to their island,
where they had already prepared a house for his
reception: at this the father, tho' every motion
put him to extreme torture, gave directions for
helping him into the boat, and when he came
on shore, was carried by the seamen and Californians, the islanders standing to receive him
in two rows; one of women and the other

of

of men. When he was feated in his houfe,
which was made of boughs of trees and had
two doors, the iflanders came in one by one,
without the leaft tumult; firft the men and then
the women. They entered by one door, and
as they paffed along, bowed their heads, that
the father might lay his hand upon them : which
he did with great affection; after which they
retired by the other; and all was performed in furprifing order. This tranfitory vifit
was the whole ceremony, after which the
iflanders gathered about the father, who endeavoured to fupport himfelf as well as poffible
under his excruciating pains, that he might receive them with all poffible affability. He recommended to them to go to the miffion del
Populo, about two or three days journey
from the neighbouring coaft, and bring with
them to their ifland an Indian Temachtian or
teacher to inftruct them. The time he ftayed
here was but fhort, being obliged to return to
the coaft for a fupply of provifions. Accordingly he re-embarked, and continued his voyage
to the mouth of the little river Caborca.

In his farther furvey of the coaft the only
convenient place he met with was a fmall and
open bay, where they anchored. From thence
the pinnace was fent to reconnoitre the coaft farther to the northward, and obferve the figns of

Pimeria

Pimeria along it, which were some sand-banks beyond Costa Brava; three men were also sent to survey it by land. These returned in a day or two, reporting that the coast all along was without any bay; and all that they had discovered remarkable, was a pit of foul water, a path, and the tracks of a mule. On this information the father immediately dispatched two seamen, who, following the track, on the third day came to the mission of Conception la Caborca, where they found father Luis Gallardi, who had been lately sent thither. They delivered him father Ugarte's letters for himself and the father missionary of San Ignacio, desiring the latter to furnish the provisions he had offered the preceding year. As he had already received the former letter sent by the Seris, he immediately set out with what provisions and necessaries he could get together, being indeed but a small quantity, both messages coming at a time, when he was unprovided: for tho' father Ugarte had informed him, how acceptable his offer was and likewise specified the time of his expedition; yet these letters the father never received, so that he concluded his voyage would not take place that year. He also collected what he could at Caborca for the assistance of the bilander, and went to the shore, where father Ugarte waited the return of his

messenmeffengers. But his pains ftill raged in all their violence, and for relief he was obliged to continue on his knees, this being the only pofture in which he found any eafe. It was now twelve days fince his pains had hindered him from going afhore; tho' this was partly owing to the roughnefs of the fea, for after he was twice put into the canoe, they were not able to land him. However, on advice, that the father miffionary of San Ignacio was coming, he was with no fmall danger as well as labour carried afhore, whence he went a league and a half to meet him; and found himfelf much eafier by this exercife.

The father was extremely concerned for the flender fupply he brought, and under this exigency meafures were taken for purchafing provifions among the neareft habitations of the Pima Indians, partly on credit, and partly by the things brought on board the bilander: meafures were alfo now taken for watering, which, notwithftanding the diftance, was done in a fhort time by the contrivance of father Ugarte, who placed the people at certain diftances; and thus the veffels were carried from one to the other. In the mean time the bilander was in continual danger from the great agitation of the fea; one of her cables was already broke, and the bowfprit, tho' of maria, a very ftrong

kind

kind of wood, was carried away by a wave, but the greateſt part of it was thrown into the bilander by the motion of the ſea. The day following, the weather proving fair, the bowſprit was fixed as well as poſſible, and the veſſels of water taken on board. However the ſhip's company were under great dejection; the croſs, placed on the bowſprit, being loſt: but was afterwards recovered by an Indian, and again fixed at the end of the bowſprit.

During theſe tranſactions, the people of the bilander ſaw at a diſtance a Californian young man, who went in the pinnace to take a ſurvey of the coaſt: they had all, for ſome time, concluded, that the whole company had periſhed either by the waves or famine, as they had only a week's proviſion aboard; and ſome of the ſhip's company had ranged the coaſt to a great diſtance north and ſouth, without being able to acquire any account of them. The Californian was followed by three of his companions, who related that after great fatigues and dangers from the boiſterous waves, they put into a large ſhallow bay, where at night they anchored in two fathom water: but in the morning found the boat quite dry, the ſea having ebbed away above two leagues: ſo that from the place where they were, they could not diſcern the water; and part of her keel was broken off.

In

In this situation four of them left the pinnace to search for water; and seeing nothing but death before them in that desert country, the provisions in the pinnace being nearly spent, they determined not to return, but keep as near the shore as possible, till they reached Yagui, in case it was not their good fortune to meet with the bilander before. On this advice water and provisions were immediately dispatched to the place; and the men in the pinnace, who at the return of the flood had with great difficulty brought her into a creek, being revived by this supply, repaired the keel, and putting to sea, joined the bilander within four days. On the second of July, they all left this dangerous situation, intending to abandon these barren coasts, which, after all the exact observations in the pinnace, afforded neither watering place, nor safe harbour; for, with regard to the bays, which were said to be marks of Pimeria, they were certainly formed by the impetuosity of the tides.

Accordingly they steered towards the coast of California, and in three days crossed the gulf, the breadth of which in those parts, does not exceed forty leagues, and came to an anchor, without entering the harbour, and sent the pinnace ashore: but at the sight of the boat the Indians came down to the shore armed, and

having

having drawn a line on the ftrand made threatening figns to thofe who were coming afhore,
if they offered to fet a foot beyond it. But our
people by figns and little prefents changed their
difpofition, fo that they came up to them in a
friendly manner, and carried them to the rancheria or watering place: and from thence to
another ftill larger, and at no great diftance.
With thefe recommendations from one to another, our people went nine leagues along the
fhore, where they found five watering places,
and at each a rancheria; all the inhabitants of
which received our people with candour and
franknefs. The bilander likewife continued
her voyage in fearch of an harbour or bay; and
after weathering a point of land which projected
a confiderable diftance into the fea, fhe came
into a large bay, where fhe anchored, the fhore
fheltering her from the fouth eaft wind, which
at that time prevailed. But here they met with
a circumftance more formidable than the wind
itfelf, namely the rapidity of the currents, which
prevented the veffel from riding with her head
to the wind, and caufed her to roll as if in a
violent ftorm. Hereupon, whilft the pinnace
went nearer the land in fearch of an harbour,
Strafort the pilot determined to go afhore in
the boat, in order to find an anchoring place
farther up the bay: the boat was foon out of
fight,

fight, and did not appear again till the next day, when fhe came along fide, but in fo fhattered a condition, that it was with the utmoft difficulty the people were taken on board.

The pilot reported, that having left the boat a day on the fand, he and his companions went up to the rancheria, where the Indians received them with all the figns of friendfhip; and that he diftributed amongft them feveral toys; but amidft thefe reciprocations of good will, the tide returned, not gradually as ufual, but with dreadful roarings; and on a fudden rofe above three fathom. The boat was in an inftant thrown among the rocks, and in a fhort time fplit into two feparate pieces from head to ftern. The Indians came up to their affiftance, and by figns expreffed their concern: and one of them in particular, gave them to underftand, that in the neighbourhood there was wood of the fame kind for building another. But this in their fituation was impracticable; the only refource was to faften the two pieces with nails taken out of the oars; with the founding line and painter, they made oakum for caulking the feams, while clay fupplied the place of pitch and tar. This took them up great part of the night, the Indians affifting them with lights, which were perceived from the bilander; and the next day at the return of the flood,

flood, they put to sea, keeping near the strand, that on any emergency they might get on shore. One of them was continually employed in throwing out the water; yet when they were near the bilander, it gained so fast upon them, that they gave themselves over for lost. Soon after the pinnace returned, without having met with any harbour in the distance of twenty leagues. They had also been in great distress for want of water, but on advancing towards the shore, they saw several Indians, and by signs informed them of their distress; and the Indians by others, that they understood them; and accordingly dispatched two women for water. When the crew saw them returning with it, they came ashore without any apprehension, and took what they judged would suffice them till they reached the bilander, where every one was impatiently expecting the issue of their survey. On this report the bilander stood again to the northward; and after some days sailing, the colour of the water was perceived to alter, being sometimes of an ashcolour, and sometimes black; but generally reddish. This last appearance gave them to understand that they were not far from the river Colorado or red river; so that to avoid the shoals, they stood away to the coast of Pimeria, the pinnace continually sounding a-head. In the middle

dle of the gulf, the water was more turbid; and near the coast the depth of it was found in some places to be seven, eight, ten fathoms and more, always varying and without any contiguous channel. They now came to an anchor near the issue of the river on the Pimeria side, where they observed two of its mouths, which ejected into the sea grass, leaves, weeds, trunks of trees, burnt logs, the timbers of cottages and the like. When the inundations ceased, the ship's company were for going up the river on discoveries; but father Ugarte opposed this as on the two preceding nights the weather had been very tempestuous with thunders and lightnings and violent rains, which had occasioned the two inundations they had observed in the river; and that as the aspect of the sky continued still threatening, another flood was to be apprehended; and should this happen when they were in the river, they must inevitably be lost. Besides, father Ugarte and several others were very ill. They therefore crossed the mouth of the Colorado at a convenient distance, and anchored in four fathom water, being continually afraid of running on the sands.

On comparing this account with the survey, taken by father Fernando Consag in 1746, it appears that of the two channels separated by an

island,

island, and through which the Colorado issues
into the sea, father Ugarte only passed that on
the east of the island, or the Pimeria side;
and that when at anchor betwixt them, he
saw at a distance the other on the west. From
the same station father Ugarte had a clear and
distinct view of the Cape of California, joining
to the neighbouring mountains, and separated
from the coast of Pimeria only by the river.
If he did not go ashore at this point of land
in order to a farther investigation, it must be
imputed partly to his indisposition, and the il-
ness of his ship's company; and partly to what
he had observed of the flood and ebb. In those
parts the tide shifts every six hours; the flood
with a frightful impetuosity rises from three
to seven fathoms, overflowing the flat country
for some leagues; and the ebb necessarily returns with the same dangerous violence: and the
bilander was without any secure anchoring
place, nor was there an harbour at hand. He
found in those waters the same noxious quality,
which has since been confirmed by father Consag, namely, that they raise blisters and cause
very sharp pains, especially in the more sensible
parts; and which are not healed for some
months. However the pilot who went on shore
in the pinnace at several parts in order to
make a complete drawing of it for his chart,

was

was equally convinced that this cape was the extremity of the gulf of California, and that the waters beyond it were thofe of the river Colorado. By the founding there appeared no figns of a channel which muft have been large and deep: but four or five fathom was the greateft depth. The bottom is of a flimy vifcid clay fticking to the anchor. There is no appearance of a channel as far as the eye can reach; which, in a northern direction, every where fees the land. The dangerous and extraordinary tides in thofe parts, as on both coafts, are a farther proof that the gulf is confined there: for had it any difcharge or outlet towards the South fea, its waters would not rife with fuch rapidity, or to fuch a height, if they were not contracted at the extremity of their courfe, and at the end of the ftreight checked by thofe of the river Colorado. In fine a council of the marinerswas held, in which it was refolved, that it was impoffible for the bilander to continue in fuch a critical ftation without any fafe harbour, in bad weather; that the pinnace being without a deck was in danger by the fury of the tides and the tempefts; and that it would be rather rafhnefs than courage to proceed. This was followed by a general fhout of buen viage. And on the 16th of July of the fame year

1721,

1721, being the day of the Triumph of the Crofs, they weighed in order to return to California.

They continued their courfe along the middle of the gulf, but fometimes ftood over to one coaft, and fometimes to another, on account of the fhoals and fmall iflands, which they were to furvey. In the mean time violent tempefts and rains came on, by which very probably they would have been loft, had they, as fome propofed, failed up the river Colorado. The father, who was in the bilander, informed the mate in the pinnace, that being without a deck, he was expofed to great danger in fuch weather, that the boat was not of much importance if the people were faved; and therefore defired he would quit her, and come on board the bilander: but the intrepid failor anfwered, that he did not fear the dangers of the fea; adding that if he would fupply him with provifions, he would return to Loretto, keeping clofe along fhore, that on any exigency they might fave themfelves. Accordingly, having received the provifions, he put off in the pinnace to continue his voyage. The bilander was now arrived at the iflands of Sal-fi-puedes, of which there is a great number, forming different channels at the entrance of a wide bay known among the divers, by that name. Here they were in fuch

danger,

danger, that being driven by the wind and currents to avoid shipwreck, they were obliged to ride at anchor several nights; at last after many tedious tacks they weathered the island of Tiburon; possibly the same that father Consag in his map calls the Angel de la Guarda, when the rapidity of the currents drove them so far to leeward, that in six hours they lost the labour of eight days. These currents run with astonishing rapidity, and their noise is equal to that of a large rapid river among rocks; nor do they run only in one direction, but set in many interfected gyrations. For as there are great numbers of islands, so the current sets in several different directions.

The continuance of the danger however abated the general fear. But what chiefly encouraged the men, was, that for three nights successively, and while the tempests continued, the cross at the mast head was illuminated with the fire called St. Elmo, which they all construed as a mark of the divine protection, and notwithstanding the opposition of the currents, they determined to make a third attempt, in which they spent eight days, when their courage began to fail, and observing a convenient place in one of the islands, they came to an anchor intending to go ashore. This was now the more necessary, as of all the ship's company only

five

five were able to keep the deck; some were attacked by the scurvy, others cruelly suffered from the violent effects of the sea-water, and father Ugarte himself was not free from the scurvy, besides his other indispositions. It was certainly by the interposition of providence, that they put into this place, a violent tempest coming on immediately after, that had not the bilander been sufficiently sheltered, and well moored, she would undoubtedly have foundered. In this harbour they continued four days, but father Ugarte's disorders increased so upon him, that he determined to go in the boat to the Seris coast: and thence if possible to proceed by land to Guaymas. But this resolution caused such a general dejection in the ship's company, that the father promised not to leave them if it cost him his life. The sick now began every day to recover; and on Saturday the 18th of August, a fair wind carried them beyond the third current of Sal-si-puedes, which runs towards the coast of California. Their joy was increased on the Sunday morning by the sight of three rainbows one above another, in the clouds over the island, which they had just weathered.

They now cheerfully continued their voyage, thinking all danger was past. But a little before they came to the bay of Conception, a

storm

ftorm came on fo fuddenly, at N. E. by N.
that they had hardly time to furl their topfails,
and take in two reefs in the forefail: at noon
it was as dark as midnight, the claps of thunder
were aftonifhing, the rain poured like a torrent
from the clouds, and the fea-broke in a frightful manner. But what increafed their terror
was, that within lefs than half a league they faw
moving towards them a water fpout. If ever
they fervently implored the protection of our
lady and the holy crofs it was now; and father Ugarte himfelf fays, that amidft all the
various dangers of the voyage, this was the day
of the greateft confternation. Providence, however, caufed the wind to fhift, by which means
the clouds difcharged themfelves on the mountains of California: and the bilander, in the
beginning of September, arrived fafely in Conception bay. From hence they went in boats
and mules to feek eafe and refrefhment after
fuch a variety of fufferings, from the benevolence
of father Siftiaga and his Indians of Mulege.
Here the fick recovered, the few who were in
health refrefhed themfelves, and in the middle
of September, they all returned to Loretto in
the bilander; and there found the pinnace
which had happily arrived fome days before
them. The advantages flowing from this furvey of the gulf, added a pleafure to the re-

membrance of paſt dangers and hardſhips.
For it now appeared that there were watering
places for ſhips at ſeveral places near the ſhore,
and Indians who readily ſhewed them to ſtrangers; while the coaſt of New Spain from Guaymas to the Seris afforded very few, and theſe
above a league from the ſhore. From the Seris
to the mouth of the river Caborca the ſhore is,
for the moſt part, ſteep and without water:
from the Caborca to the Colorado, are only
three watering places, and little or no paſture
ground, the ſhore for many leagues being
ſandy and barren, and conſequently deſolate,
ſo that not an Indian is to be ſeen. The ſub-
ſequent ſurvey of the coaſt of California by father Conſag, confirms father Ugarte's obſerva-
tions. Another and no ſmall advantage was,
the obſervation made of the numbers and ge-
neroſity of the Cochimies along the coaſt of
California above the Indians of the oppoſite
ſhore, and even above thoſe of the ſame peninſula. For thoſe who inhabited the Seris and
Tepocas, tho' the father went among them,
and offered them any ſatisfaction, he could not
prevail upon them to aſſiſt him with any thing,
tho' they ſaw the ſhip's company were in the
greateſt diſtreſs: but when every body was hard
at work, they with great compoſure, lay ſlug-
giſhly on the ground; nor have they during the
                                                    forty

forty years they have known the fathers, ever
ſhewed them the leaſt civility. A very liberal
equivalent was offered them for ſome coarſe
earthen pots, but they would not part with them
on any conſideration. Whereas the northern
Californians, on the occaſions before related,
and many others, always ſhewed the greateſt
candor and courteſy : and tho' they had never
known the fahers, nor ſeen any veſſels on their
coaſt, they came voluntarily with their little preſents before any thing had been given them.
And when they found that their gueſts were
not enemies, they with great alacrity aſſiſted
them with every thing in their power, and cheerfully lent a hand to eaſe them in their labours.
They furniſhed the bilander's people with as
many pots as they wanted, without requiring
any return, and theſe of as neat workmanſhip
as if they had been turned. Father Ugarte
endeavoured to ſave ſome, that the other miſſionaries might ſee them. I mention this circum-
ſtance becauſe, as I have obſerved in another
place *, it does not appear that the Indians of
any other diſtrict of California, had the leaſt
notion of turning clay to ſuch uſes. The ſame
is confirmed by captain Woods Rogers in his
voyage to the South ſea, where he alſo charges
the Californians of the ſouth, with the ſame

* Part. I. ſect. VI.

cowar-

cowardice and floth, which father Ugarte obferved in the Seris. But an advantage ftill greater than the former is, that by this furvey, they difcovered the many grofs errors of the ancient charts, maps, and journals, which placed iflands, rivers, bays, and harbours, where there are none. And on the contrary, omitted thofe which are actually to be found on the two coafts of the gulf of California.

The extract of this voyage, which I have before me, does not enter into the particulars of every circumftance; for I fhould have copied thefe with more fatisfaction, as affording more ufeful knowledge than is to be found in all others of that kind; fo that I muft content myfelf with faying, that this voyage anfwered its principal intention, which was to afcertain whether California was an ifland, or a peninfula joined to the continent of New Spain. It now evidently appeared to be a peninfula, feparated from Pimeria, only by the river Colorado. The opinion therefore entertained by fome at Mexico, who afferted that the galleons from the Philippine iflands paffed through a channel into the gulf of California, in their voyage to New Spain, was entirely groundlefs. It alfo appeared, that if there had been a communication betwixt the gulf and the South fea, the voyage this way, on account

count of the tempeftuous weather, the fhallow-
nefs of the water, the narrownefs of the channel, the rapidity, and various directions of
the currents, would have been absolutely impracticable to fuch large fhips as the Philippine
galleons.

Thus the only method of providing a receptacle for thefe fhips, appeared to be the fettling
a colony and garrifon, at fome convenient harbour of the fouth coaft. And in order to fecure it from any danger on the land fide, to
extend the miffions towards the harbour, and
by that means reduce the inhabitants of both
coafts of the gulf. We may therefore account
for the many unfuccefsful attempts that we
have related in the foregoing parts of this
work, exclufive of others made at different pe-
riods of time with lefs noife and expence, but
equally unfortunate. About this time alfo,
father Tamaral, at different times, furveyed
great part of the coaft northward from his
miffion of Puriffima, and almoft the whole of
it towards Cape San Lucas, the viceroy having,
in a very particular manner, directed him to
look out for harbours and lands, where colonies and garrifons might be conveniently fettled ; but all proved ineffectual. With the
fame intention father Ugarte, on his arrival at
Loretto, ordered preparations to be made for

a new attempt, and for making a furvey of
the fouth coaſt as far north as poſſible. By
his order, the captain of the garriſon went with
a party of foldiers to the miſſion of Santa Roſalia de Mulege; and from thence, with father
Sebaſtian de Siſtiaga, to that of Guadalupe,
where father Everard Helen was fettled. On
the 19th of November of the fame year 1721,
they departed from Guadalupe to the coaſt,
which they traced beyond the 28th degree of
latitude. And tho', in this excurſion, they
fuffered in feveral reſpects, they had the fatiffaction of finding three feveral harbours, with
good watering-places, and a fufficiency of
wood, but the foil too barren for culture. The
largeſt and moſt fecure harbour, which alfo
had the beſt water, was not far from the Indian
village of San Miguel, with the miſſion of San
Xavier; and from whence the ſhips might be
fupplied with neceſſaries.

With theſe agreeable difcoveries they returned to Loretto, where father Ugarte drew up
a narrative of his voyage, adding the pilot
Strafort's map and journal. Father Siſtiaga
likewife compofed an account of his difcoveries, with draughts of the harbours he had
met with; all which were fent to Mexico to
be prefented to the viceroy, that he might
take what meaſures he ſhould think proper,
                                                        and

and tranfmit the feveral papers to his majefty, and the fupreme council of the Indies. Whether thefe journals, maps, and narratives ever reached Madrid, I cannot pretend to fay; but this unfortunate truth is well known, that nothing was ordered by either government, in confequence of them. It is proper alfo to obferve here, that tho' diligent fearch was made after thefe papers in Madrid, they could not be found; nor could any entreaty prevail to have them remitted for Mexico. I am fenfible it would be a great fatisfaction to the curious reader to find here the whole journal of father Ugarte, and the narrative of the fathers who difcovered the feveral harbours, with a diftinct account of the latitudes of every headland; the fituation and views of the iflands, coafts, harbours, and bays; their obfervations on the fhoals, anchoring places, tides, currents, variations of the needle, &c. The charts, at leaft, drawn in thefe expeditions, are effentially neceffary to form a complete idea of the difcoveries; and, it may be added, that fuch maps, when accurate, are the principal advantage of thefe enterprizes. But notwithftanding all the means of information I enjoy, I find myfelf under a neceffity of being the firft, and the moft interefted in complaining of this deficiency; but I ftill comfort myfelf, that

no

no diligence has been wanting to retrieve them; and still hope, that some time or other, if what I at present offer proves of any utility, and meets with the approbation of the publick, these vacuities will be filled up; and his majesty's subjects enjoy all the knowledge of these countries, as the interests of the kingdom and church require.

S E C T. XVI.

The mission de Nuestra Senora de los Dolores del Sur founded by father Guillen, and that of St. Jago de los Coras, by father Napoli.

The care of general enterprizes, undertaken pursuant to the orders of his majesty, and his ministers, and for forming others for the advancement of the conquest, did not hinder the particular zeal of every missionary, in his district, for promoting religious knowledge and practice among his parishioners; for increasing the number of missions, and extending these christian settlements as far as circumstances would permit. It was evident from the foundations, the progresses and surveys, taken northwards by sea and land, that the northern parts were less barren, and abounded more in

fresh

frefh water, than the fouthern. It was alfo found, that the nations and people of the north were much more docile; of better intellects; more peaceable and faithful; lefs vicious and petulant; and, confequently, naturally fitter for the reception of the gofpel, and conforming to its precepts, than thofe of the fouth. On the contrary, the miffion de la Paz had fent an account, that the whole Pericu nation, with its feveral branches of Guaycuros, Uchities, Coras and iflanders were implacably vindictive, at continual wars, and by treachery, and open violence, conftantly deftroying one another; that unlefs they were all univerfally made chriftians, and brought to a folid reconciliation, there could be no fecurity among them; and that a partial converfion would only increafe the diforders. Likewife that the other vices of floth, ingratitude, and fraud, were arrived at a greater height among this fouthern people, efpecially a brutal appetite, being not only permitted, but making a boaft, and even a profit of polygamy.

But the fame reafons which feem to entitle the northern people to the preference, rendered it neceffary to attend firft to that of the Pericues. For no garrifon being obtained, as had been endeavoured, for la Paz; and the twenty-five foldiers at Loretto not being fufficient for the

neceffary

neceſſary eſcortes, journies, and defence of the
countries, ſo diſtant from each other; the whole
conqueſt, towards the north, was expoſed, till
ſeveral nations of the ſouth ſhould be reconciled and humanized. Beſides, the Uchities,
who live betwixt La Paz and Loretto, had in-
ſulted ſome chriſtian Indians on their way, between theſe two places, as if they intended to
cut off all communication by land between the
two miſſions : the Coras, or thoſe who lived at
the extremity of the peninſula, near Cape San
Lucas, were every day moleſting their old
enemies the Guaycuros of **La Paz,** and
neighbourhood, the inhabitants of the its
iſlands of the San Joſeph, Eſpiritu Santo,
Ceralvo, and others, betwixt Loretto and
La Paz, tho' by father Ugarte reconciled
to the Guaycuros, renewed their former depredations in theſe parts ; and the quantity of
maize, pozoli, knives, and toys at **La Paz,**
were with them incentives to avarice, inſtead
of producing moderation and reſpect. Theſe
iſlanders had three times pillaged the miſſion of
San Juan Baptiſta Ligui, or Malibat, in the
abſence of father Guillen the miſſionary, without leaving any thing behind them ; and tho'
the captain and ſoldiers of the garriſon went
in purſuit of them, killed three or four, took
fourteen boats, and eleven men, who, after
being

being kindly entertained at Loretto, were sent back to their ifland, as a teftimony of friend-fhip and kindnefs; yet their pretended recon-ciliation lafted no longer than their fear, or whilft this fuppreffed their rancour againft the inhabitants of the fhore, or were not in want of little utenfils. Thus the only remedy was to enter on a reduction of the Uchities and Coras, who lived on each fide of La Paz; and gain the affections of the iflanders. To this great end, in the fame year 1721, the founda-tion of two new miffions was undertaken, at the fame time that the above furveys of the coaft and gulf were making by land and fea.

The fund of the miffion of San Juan Ligui, or Malibat had, as we have already noted, ceafed by the failure of its endower Don Juan Baptifta Lopes; and tho' father Guillen and the other miffionaries were fupplied for them-felves and their Indians, it was by ftrict fa-vings of the expences, and ftraitening indivi-duals for the fake of the general caufe. Be-fides, the village and rancherias of Malibat had been extremely thinned by a dreadful epi-demia, and the few Indians, who remained at every abfence of the father, lived in fuch con-tinual dread of new inroads from the iflanders, that, for fear, they withdrew from the village. At this time, that religious nobleman the mar-

quis de Villa Puente, endowed two miffions to
be founded between cape San Lucas and Loretto. On which it was refolved that father
Guillen fhould leave San Juan de Malibat for
the vifitation town, and found a new miffion
betwixt the Uchities and Guaycuros, the reduction of whom was of fuch immediate concern. Accordingly in the year 1721, the father fettled among them, and immediately
laid the foundations of a church, a village,
and other buildings neceffary to a new miffion.
In the month of Auguft he fixed his refidence
along the fhore of Apate, 40 leagues from
Loretto by fea, and above 60 by land, on
account of the unavoidable circuit of the
mountains. The miffion was dedicated to
Nueftra Senora de los Dolores, with the ad-
dition of del Sur, to diftinguifh it from another
miffion of that name in the north. The hardfhips which father Guillen underwent in this
department, the moft barren and inconvenient
of all California, and the zeal and incredible
labour with which he cultivated this vineyard of
his mafter, were never exceeded; and the confequences refulting from them more ufeful and
beneficial than thofe of any other in California.
In the year 1744, at the direction of his fuperiors, he fent a fhort account of the ftate of
his miffion. It is written with great referve
and

and humility; and shews at once his virtue, great abilities, and penetrating judgment. This was the thirtieth year of his serving as missionary in California, where he arrived in the year 1714, after the deplorable shipwreck, in which his faithful companion father Guisi was drowned.

The mission of Los Dolores was founded purely for the conveniency of the Indians, but afterwards removed from the shore to a place called Tanuetia, 10 leagues from the gulf, and 25 from the South sea. The father sought the families of the Indians on both sides among the caves, woods, and recesses of those craggy mountains, and assembled them into six villages, Nuestra Senora de los Dolores, La Conception de Nuestra Senora, La Incarnation, La Trinidad, La Redemption, and La Resurrection; which had been inhabited by the Indians of Malibat, before they quitted this part of the country. He likewise converted to the faith other Indians, whom he formed into three villages; and of these was erected the new mission of San Luis Gonzaga, on the endowment of the count de St. Jago, who lived at Mexico; and in the year 1737, a particular missionary was appointed for it. Lastly, he instructed and converted all the other heathens of the south coast, from the mission of San Xavier

Xavier to the nation of the Coras. They were all regiftered as catechumens, and well difpofed to be incorporated in another miffion, which was to be founded that year; and was the more neceffary from its being impoffible, confidering the great diftances, and the nature of the country, to give proper inftruction and relief to all. Thus by him alone were brought to chriftianity, all the inhabitants for above 40 leagues of the peninfula, from the one coaft to the other; yet in all this tract, the foil is fo rocky and barren, that no place could be found for fowing any grain, except a little maize at Aparte, barely fufficient for the Indians there. This fhews the extreme indigence of the Indians in thefe parts; and likewife the inability of the miffionaries to give them any relief. Yet his labours were fo fuccefsful here, that, amidft all the fubfequent rebellions of the fouth, father Guillen's Guaycuros, and Uchities, once fo turbulent, are now, contrary to the example and ftrong inftigation of the Periques and Coras, not only firm in the profeffion of the faith, but the miffion de los Dolores del Sur, was the afylum, where the refugee fathers, and Indians, met with an affectionate reception.

For the reafons already fpecified, there was founded, during the fame year, another miffion, endowed

endowed by the marquis de la Puente, in the nation of the Coras, not far from Cape San Lucas. This the father superior Ugarte was very solicitous of establishing; and, accordingly, before he undertook to survey the gulf, he had left directions, with every thing necessary, that father Ignacio Maria Napoli should go to La Paz, and from thence to the bay of Palmas, the place chosen for the new mission. Loretto, at that time, laboured under a great scarcity of provisions; but the bark with the provisions and supplies being soon expected from New Spain, father Ugarte impowered the new missionary to take what should be sent for his mission of San Xavier, together with whatever else he stood in need of, and proceed in the bark to his station, carefully conforming to the instructions which he had given him with regard to his actions, on all occasions. The bark arrived in the middle of July; and on the 21st of the same month, father Rapoli embarking with captain Don Estevan Rodrigues, and four soldiers, happily arrived at La Paz, on the 2d of August. At his landing, the Indians of the mission received him with great veneration, kissing his hand on their knees, and in procession conducted him with the captain and soldiers to the church, where father Jayme Bravo was waiting for him. The bark

was

was difmiffed for the coaft of Cinaloa to load maize for Loretto; fo that to convey the neceffaries to the bay of Palmas, they were obliged to borrow the boats belonging to general Rezaval's bilander, which was come up the bay to fifh for pearls. The fathers and foldiers went by land, in order to clear a way for La Paz, and invite to the miffion what Indians they fhould meet with. Eight days were fpent in reaching the bay, where they arrived on the 24th of Auguft; but all the Indians had withdrawn farther up the country, and the rancherias they met with in the way, were all abandoned. The boats with the neceffaries did not arrive till five days after they came to the bay, which, with the retreat of the Indians, gave father Napoli great uneafinefs. Befides, his extreme pains, occafioned by a violent fall from his mule, when he remained for fome time fenfelefs, and, by his company, was given over for dead.

One evening, as he was walking at fome diftance from the tent, to view the fhore, he faw furioufly running towards him, a company of naked Indians, headed by one, who, befides his extraordinary ftature and bulk, was painted all over black and red. He was partly covered with a kind of hair cloak; feveral deers feet were hanging about his waift; in one hand he held

held a fan of feathers, and in the other a bow
with an arrow on it. The terror of his frightful howlings, accompanied with thofe of his
followers, was increafed by their threatening
geftures. Father Napoli now thought that his
laft hour was inevitably come; and, lifting up
his heart to God, he fervently offered to him
the facrifice of his life, imploring that his fins
might be forgiven. After this, he boldly advanced towards the Indians, fuppreffing as
much as poffible his natural timidity, agreeable to the inftructions given him of never betraying the leaft fear. At firft, having never
heard any thing of the drefs of the Californian
forcerers, he was fhocked at his frightful appearance, and even doubted whether it was
not the devil himfelf, in a vifible form, leading
on the Indians to deftroy him as the meffenger
of Chrift. But foon recovering from his firft
aftonifhment, he approached him with a look
of contempt; fignifying, at the fame time, by
figns to the Indians, that he took it ill, they
fhould intend him any harm; and then with
the moft endearing marks of love diftributed a-
mong them feveral trifling articles he had
about him; inviting them to the camp, where
he would give them more. This kindnefs of
the father had its defired effect; they kept him
company, till by degrees he brought them to

the tent; where, after being liberally treated,
some provisions and little utensils were given
them, and others sent to those who remained in
their rancherias, as tokens of peace and friendship. The Indians departed highly satisfied;
but desired, if they would have them return,
to hide the beasts, and a dog, which, as they
had never seen before, they were much fright-
ened at. The day following they came in
little troops to the number of five hundred,
bringing such presents as the country afforded,
which were returned with pozoli, sackcloth-
frocks, razors, and the like, which had been
got ready for this purpose. It was now five
days since they had pitched the tent, and
without any account of the boat, the loss of
which would have reduced them to the utmost
extremity. But they had landed four days before, and waited for the rest of the company,
who came by land, in a little lake, a few
leagues off, thinking that had been the place
appointed for the rendezvous. The first account of them was from the Indians; and they
being acquainted on what part of the shore
the father was, the goods were landed, and a
survey taken of the country, in order for settling the mission. Besides several thickets of
palm-trees, and places over-grown with sedge,
there were near the sea several ponds of fresh
water,

water, as likewife a brook, tho' thefe were by
no means convenient watering-places. They
likewife met with fome fpots of ground that
promifed very well for pafture and tillage; yet on
account of the nearnefs of La Paz, and the facility
of receiving fupplies, the father determined to
found the miffion at the place where they firft
pitched their tent. Accordingly the ground
was cleared, and the little village began to af-
fume fome form; when, on a fudden, all the
Indians difappeared, and not one was feen for
a whole day.   The father, at a lofs what
could occafion this hafty change, determined,
in the evening, to go in queft of them, with
only a foldier, and an unfkilful interpreter.
He found out fome, who, on his complaining
in an affectionate manner, made no difficulty
of acquainting him with the true caufe of their
fear. The Coras were engaged in an inveterate war with the Guaycuros of La Paz; and the
father had come with foldiers from the territory of the latter, in which there was already a
miffion. The Coras had feen a furvey taken
of the whole country, and walls making for
the church; which, tho' only of earth, and ill
put together, the Indians concluded were
defigned for fome fortrefs. Laftly, the father
had brought with him fome Guaycuros; and
three of thefe had, by the father's orders, gone

that day along the open road to La Paz, to con-
voy from thence a mule loaded with maize.

Thefe particulars raifed a fufpicion in the
Coras, that the Guaycuros were come to maffa-
cre all the nation ; that this was the end of the
taking a view of the country ; of their treating
them, and defiring to fee them every day;
that they were building walls for their fecurity,
and that, reckoning themfelves fure of the fuccefs of the attempt, they had fent for all the
nation of the Guaycuros to come and join in it ;
and thus falling on them fuddenly deftroy
them root and branch. The father took fuch
pains to remove their fufpicion and quiet them,
that many came with him to the tent and ar-
bour made of palm leaves, where the foldiers
kept guard. On the other hand the more fear-
ful Indians lighted feveral fires, that they might
better perceive their enemies, if they fhould
attempt to deftroy them. The next morning
their fears returned a fecond time, that for two
days not one of them was to be feen. And
now father Bravo who had a tolerable knowledge of the Guyacuri tongue, and could be
well underftood by the Coras, was fo far from
being of any fervice in this exigency, that he
did the greateft hurt, being looked upon as the
father, head, and leader of their enemies. The
mule which had been detained with the maize
came

came up; and tho' the Indians at a distance saw the reality of what father Napoli had told them, they would not return to their dwellings. It was in vain to go after them, as they immediately betook themselves to flight. At last however, men and women with their children returned continually, and even entreated that their children might be baptized like those of La Paz; and that they might be friends for ever. And thus a peace was concluded betwixt the Guaycuros and Coras: which reconciliation was allowed to be celebrated with their usual festivities and dancings. The fourth of September, father Napoli baptized twenty nine children; after which the women were continually coming to him, and begging the like favour for their children. Thus the inhabitants of this country, formerly so suspicious, were now never easy, but when with the fathers.

Every thing that had been brought, even to the furniture of the altar, had now been distributed to the Indians for gaining their affections, so that there scarce remained a sufficiency of provisions for returning to La Paz, to procure a new supply. Accordingly, leaving the house of palm-trees, and a little furniture in the care of some of the eldest, with many assurances from father Napoli of a speedy return, they set

out

out by a new way, in order to make a more accurate furvey of the country.

Father Napoli ftaid two months at the miffion of La Paz, waiting for provifions and applying himfelf to the language of the Coras; a tafk of the utmoft difficulty, tho' abfolutely neceffary to be performed. Whilft the fathers were abfent from Palmas bay, forty men from the ifland of Cerralvo, oppofite to the bay of La Paz, landed; and finding the miffion without a father or guard, they fell upon a rancheria, killed fix young children, two women and a man, and took a young man prifoner; after which they pillaged the rancheria of all its ftores and furniture. Nor had the church and chapel efcaped, had not the ravagers been afraid that on any longer ftay, the whole nation of the Guaycuros, would be in arms againft them. However the captain with a party of foldiers went in two boats to the ifland of Cerralvo: and tho' the iflanders retired among the caves and rocks, our men killed two or three of them, which, with the firing of their pieces, proved a terrible warning to them for the future. The captain immediately marched for Loretto, and in November father Napoli returned to Palmas bay; which, however, he did not think fit to make the feat of the miffion, on account of

its

its great diftance from La Paz, at that time the only place for fupplies.

Accordingly he made choice of a fpot of ground called St. Anne, lying up the country thirty leagues from La Paz, and five from the gulf, where he built a chapel and a fmall houfe; and brought the neareft rancherias to the belief and regular practice of chriftianity. In the year 1723, he built a church in a place fomething farther from the fea, intending to alter the feat of the miffion; but the whole mifcarried by an incident which it was impoffible to prevent. The church was now fo far finifhed that the beams and rafters were laid for the roof; and whilft the father was affifting a dying perfon, one of thofe terrible hurricanes ufual in this country arofe; at which the Indians fled for fhelter to the church; but the roof being but imperfectly fettled, and the walls of themfelves, but weak and not thoroughly dried, the force of the wind blew down the whole building, by which fome Indians were killed, others maimed, and the living frantick with dread and horror. Father Napoli at the noife haftened to the place, and behaved with all the tendernefs of an afflicted father: but this accident proved the foundation of a confpiracy among the relations of thofe who were killed; and he every day faw the beginning and period of fuch combinations from

leffer

leſſer motives : but their rage was now wholly
bent againſt the father, as the murderer of
their friends.   They were however ſoon ap-
peaſed, when the ſurvivors informed them that
they had retired thither of their own accord,
without being bid by any one.   However, the
church was rebuilt in a more convenient part
which afforded water, not only for drinking,
but for fertilizing ſome little ſpots for ſowing
in the neighbourhood, and was dedicated to
St. James the apoſtle.   Some ground having
been cleared for ſowing maize, it was found to
ahſwer very well.   The like unhappily cannot
be ſaid of the ſpiritual ſeed : this giddy, ſloth-
ful, brutiſh people ſhewing a great reluctancy
to the pure doctrine of the goſpel : and tho'
the father neglected no part of a faithful miniſter, the whole number of thoſe he baptized
amounted to no more than ninety adults, and
about four hundred children. In the year 1726,
father Napoli being appointed for the miſſions
on the other ſide ; was ſucceeded by father Lorenzo Carranzo, whoſe blood was ſhed in this
wilderneſs, over-run with the moſt abominable
corruptions; as we ſhall hereafter more particularly relate.

S E C T. XVII.

Foundation of the northern miſſion of San
   Ignacio by father Luyando and its progreſſes. Death of the fathers Piccolo
   and Ugarte. Inſurrections of the Pericues, and foundation of the miſſion of
   St. Joſeph at cape San Lucas, by father
   Tamaral.

Ever ſince the year 1706, it had been greatly
deſired that a miſſion ſhould be founded in the
N. beyond that of Nueſtra Senora de Guadalupe in the country of Kada-Kaaman, i. e.
Sedgebrook, among the Sierra de San Vicente
in the latitude of twenty eight degrees, forty
leagues S. E. of Santa Roſalia Mulege, and
twenty five S. of Guadalupe. The Cochimi
Indians of that diſtrict had, with all the ſigns of
ſincerity, expreſſed a deſire of becoming chriſtians, on the occaſion of father Piccolo's viſit
in the ſame year ; but from the want both of
inſtructors and funds, together with the immediate neceſſity of reducing the Edues and Pericues in the S. occaſioned the work, however
deſirable, to be delayed. The neighbouring
miſſionaries, however viſited them occaſionally
to cheriſh their good diſpoſitions, till the
year

year 1728. In the preceding year there arrived at Loretto, father Juan Baptista Luyando
a Mexican Jefuit of moft excellent parts and
qualities, who not only delivered up his fortune
into the hands of his fuperiors, for the foundation of a miffion in California, but alfo offered
in perfon to be himfelf the founder. Accordingly, in January 1728, he fet out from Loretto, accompanied by nine foldiers, and on the
20th of the fame month, came to the place
which had been marked out for the feat of this
miffion, by father Siftiaga, of Santa Rofalia Mulege, who for fome months before had vifited
the Indians to acquaint them with the defign,
and prepare their minds for giving the father
a favourable reception. Accordingly, father
Luyando was received by the natives with all
the appearance of fatisfaction, and in a few
days he found about him five hundred perfons
from feveral rancherias. He now entered on
his office, which was the eafier, as fome were
already acquainted with their catechifm, and
moft had heard father Siftiaga. And they applied themfelves with fuch affiduity, to imbibe
his inftructions in the doctrinal and practical
parts of the chriftian religion, that in a little
time he had the pleafure of perceiving from the
ftability of their good difpofitions, that he might
fafely adminifter baptifm to the adults, efpecially

cially as they readily complied with the preliminary of breaking and burning all the superstitious implements of their forcerers. For above fix months the father was enabled to support near five hundred catechumens: for tho' fome after baptifm returned to their rancherias, they were abundantly replaced, that he began to be under apprehenfions of the provifions failing; therefore that nothing might be wanting in him towards the completion of a work fo happily begun, he difmiffed feven foldiers with letters, earneftly requefting a fpeedy fupply from Loretto, and thus remained with only two guards. It muft be faid to the praife of the foldiers, that feeing the father fo taken up in the immediate functions of his office, and with fo much fuccefs, they voluntarily took upon themfelves the labour of building a church and a houfe, which, by the help of the Indians who readily lent a hand to whatever they were directed, the church was nearly finifhed before the foldiers fet out on their return, and the dedication of it performed on Chriftmas day that year.

As thefe fucceffes filled the miffionary's heart with joy, fo they animated him readily to take under his inftruction, all who came to the feat of the miffion, and likewife to make excurfions on all quarters in fearch of new Indians.

He

He was particularly fent for once a great way
off, by one who had been bit by a viper: and
tho' both the foldier and the fervant who underftood the language were abfent, he ventured
himfelf with only one of the natives, who had
been already baptized.   On his arrival at the
place, he found a large rancheria of favages,
who had never fo much as feen an European
or a horfe: accordingly they were at firft greatly terrified, but the prefents the father brought
with him and his graceful carriage, foon removed their fears: and they all came about
him offering him all they had.

This docility of the Cochimes, together with
the vivacity, genius, and activity of body, in
which they furpafs all the other nations, enabled
the miffionary to make great improvements in
their country.   This diftrict is very proper for
agriculture, both on account of the foftnefs of
the earth, and the eafinefs of procuring water,
fo that a large colony might eafily fubfift there;
and the Indians be no longer under a neceffity of
roving among the woods and mountains for
fupport. Father Siftiaga had before fown maize
and wheat, which in the firft year yielded together a hundred bufhels: but in the fourth
and laft year of father Luyando, the harveft,
every fort of grain included, amounted to a
thoufand bufhels.   The confequence of this,

was a more eafy and plentiful fupply to the
ndians, who, being lefs brutifh than their neighbours, willingly affifted in the labour, which
they faw was entirely for their benefit. Father
Helen, at another entrance, had already taught
them to cultivate feveral forts of garden vegetables, which he himfelf had planted: and
father Luyando laid out a fpot of ground for a
garden, where exotick plants, in that barren
land throve very well, and others which were
natives of it improved under his culture. He
likewife planted five hundred vines, together
with olive-trees, fig-trees, and fugar-canes,
which have fince proved of great advantage to
a miffion fo remote, and not a little contributed to the extraordinary increafe of it, and the
improvement of real chriftianity among the
Indians. The father was now defirous of af-
fembling the Indians in villages, built in the
moft convenient place for the neighbouring
rancherias, with a chapel in each, that they
might there daily perform their devotions. He
likewife taught them to make little houfes of
adobes and boughs of trees, tho' being always
ufed to the open air, it was with great difficulty they could be reconciled to live in them.
In the parts fit for paftures, he likewife endeavoured to breed great and fmall cattle for
the ufe of the miffion.

Thus

Thus every thing wore a very pleasing aspect; but the great enemy to the peace and happiness of mankind, instigated the Indians to oppose the tranquility of the mission, and render all the pains of the father abortive. Accordingly, eight of these savages taking advantage of a dark night murdered a catechumen near the father's cottage, probably because the missionary shewed a great regard to him for his amiable dispositions. It was necessary however not to take notice of this barbarous act, lest greater mischief should ensue; but it did not escape the divine vengeance, all the eight miserably dying in the epidemia of the following year 1729. Another rancheria obstinately refused to come to the mission; and on the baptism of the three first adults, sought for them in order to destroy them, which they would certainly have effected, had not they taken refuge in the father's house: two years they persisted in this stubborn humour, till their depravity was overcome by the patience, gentleness, and liberality of the father: but it was not till seven years after, that those advanced in years embraced the christian religion. The old men indeed, in every rancheria expressed the greatest acrimony against christianity: and as these were generally the sorcerers, priests, and teachers, or rather deceivers of the rancherias,

rias, it is no wonder that they fhould oppofe the progrefs of chriftianity, which put a period to all their profits and power: their lives alfo were profligate; their brutifh cuftoms and favage manner of living had taken deeper root in them; their attendance at church and devout exercifes, was a more painful conftraint on them; and having been the refpected teachers of the nation, they could not prevail on themfelves to be fcholars to ftrangers, or ftand among boys, and even be ridiculed by them for their abfurd doctrines.

Amidft thefe various tranfactions, the miffion went on very profperoufly, which was in a great meafure owing to the docility and candour of thefe Indians, who ufed frankly to acquaint father Luyando with whatever they faw amifs in their countrymen: fo that he eafily prevailed upon them, in order to facilitate his vifiting them in the rancherias, and afterwards in the villages which were building, to clear ways for them to the feat of the miffion: and for their encouragement, he propofed rewards which he beftowed on thofe who diftinguifhed themfelves in the work.

Some wild Indians of the N. inftigated by malice, at the flourifhing ftate of the miffion, and the tranquility enjoyed by the converted tribe, fell upon a chriftian rancheria, killing two In-

diars.

dians, and a little girl, all the others having fled to the seat of the miffion. The chriftians of the other rancherias were for taking arms againft the invaders, but the father fearing it might kindle a perpetual war, entreated them to forbear, and patiently forgive injuries as became chriftians. He flattered himfelf that this tranquility and forbearance would have a good effect on the enemy, and induce them by degrees to receive the gofpel; to forward which, he fent them fome meffages and prefents: but experience fhewed his miftake; and that thefe barbarians are firft to be quelled by force, as they afterwards readily believe that whatever kindnefs is done them, proceeds from love: whereas, otherwife they attribute it to weaknefs and cowardice; mildnefs and prefents only increafing their infolence. Accordingly the invaders from the mild meffages and prefents, concluded the father and his Indians were in a terrible confternation: and this animated them to attack other rancherias; plundering where-ever they came, killing or driving the chriftians before them, and threatening the feat of the miffion. As the father had only two foldiers with him and the Indians were terrified and unarmed, he judged it advifable to withdraw to the miffion of Guadalupe, where father Siftiaga officiated. From hence both the fathers returned to San Ignacio, where

where it was refolved vigoroufly to march a-
gainft the enemy, without waiting for foldiers
from Loretto, which was feventy leagues diftant. Accordingly, the chriftian rancherias
were fummoned; and arms given them, with
great noife and hurry both to raife the fpirits of
the chriftians, and intimidate the favages, by
the great and tumultuous preparatives for war,
according to the ancient cuftom of California:
fome made bows; others were fharpening pieces
of ftone for the arrows; fome went to cut wood
for fpears, which till then had not been known
in this country, and at the ends of which the
foldiers fixed large knives, that had been
brought to diftribute among the miffions. The
very women made bags and nets for carrying
the provifions, roafted maize, and baked bifket.
The preparations being finifhed, the people
were reviewed and found to be above feven
hundred men fit for action: but there not
being provifions for fuch a number, thofe of
weak conftitutions were difcharged, fo that only
three hundred and fifty ftout men remained for
the expedition. But thefe were of different
rancherias, and the cuftom was for every one
to chufe their captain, which, at prefent, would
have given rife to fatal confufion. The fathers
therefore acquainted them, that it was proper
for all to be under one command: that there-

fore two captains fhould be appointed ; one by
them, and the other by the fathers ; both of
their nation, men of courage and conduct and
well acquainted with the country. Accordingly,
they chofe one among them of great reputation : and the perfon appointed by the fathers,
was the governor of the village that year, a
young man of good parts and faithful, who
had been brought up at Loretto, whither father Ugarte carried him when a child at the
time of cutting the timber for the bilander.
The whole army thus equiped, marched in
queft of the enemy, and the fcouts foon brought
advice that they waited for them by a watering
place near the fkirts of the mountains. On this
advice it was determined to attack them during
the night. Accordingly they marched up to them,
and furrounded them on all fides ; after which
they gradually approached them with the greateft filence, left they fhould give them any
alarm. At fun-rife the Indians, who on all
fides had hem'd in their enemies, fet up a
dreadful fhout of war, which awaked the favages, who were fleeping without any apprehenfion of danger. At this fhout they ftarted on
their feet, fought confufedly about for their arms,
while the other advanced on all fides in good
order ; fo that the enemy, finding themfelves
furrounded by a fuperior force, and their re-

treat cut off, laid down their arms as a sign of submission. Two only found means to escape; and giving advice of the defeat to a few of another rancheria, they precipitately fled to their own country, so that the remainder, to the number of thirty four, were easily made prisoners: and after the country had been reconnoitred to know if it was clear of the enemies, our people returned to San Ignacio, which they entered with their prisoners in a kind of triumph. The fathers led the victorious army to the church, where thanks were returned for this victory gained without shedding any blood, or even discharging a single arrow. The men also were entertained, and next day all the people were assembled: and the soldiers and governors sitting as judges, the prisoners were brought to tryal; where, being convicted of rebellion, robberies, and murders, they were sentenced to be removed to Loretto as guilty of capital crimes. Sentence being passed, they were remanded to prison very much dejected, whilst many of the new christians danced for joy, thinking they should now have the pleasure of killing their enemies and revenging themselves. But the fathers came up, and assured the captives that they should not die; made them some presents, and mildly reproved the exultations of the others; taking occasion to instruct them

in

in the duties of charity, and chriſtian compaſ-
ſion, forgiveneſs and living peaceably with all
men.   The next day the court ſat again at the
requeſt of the fathers, who brought with them
many Indians to deſire the ſoldiers that they
would ſoften their ſentence without inflicting
death, or ſending the priſoners to Loretto.   Accordingly each was to receive a certain number
of laſhes.   The execution began with the principal murderer : but the fathers again interced-
ed that the puniſhment ſhould be limited to
him, and the reſt pardon'd, which was complied with; and the priſoners being deprived of their
arms, which were diſtributed among the leading men of the forces, as monuments of the
victory, were diſcharged.   This extraordinary
lenity had a very good effect among the ſavages :
the chriſtians being inſtructed, and the gentiles
filled with affection for the fathers and their law,
which enjoined ſuch mild treatment.   They
were detained ſome days, but at full liberty
that they might ſee the good behaviour and
conformable way of living of the Indians of the
miſſion.   They begged of the fathers that they
would baptize them and their ſons, but it was
thought proper to refuſe them, both to augment
their deſire and to try their ſincerity.   They
were diſmiſſed with great affection : but they
ſoon returned, requeſting that at leaſt their
                                    children

children might be baptized, as otherwife they fhould think that the fathers did not love them; and that the chriftians intended to carry on a fecond war. In this they were gratify'd, except a fon of the principal murderer, or head of the confpiracy, who, like the reft, went away very difconfolate. But returning a fecond time with his little fon in his arms, begging with tears, that he might be baptized if they killed him; accordingly the child was baptized, and he chearfully went away to rejoin his countrymen. A few months after, all the former prifoners, with their relations and families, and even decrepit old men, came to be inftructed in order to baptifm; which, at a proper time, was adminiftered to all.

This victory was of great fervice to the caufe of chriftianity, by intimidating the gentiles and recommending the law which the ftrangers preached, to their favourable receptions, fo that a free paffage was now opened towards the nations of the North. But father Luyando's health was fo impair'd by fatigues, that he was obliged to quit the miffion which he had founded with his fortune, and improved by his zeal and abilities. He was fucceeded by father Siftiaga the indefatigable miffionary of Santa Rofalia Mulege.

At

At the same time California lost two of its most ancient labourers: the first was father Francisco Maria Piccolo, who, full of days, ended his labours in the royal garrison of Loretto, on the 22d of February 1729, in the 79th year of his age; and the 32d from his coming to California. In the following year 1730, at the village of San Pablo belonging to the mission of San Xavier, father Juan Ugarte quietly breathed his last in his 70th year, after having served 30 as a missionary in California.

In the mean time the southern nations were every day shewing those turbulent, lawless, and treacherous dispositions, of which, from the beginning they had given too many proofs. And notwithstanding father Guillen at Dolores, Father Bravo at La Paz, and father Napoli at San Jago; and since them their successors, had civilized many of the Uchiti, Guaycuros, and the Coras; and brought them within the pale of the church; yet even in those and the adjacent nations, great numbers of gentiles remained, who were constantly insulting the christians; many of whom, were daily less fond of the rational and orderly life to which they were now brought, and even making no secret of their disgust; fomenting seditions and infecting those who remained quiet in the faith. In the year 1723, all the three missions being recently

cently founded, the captain of the garrison with
some soldiers made a progress about the country
to terrify those who molested their neighbours.
The Coras of cape San Lucas very earnestly desired that the father might be sent to make
them christians; but others who had already
embraced the faith, gave him sufficient trouble,
and a gentile accidentally wounded him in the
shoulder with an arrow. Yet he bravely concealed it for two months, whilst he was under
cure at La Paz, that the accident was not to
be so much as known to the faithful Indians
of Loretto, with whom however it was proper
to use such precautions.

In the year 1725, the captain was obliged a
second time to march with an armed force to
some rancherias of Uchities and Guaycuros, who
were withdrawn towards the opposite coast, but
without killing a man. These and some Coras
had in the year 1719, renewed their outrages,
chiefly at the instigation of some Mulattoes and
Mestizos left on those coasts by foreign privateers, who happened to touch there. These
were the leaven which corrupted the simplicity
of those Indians, of themselves too susceptible of
bad impressions. For as captain don Estevan
Rodrigues observes in his journal, "the natives here are so naturally uneasy, turbulent, and
factious, that unless a party of the garrison goes

H 4 every

every year to fupprefs their commotions and
check their infolence, there would be no living
in fafety." The captain was employed in
this furvey from March to September of that
year, when fome rancherias of cape San Lucas
again urged them to fend them fathers. But
they were now obliged to have recourfe to fome
flight punifhment. The good difpofitions of
fome for receiving the faith; the continual
dread of invafions from others; and of the
defertion of new converts, rendered it abfolutely neceffary to haften the foundation of
other miffions among the Pericues, in order
to fecure the reduction of the peninfula as far
as the cape above mentioned.

This total converfion of the Indians, the
marquis de Villa Puente, a moft munificent benefactor to thefe miffions, had very much at
heart; he made an offer of eftablifhing one in
the neighbourhood of cape San Lucas, and, animated by his example, his coufin donna Rofa
de la Penna, fifter to the marchionefs of Villa
Puente, a lady of eminent virtues, and exemplary charity, to endow another intended to be
founded in Las Palmas bay, the original fituation of the miffion of San Jago de los Coras,
fince removed to fuch a diftance, that the miffionary could by no means attend the neceffities and inftruction of thefe Indians; and their
indo-

indocility and turbulency rendered it ſtill more difficult and diſcouraging.

The agent for California at Mexico, was father Joſeph de Echeveria, who, on the loſs of the bark in 1729 with all the proviſions, the people with great difficulty ſaving themſelves in a boat, went over to Cinaloa to purchaſe a-nother veſſel, and make preparations for a freſh ſupply. In this he was engaged when the fa-ther general Tamburini's nomination of him for viſitor general of all the miſſions of the Je-ſuits arrived from Rome. On receipt of this order, he prepared to begin his viſitation with thoſe of California, whoſe agent he had been for ſeveral years : and purpoſing to accompliſh the foundation of the two new miſſions in the South, for which the endowments had been al-ready offered, he embarked at Ahome in the Triumph of the Croſs, which, on the ninth day being the 27th of October, happily landed him in San Dionyſio or Loretto bay.

A few days after his arrival, he was ſeized with a malignant fever, ſo that his life was de-ſpaired of ; but providence was pleaſed to reſtore his health : he did not however ſtay till it was confirmed, but left Loretto to proceed on his viſitation of the northern miſſions, having with him only the enſign, a ſoldier named Acoſta, and a few Indians. The good father's heart

over-

overflowed with joy at feeing the œconomy of the miffions, the knowledge, devotion, and regular behaviour of the Indians, the zeal and charity of the miffionaries, their labours and patience in forming and attending on their parifhioners, under all the inconveniencies and hardfhips of that wild folitude; and laftly the great progrefs chriftianity had made in fo fhort a time. In a letter dated the 10th of February 1730, he has thefe expreffions. " The fever having by the goodnefs of God left me, I fet out to vifit the miffions, beginning with San Xavier to San Ignacio del Norte, which is the laft, and from hence about eighty leagues. The whole journey took me up forty eight days, the cold being feverer here than at Guapango in January. But I was well rewarded for all thefe fatigues, were it only in feeing the fervour of thefe new chriftian eftablifhments. And the leaft I could do was to fhed tears of joy at fo frequently hearing God praifed from the mouths of poor creatures, who very lately did not fo much as know whether there was any fuch Being." In the fame letter he gives a detail of the particulars he obferved in every miffion; their polity and the fatigues of the fathers.

Father Echeveria now prepared for vifiting the fouthern parts of California, where he was defirous of founding two new miffions among the Coras; but only that of San Jofeph del Cabo could then take place. Father Sigifmund Taraval appointed miffionary for the other, which had been projected under the name of Santa Rofa, in honour of the foundrefs not arriving till May 1730: befides the deaths of the fathers Piccoli and Ugarte; and the retreat of fathers Helen, Bravo & Napoli, occafioned by the ill ftate of their health, rendered it neceffary to employ the new labourers in fuch fettlements as were deftitute.

The intended miffion, near cape San Lucas, required a perfon of confummate virtue, intrepid zeal, great fagacity, and addrefs: fuch was father Nicholas Tamaral, founder of the miffion of La Puriffima Conception; and he fortunately was appointed for founding that of San Jofeph del Cabo. According he embarked the 10th of March, with the father vifitor, leaving directions that father Taraval, on his arrival, fhould immediately go and officiate at La Puriffima; and, having a fair wind, in nine days, they arrived in the bay of La Paz, where they were received with the moft cordial affection by father William Gordon, fucceffor to father Bravo, at El Pilar de la

Paz;

Paz; and with him they folemnly celebrated the feftival of the patriarch San Jofeph.

The tranquility and chriftian deportment of the Guaycuros of this miffion, before fo much dreaded, filled the fathers with the moft pleaf-ing fatisfaction. They next vifited the miffion of San Jago de los Coras, and from thence continued their journey to cape San Lucas, the fouthern extremity of California, in the neighbourhood of which they intended to found the new miffion of San Jofeph. At fome diftance from the cape, they found a verdant fpot, fhaded by the circumjacent mountains, and thro' it ran two rivulets, which joined each other a little before they difcharged them-felves into the fea, which is about a league from the fpot abovementioned; and on the fhore were feveral lakes, abounding with fifh, and furrounded with withered ftocks of palm-trees, the Indians having lopped off their branches. Near one of thefe frefh-water lakes, in a level fpot, a good foil, and defended from inundations, the fathers appointed for the feat of the miffion; and accordingly a chapel and houfe, covered with rufhes and fedge, of which the coaft afforded great plenty, were foon run up. The fathers, from the account given by the captain of the garrifon of the num-bers, and repeated defires of the Indians of having a father among them, expected that they would have flocked to them, but very few were seen; and, during the three weeks that the father visitor continued there, scarce twenty families came into the mission. With these, however, father Tamaral entered on his charge, instructing them in the doctrines of the christian religion. The Indians, on being asked whither the rest of their countrymen were retired, answered they all had died of an epidemia: but this was an equivocation, proceeding from their fear, for as soon as the father visitor, with his two soldiers attending him, were gone, and father Tamaral left with only two others, the Indians repaired to him by multitudes; and the reason for their not appearing sooner, was a persuasion, that the fathers were come with soldiers and armed men, to punish some disturbances and assaults on the missions of San Jago, and La Paz. Matters being thus accommodated, the father took a journey thro' the country, in search of the rancherias, and a more convenient spot for the seat of the mission; the first situation being infested with muskettos, and other troublesome insects, to an intolerable degree; it was also close and hot; the country damp, and water for the little arable ground very uncertain. These circumstances were sufficient to prevail on them to remove the mission

to

to another spot, 5 leagues from the sea, where a church and house were immediately built, as well as circumstances would permit; and afterwards, by incessant labours, several roving rancherias were assembled and distributed into two villages; where they were instructed with such success, that in one year only he baptized a thousand and thirty-six souls. He likewise attended to promote the temporal welfare of the mission, as being in some measure the foundation of its progress and security; but the death of this missionary has deprived us of the particular accounts of the following years.

S E C T. XVIII.

Survey of the islands of Dolores, by father Taraval. Account of others formed by the channel of Santa Barbara, in the South sea. Foundation of the mission of Santa Rosa, by that father. Insurrection of the Coras, for want of a garrison.

Two months after the fathers Echeveria and Tamaral had set out on the preceding expedition, father Sigismund Taraval, nominated for founding, among the Coras, the proposed mission of Santa Rosa, arrived in Loretto bay

in

in May 1730. This father was possessed of all the qualifications requisite for an enterprise of such difficulty. He was only in the 30th year of his age; but his mind was adorned with all the sciences and learning, requisite to the discharge of his function. He was born at Todi, in the Milanese, being the son of don Miguel de Taraval by donna Teresa de Andrade. His father had served with the greatest reputation in the army, where he died of his wounds, in quality of lieutenant general, to which his merit had raised him. His son, at eighteen years of age, took the habit of the order in the college of Ocana, where he was a boarder. He went thro' his noviciate at Madrid, and having afterwards happily distinguished himself in the sublimer sciences, in the college of Alcala de Henarez, under father Alexandro Laguna, he was sent to finish his studies at Mexico, where his distinguished talents procured him to be appointed founder of a new mission in California. The father provincial Juan Antonio de Oviedo also recommended to him the collecting of materials, for a history of the whole mission, from its beginning; and to his attention and judgment, most of the particulars in this narrative are owing.

This year the mission of Santa Rosa could not well be undertaken. Father Taraval, according

cording to the orders left at Loretto, by the father vifitor Echeveria, going to the miffion of La Puriffima to officiate, during the abfence of father Taramal, who undertook to furvey the iflands lying near the coaft.

He fet out, accompanied with fome Indians, on the feftival of San Xavier, and after travelling fix days came to a point of land, or cape on the coaft of Anawa, where a vaft bay, many leagues in breadth, begins, and to which he gave the name of San Xavier. From this place they difcerned two iflands, fix or feven leagues from the coaft; and having made a raft of timber, which they formed near the fhore, they went over to the firft ifland, by the natives called Afegua, i. e. the bird ifland. This is very fmall; not above hal a mile in length, and lefs in breadth, without a fingle inhabitant, being abfolutely deftitute both of verdure and frefh water. Prodigious flight of birds frequent it, and from thence it derives its name. Among thefe, befides the known fpecies, are two remarkable; one fomething bigger than a fparrow, but quite black; they live all day in the fea, and at night repair to the land, where they have nefts, which they make, by digging burrows in the ground, like rabbits; but being only four feet deep, they are eafily caught. The other is of the bignefs

of

of a goose, with black wings, a white breast and claws, and a beak resembling those of the birds of prey. These, like the former, make their nests in the ground, but three or four yards below the surface, and never visit them but in a calm, living day and night in the sea, while the rough weather lasts. The Indians of the coast, and those of the neighbouring islands, often come hither to catch these birds.

The other island, in the country language, is called Amalgua, i. e. fog island: and lies about 4 or 5 leagues from the former. They walked over this island also; and found it to be nearly triangular: the distance from the western to the northern point, is two days journey, and one a-cross it, in the narrowest part. In the middle of it is a conical mountain, of a considerable height; it has fresh water-springs; and in three little bays are several pits, dug by the Indians; but the anchoring-places are narrow, and without any shelter from the sea, which on these coasts runs very high. It also affords some deer, tho' smaller than those of California, but the hair longer and closer: likewise rabbits; and among these a black kind, very small, but their fur softer than that of a beaver, numbers of which are found here, and, many of them killed by the Indians. This island is also much frequented by sea-wolves, of different kinds ; likewife a great variety of birds. On thefe the Indians live ; and, inftead of bread, they ufe the mefcales, which are here much more juicy than the manfos of California. Along the fhore are found, among other fhells, fome of the azure kind, of a moft exquifite beauty. In this fea likewife are feen whales, which the Indians often kill with harpoons.

From the high mountain in the ifland, you have a view of two other fmall iflands lying to the weftward, at the diftance of 8 or 10 leagues. There are alfo in the large bay of San Xavier, three other fmall iflands, the haunts only of fea-wolves and beavers. To all thefe iflands, the father gave the name of Los Dolores. Further to the northward, they faw other large iflands, which appear to be three days failing beyond the bay. It was believed, that thofe were the iflands which formed the channel of Santa Barbara, and that the firft of them was furveyed by captain Vifcaino, and called Santa Catalina ; but thefe iflands lay at fuch a diftance, that it was impoffible to count their number, or defcribe their fituation.

The inhabitants of Amalgua know nothing of thefe iflands, the old forcerers ftrictly prohibiting, not only an intercourfe with their inhabitants, but even their looking towards them. The few inhabitants

they

they found, were eafily perfuaded to come to San Ignacio, in order to be inftructed in the chriftian religion. The only one that oppofed it was a forcerer; and they were for leaving him alone on the ifland, his very wife intending to go with the reft. But feeing them all preparing to depart, his obftinacy abated, and he at laft confented to make one of the company. Foul weather obliged them to put in at the defert ifland of Afegua, where they were obliged to ftay feveral days; but on the return of fair weather, they made for the continent, meeting only with one misfortune, which happened in the following manner. As they were coafting along the fhore, they faw on the fand banks, a great number of fea-wolves; and the Indian forcerer, who was continually betraying his difcontent, relying on his dexterity, leaped into the water, and fwam towards the banks, in order to kill a wolf, but they all retired at his approach. The Indian, on this, endeavoured to return to the bark, but as he was fwimming back, a fhark, in fight of the whole company, feized him: however, by an extraordinary activity, natural to thefe people, he cleared himfelf, tho' wounded, and threw blood at the fhark, by way of fport; but the voracious fifh feized him a fecond time, with infuperable violence, and at once darted down with him to the bottom; his companions, tho' very much affected, not being able to help him.

No mention is made of these small islands, comprehended under the new name of Los Dolores, in the narrative of capt. Sebastian Viscaino's voyage; either because his squadron had no sight of them, possibly, passing by them in the night; or, in his course from the harbour of San Diego, to the new bay, lately called San Xavier, he kept at too great a distance from the coast. Opposite to this bay, the captain, in his passage to Puerto de Monte Rey, had a view of the island, which he called Santa Cathalina; and the others which formed the channel of Santa Barbara. Of these islands, all the account and information which father Taraval could get, was only a distant view, which he took of it from the mountain in the island of Amalgua. For neither its inhabitants, nor those of cape San Xavier, have any intercourse with the inhabitants of this island, nor with those of the continent, on the other side of the bay. We have already seen, part I. sect. VII. how different father Taraval's accounts of the belief, religion, and rites of the islanders of Amalgua, are from those in captain Viscaino's relation, in the same particulars, among the islanders of Santa Cathalina.

It

It would indeed be very proper to take a more accurate survey of those islands, which were seen by captain Viscaino, and likewise of the coasts of the continent, as far as the Sierra de Santa Lucia, which the Philippine ships have sight of; for he found the people very tractable, tho he was not able to stay with them. But however desirable such a survey may be, it has hitherto been found impossible to be taken, on account of the great distance betwixt the mission of San Ignacio, and the channel of Santa Barbara.

The time was now arrived for father Taraval, by order of father Clement Guillen, the new visitor, to found the mission of Santa Rosa, his first destination in the bay of Palmas, near the cape of California; and like the mission of San Joseph of cape San Lucas, inhabited by the Coras. This mission was necessary as the Coras of those parts could not be superintended from the mission of San Jago tho' the nearest, both as the greatest part of this mission were Guaycuros, but chiefly as the savage, turbulent, and deceitful humour of these Indians required a greater number of missionaries; and their continual presence at their residences, in order to secure the reduction of them, and prevent rebellions : for which however such prudent measures did not prove sufficient. Ac-

cord-

cordingly, every thing neceffary for the new foundation being provided at Loretto, father Sigifmund went to the bay of La Paz; and thence to the miffion of St. Jago at Palmas bay; near which his new miffion was begun on the fpot, where, fome years before, father Napoli had laid the foundation of that of St. Jago. The Indians of this coaft he found civilized beyond expectation, which was partly owing to the diligence of father Napoli, and partly to fome vifits which the fathers Carranco and Tamaral had paid them from their miffions. But fome of the Indians who were wedded to their beaftly manner of living, made fuch oppofitions to his meafures, that it would have been highly imprudent to have difmiffed the three foldiers that attended him. His affiduity and addrefs were however fo remarkable, that before the conclufion of the year, he had baptized the greater part of the gentiles within his diftrict, of every age: and to their affection and fidelity he owed his life in the general revolt of the nation. There had appeared fome intimations of this revolt in the two miffions of St. Jago and San Jofeph, in the fame year 1733, and beginning of 1734. The Indian governor of San Jago, by the Indians called Boton, who had been promoted to that poft, becaufe of his intereft with his countrymen, on

account

account of his superior capacity, and as born of a Mulatto and an Indian.

It was also thought that by laying an obligation on him to behave as became a christian, he would abhor his way of living; but in this they were mistaken, for he returned to his former excesses; and as private exhortations were of no consequence, it was necessary to give him a publick reprimand. This also had no effect; so that father Carranco thought it necessary to depose him and chastise him publickly. This instead of bringing him to a sense of his guilt, filled him with such rancour, that he frequently attempted to spirit up the new christians to kill the father; and being joined by some discontented Indians, he would certainly have succeeded, had not the father, on timely advice of his intention, been on his guard. This seduction, however threw the whole mission into a flame. And the cessation of these disturbances was principally owing to his departure to the rancherias of San Joseph del Cabo, which were still gentiles: the chief of one of these was a Mulatto named Chicori; who lived in an abandoned manner, with a great number of wives. Among these was a young woman, who, on coming to the mission, was instructed by father Tamaral: and after she became a christian, was robbed, and forcibly

carried

carried away by the Mulatto to Yeneca, the
name of the rancheria, But the father to a-
void ftill greater evils, winked at this enormity
for fome time; but having at laft an opportunity of going to Yeneca, he mildly complained
to the Mulatto of the robbery. The other
haughtily anfwered that fhe was his wife, and
therefore he had a right to bring her away : the
father replied that if fhe had been his only one
he would not have detained her in the miffion,
nor proceeded to baptize her fo foon ; but that
having many others, it was unjuft to force the
young woman back. He proceeded to exhort
him alfo to become a chriftian, and painted the
turpitude of that floth and debauchery in which
he lived, in the moft glaring colours. In fhort
the father tried every method to induce him
to embrace the chriftian faith; but the Indian
grew more obdurate ; and fearing to be forfaken
by others of his wives, he determined to murder
the father the firft opportunity, and ftir up the
Californians to deftroy all miffionaries.

Such were the fentiments of the Mulatto
Chicori, when the perverfe Boton, with no better defign, came to his rancheria, having left
the Indians of the miffion of San Jago in a
great ferment. The plots of both being unknown to the miffionaries, father Tamaral came
without the leaft apprehenfion from cape San
Lucas

Lucas to affift father Carranco in quieting the difturbances of the miffion, which, by the abfence of the incendiary Boton, was not attended with any great difficulty; fo that by the good management and prudent conduct of the two fathers, all animofities ceafed, the Indians returned to their former obedience, and tranquillity was again reftored. Things being thus happily fettled, father Tamaral was defirous of returning to his miffion of San Jofeph; but fome faithful Indians of San Jago advifed him to defer his journey, for Boton and Chicori were waiting for him in certain parts with two bodies of men. The difagreeable news was confirmed by fome Indians, whom the fathers fent privately to reconnoitre thefe places. This account being confirmed, father Tamaral fent meffages by other roads to his chriftians and catechumens of San Jofeph, that they fhould immediately arm and march in queft of the enemy, who, on feeing fuch numbers coming armed, hid themfelves; fo that father Tamaral's faithful parifhioners finding no body to oppofe him, burnt their arbours, after taking what wretched plunder they found in them. After this expedition father Tamaral, efcorted by his Indians, of whom many were ftill gentiles, returned to his miffion of cape San Lucas, without meeting with the leaft difturbance from

the

the seditious Californians : and the two heads of the conspiracy, seeing their followers extremely diminished, thought proper on the miscarriage of their design, left both missions should fall on them, to make their submission.

Accordingly, they begged for peace, and promised a suitable behaviour for the future. The fathers who laboured entirely for their conversion, readily consented. And in the beginning of the year 1734, a peace was concluded with great rejoicings. But this peace, which had at first all the appearance of being lasting, was of very short continuance.

This defection of the Californians and other smaller disturbances, with which the fathers saw themselves every day menaced, by the pride of the Indians, and the practices of those whom, on account of their brutish excesses, there was a necessity of correcting, arose chiefly from the want of an escorte of soldiers, and of a garrison in the bay de La Paz, or some other part betwixt it and cape San Lucas, to which recourse might have been had in case of necessity. The fathers had only one soldier for a guard ; and at the time of these tumults were without any ; the garrison consisting of so few, and the necessity of supplying other new missions on the frontiers of the gentiles, not permitting any to remain in these missions. The garrison of Loretto,

Loretto, which was above one hundred leagues from hence, could be of no service; besides to the factious, fickle, and treacherous difposition of the Pericues, such a check was much more neceffary than to the northern Indians. And this was the reafon which induced father Bravo to move the marquis de Valero the viceroy to form a new garrifon at La Paz, for fecuring the remaining part to the fouthward: and though at firft a refolution was accordingly taken, yet this falutary purpofe was defeated in the manner we have already mentioned.

SECT. XIX.

The Philippine galleon comes for the firft time to cape San Lucas. The fhips company are refrefhed, and the fick cured. The fathers Carranco and Tamaral fuffer martyrdom by the hands of the Pericues. Father Taraval efcapes. Four miffions deftroyed.

No fooner had the peace been concluded with the rebels than they openly confeffed their intention of maffacring all the miffionaries. And foon after, in the month of January 1734, fome Indians who had been fifhing off cape San Lucas, came running to the feat of the miffion

fion of San Jofeph, with news that a very large
fhip was come thither. The father fent other
Indians for a more particular account: but on
their arrival the fhip was under fail, tho' within fight. And foon after they faw her ftand
in and come to an anchor in San Bernabé
bay, where a party of men with fire arms came
afhore for water. A young man of Loretto who
had been fent by the father, went up and fpoke
with the feamen. From them he underftood
that the fhip he faw, was the Philippine galleon; and he informed them that there was a
new miffion erected in the neighbourhood; on
which the people fhewed a great deal of joy,
and went immediately to make a report of it to
don Geronimo Montero, captain of the galleon.
The fhip, at making the cape, had only water
for two days, the rains by which they are fupplied in their paffage from Manila to Acapu-
co having in a great meafure failed: and this
had obliged them to touch at the harbour joining to cape San Lucas; but finding it too fmall,
ftood into San Bernabé's bay. But their want of
water was not the only misfortune that obliged
them to put in here; a great many were down
with the fcurvy, the only remedy for which is
to be removed on fhore, and live upon pitahayas,
acid fruits, and frefh meat: which the Indians generally barter for other things. Father Tamaral
being

being made acquainted with thefe circumftances by his Indians, immediately went to the
fhore, ordering that the greateft part of the
cattle fhould be brought thither; and likewife
to gather as many pitahayas, and other wild
fruits and berries as could be found. After
taking thefe meafures, he fent his compliments to the captain, with an offer to affift his
people with whatever his poor miffion afforded;
acquainting him, at the fame time, with the
order he had given for the frefh meat and pitahayas for thofe who had the fcurvy; and
every thing was immediately fent aboard on its
coming to the fhore. The Indians, encouraged
by the father, helped the feamen in filling their
cafks with water; and all who came on fhore
partook of the father's welcome charity, which
was accompanied with the moft winning fweetnefs and courtefy. The captain, with the
whole fhip's company, formally returned their
thanks to the miffionary; and, in return for his
extraordinary kindnefs, fent him a prefent of
fome goods. This refrefhment was fo feafon-
able, that, of the great number of fcorbutick
patients, all recovered by the known remedy of
the pitahayas, frefh meat, and being afhore during
the time of watering. Three indeed were fo
far gone in the diftemper, that there was a neceffity of leaving them in California. Thefe

were

were don Jofeph Francifco de Baytos, captain of marines, don Antonio de Herrera,
boatfwain of the galleon, and the moft reve-
rend father, Domingo de Horbigofo, of the
order of San Auguftine, who was going to
Mexico, as prefident of the hofpital of Santo
Thomas de Villa Nueva, and agent general
in New Spain for his province of the Philippine iflands. Thefe three, on their coming
afhore, were in fo deplorable a condition, that,
notwithftanding the poverty of the miffion, they
determined to continue there, committing themfelves to the charity of father Tamaral; to
whom the captain in a letter recommended
them all; and the father commiffary Mathias
de Ibarra, in a particular manner, father Horbigofo of the fame order. The captain alfo
wrote to father Tamaral, that as a miffion was
now founded, near cape San Lucas, and the
Indians converted to the catholick faith, the
Philippine fhips, for the future, would always
put in there, as he would procure orders for
that purpofe from the government, having
fo recently experienced the neceffity of touching
at that port, the only one in the whole paffage
from Manila to Acapulco, both for watering,
the recovery of the fick, and refrefhment of
the healthy; defiring that there might, in the
following years, be a greater quantity of
cattle

cattle and provisions kept in readiness for those purposes. This the father promised should be carefully observed; and the watering being completed, the galleon sailed from San Bernabé bay with a fair wind.

The three patients who remained under the care of father Tamaral, found every thing they could desire for their cure and relief. The most tender mother could not exert herself more for a favourite son, than the father did for his three patients. He not only expended his own store, but sent to request of the fathers of the other missions in the neighbourhood, that they would spare him the best of their provisions for the relief of these three distressed strangers. He spent the days and nights at the seat of his mission; and by his skill and diligence all three recovered from that dangerous distemper. But don Antonio de Herrera was seized with another distemper, which, being augmented by the scurvy, proved mortal. The father buried him in his church, with all the decency the place would admit of, and proceeded to take an inventory before captain Baytos, and father Horbigofo, in order to deliver them, that they might execute his will in New Spain. Such was the noble temper of this father, that they could not prevail upon him to accept of the least gratuity for his

care of the deceased, tho' it was his express
will. Thus he will for ever remain a remarkable instance of disinterestedness, which in
America is still more singular and admirable,
the fatal thirst of riches being there more vehement, that absurd passion, which renders
men incapable of enjoying their present possessions, or of ceasing from the laborious pur-
suits, after that which they never will know
how to enjoy.

Father Horbigoso, charmed with such benevolence and disinterestedness, has perpetuated it
by the very honourable mention he makes of the
father in his account of the galleon's voyage.
He wrote it at the mission of San Joseph : but
it overflows with such affectionate gratitude and
sublime encomiums on the society and father
Tamaral, that modesty will not allow me to insert
it here. It is sufficient for the reputation of
the father to copy the latter part of his panegy-
rick : " therefore the Philippines have just
cause to be thankful for having guided them
to this city of refuge, and its so benevolent and
disinterested a ruler, by whom all their wants
were liberally supplied. And it would be very
proper that a vessel built in the same manner
as those for making signals, should be sent hither, both for the greater dispatch in watering
and supplying the galleon, and for the more
speedy

fpeedy conveyance of fuch paffengers as are fent
afhore fick and afterwards recover, to the harbour of La Paz, and from thence over to the
oppofite fide: for otherwife I am of opinion
that thefe fervices, tho' of the greateft importance, will be attended with prodigious difficulties and delays, there being no timber for
building fuch a veffel."

This was the firft time fince the beginning
of the reduction of California by father Salva-
Tierra, that the Philippine fhip had touched
there. Father Tamaral, whom the viceroy, the
marquis de Valero had fo ftrictly charged to
go in queft of a proper port, and who accordingly in his miffion of La Puriffima had without any fuccefs ufed the endeavours which we
have already related, had now the pleafure of
feeing the faid fhip come to his miffion, and of
refrefhing the feamen and paffengers in the manner above mentioned.

Don Geronymo Montero, on his arrival at
Mexico, made a report of his voyage to the
viceroy: and tho' orders were given that the
fhips in the fucceeding years, fhould make ufe
of fo commodious a port, there being no other
all along the northern coaft of the South fea;
yet this account was not generally approved of
in New Spain, by thofe, who, through private
intereft, looked with a jealous eye on the trade

to the Philippine iflands; and on every meafure which tended to its conveniency and increafe; and likewife by others who alfo from felfifh motives oppofed the miffions of California. The warm difputes then on foot relating to the tonnage and cargo of the galleon in her voyage out and home, diverted the thoughts of many from the more exalted confiderations of the common good; the great conveniency of the harbour had been proved from experience in the late voyage: it feemed proper to fecure it; and with it the miffions and miffionaries in the fouth of California; by erecting the new garrifon according to his majefty's exprefs orders. This was now earneftly folicited at Mexico: and this favourable juncture feemed to promife a happy iffue; but petitions fo well founded had no effect; and the miffionaries and miffions remained expofed and undefended as before.

At Manila, indeed, it was ordered that the galleon fhould touch at cape San Lucas, which fhe did the following year, as we fhall mention in its proper place: for captain Montero returning to Manila before the fhip failed, this article was added to his inftructions.

In the mean time father Horbigofo and captain Baytos, were by the care of father Tamaral entirely recovered: and on advice of this, a veffel came from La Paz to cape San Lucas,

in

in order to carry them to La Paz bay; whence in April they proceeded in a bark to Matanchel, and from thence to Mexico. The fathers continued their labours with the indocible favages of the fouth; father Tamaral in St. Jofeph; father Carranco in St. Jago; father Taraval in Santa Rofa; father Clemente Guillen appointed vifitor and fuperior of Dolores; and father Gordon at el Pilar de la Paz. The latter in the fummer of the fame year 1734, was obliged to go to Loretto, to haften the fupplies for his miffion and the others in the fouth, leaving it to the care of his fafe-guard don Manuel Andres Romero. The chriftian Indians and catechumens to appearance behaved very quietly, excepting fome fmall ferments which were eafily allayed; and there feemed no reafon to apprehend any thing from the gentiles: but under the afhes of this apparent tranquility, the fire of a general rebellion was gathering head; and in the autumn of the fame year it burft out to the total deftruction of four miffions, and the imminent danger of all.

This dreadful rebellion, as appeared afterwards, did not arife from any particular motive or irritating accident; the origin of the rancour of the Indians againft the fathers, being no other than their averfion to the new doctrine, which deprived them of their plurality of wives,

and

and required them to live in a regularity and decency incompatible with their brutish licentiousness. This afterwards sufficiently appeared; and the principal incendiaries owned it. The destructive plot was first formed in the rancherias towards the south coast betwixt St. Jago and St. Joseph, by the insidious suggestions of Boton and Chicori, who either were never sincerely reconciled, or soon reassumed their former hatred and malignancy against the fathers. And that they might not be disturbed in their excesses by new reprimands, they resolved at once to shake off the yoke of the missionaries. The conspiracy, with singular dissimulation and secrecy, spread itself among several rancherias of all the five southern missions: and the mutinous party increased every where, without the missionaries having the least suspicion of it. When they thought themselves sufficiently strong, being joined by many new converts, who however came to the exercises and meals at the missions, they consulted on putting their design in execution. All they feared was the soldiers, on account of their firearms; tho' the number of these was very small, father Taraval having at Santa Rosa, though a mission newly founded, but three; at La Paz there was only one; at St Jago, two invalid Mestizos of New Spain supplied the place of

soldiers;

foldiers; and St. Jofeph del Cabo was without any. This obftacle they endeavoured to remove by ftratagem; and in the beginning of September, meeting with one of the foldiers which accompanied father Taraval, they came on him unawares and murdered him. Some of them went to the father, telling him that there was a foldier fuddenly taken ill in the wood; and defired that he would come to confefs him, or fend fome foldier to bring him: but befides the oddnefs of the meffage, they betrayed fuch a confufion, that the father, who had received fome vague intelligence of the confpiracy, knew what they had done, and by queftioning them clofe, came to difcover, that there actually was a defign on foot for murdering the father and the foldiers by dividing their ftrength, and drawing him afide from his Indians. For this reafon he declined going or fending a fecond foldier; and foon after the murder of the former reached his ears. Within fome days they killed at La Paz don Manuel Andres Romero; and the fact for fome days remained a fecret. Thefe fucceffes increafed the infolence of the confpirators, fo that now the rebellion became more vifible, efpecially in the territory of St. Jago; yet the miffionaries did not confider it as any thing more than what was ufual in new miffions.

About

About this time a foldier of Loretto came to
the miffion of St. Jofeph del Cabo, as a fafe-
guard to father Tamaral, and likewife to bleed
and affift him, the wants and labours of the
miffionary having brought on him a dangerous
difeafe. The foldier had obferved fome figns of
rebellion in the territory of St. Jago; and faw
them confirmed by others in that of St. Jofeph.
He acquainted father Tamaral of this : and re-
folutely told him that the danger was too great
to ftay there any longer, and that he would
take upon him to carry him fafe to La Paz.
The father full of that intrepidity common to
a native of Seville, endeavoured to remove the
foldier's apprehenfions, but he anfwered that he
would not ftay there to perifh; and as he could
not bring the father into his meafures, he left
him to himfelf, and made the beft of his way
to La Paz; and when within a proper diftance of
that place he difcharged his piece as the ufual
fignal, but no anfwer was made : on this he
walked up to the houfe and called aloud to the
foldier, but ftill there was no anfwer, nor could he
fee any Indian of whom to enquire : but on
going into the houfe he faw fome traces of
blood, the portmanteau empty, and fome fragments of utenfils and furniture fcattered up and
down the floor. Judging from thefe evident
figns that Romero the foldier had been murdered,

dered, he immediately fled to the miſſion of Dolores which was above ſixty leagues diſtant.

Here he acquainted the ſuperior father Guillen of the diſaſter he had ſeen, and of the danger of the other miſſionaries. The father was not entirely unapprized of this, ſome rancherias of his miſſion having been diſturbed by a gang of the conſpirators, who forcibly carried off ſeveral Indians. But on the intelligence of the ſoldier, he diſpatched meſſengers to the three fathers, that they ſhould withdraw to Dolores. Soon after letters were brought him from father Carranco informing him, that a certain diſcovery had been made of a plot breaking out among the Pericues, and deſired his orders. Father Guillen ſent away freſh letters, that they ſhould all go to La Paz, whither he ſent a canoe with ſeventeen Indians of known fidelity ; but neither of the letters came to hand, the conſpirators having poſſeſſed themſelves of all the paſſes ; and even had thoſe orders reached them, probably it would have been too late. At the ſame time father Carranco ſent a body of chriſtians in all appearance very faithful, to father Tamaral at the miſſion of St. Joſeph, adviſing him of the commotions and evident ſigns of a general plot, entreating him that, being alone, and without a ſafeguard, he would come to his miſſion, where they

K 4 might

might confult on the beft meafures to be taken
in fuch a critical juncture. Father Tamaral fent
him for anfwer, that in his miffion no fuch
figns had appeared; that he looked on thofe
apprehenfions to be partly owing to the timidity of thofe who brought fuch information;
and partly to the wiles of the common enemy
for difturbing them and impeding the labours
of the miffions; that he trufted in God whom
he defired to ferve both in life and death;
but did not think himfelf worthy of martyrdom, nor in fuch dangerous circumftances as would juftify his abandoning his miffion, efpecially as in the former difturbances
his people had given evident proofs of their
fidelity. This letter was afterwards found
among the broken remnants of father Carranco's effects. Father Tamaral thus remained
alone in his miffion, having difmiffed the Indians fent from St. Jago. Thefe on their return from the miffion of St. Jofeph fell in
with fome parties of the rebels, who afked them
from whence and from whom they came.
They anfwered that they had gone by father
Carranco's direction to father Tamaral in order to
bring him to St. Jago: for the father, added
they, already knows of your defigns to kill
them: the boy in his houfe who tells him
every thing, gave him notice of it. The intention

tention of the rebels was firſt to murder father Tamaral, as quite defencelefs; and then to proceed to the other miſſions: hoping to extirpate the fathers out of the peninſula. But hearing that father Carranco was acquainted with their deſign, they altered their meaſures; and went to diſpatch him firſt, that he might not eſcape, or ſend for any ſoldiers. This they openly mentioned to the chriſtians of St. Jago, who, after a few ſolicitations mixed with threatenings, contrary to the fidelity they owed to God and the father, joined the rebels, directing their courſe to St. Jago in order to take away the life of their beſt benefactor.

They came to the ſeat of the miſſion on Friday the firſt of October, betwixt ſix and ſeven in the morning, when father Lorenzo Carranco had juſt concluded maſs, and was retired to other devotional offices in his chamber. Their firſt queſtion was, whether the two Meſtizos, the father's guards, were in the village: and were informed that a little before, they went out to fetch two beaſts for the ordinary expence of the miſſions, the catechumens, children, old men, &c. Neverthelefs the foreign conſpirators fearing the father, tho' alone, kept at a diſtance from the houſe, whilſt ſome of their meſſengers who were inhabitants of the miſſion, went in under pretence

tence of making a report of their proceedings.
The father who was then on his knees, at their
coming in, arose and received them very affec-
tionately. He expressed his wonder that father
Tamaral was not come with them, and asked
if they brought no letter: they said yes; and
gave it to him. Upon which he began to read
it; but when he was most absorbed in attention,
the whole body of conspirators rushed suddenly
into the house, and two of them falling on the
father, seized him and dragged him out between
the house and the church, where those two held
him by his gown, while the others stabbed him
with arrows: the father in the mean time
sending up fervent ejaculations to heaven, and
offering to God for his own faults, and those
of his Indians, the pure sacrifice of his life.
The cowardly wretches, when they saw there
was nothing to fear, finished their bloody purpose with sticks and stones. In the mean time
one of them happening to cast his eye towards
the house, and seeing in it the little Indian boy
who waited on the father, crying bitterly for the
cruel usage of his dear master, said to him, what
do you cry for? now go and tell the father
what is doing in the rancherias. Another added; since he loved the father, it is reasonable he
should go and keep him company. Then taking him by the feet, they dashed his head against
the

the walls of the house, and the floor, and when he was dead, threw him to the place where the others were stoning and beating the cold body of the venerable Carranco.

The noise of these violent proceedings brought together the Indians of both sexes and all ages : and though some were displeased with such inhumanity, they could not with safety interpose, especially as among the murderers, they observed some of the principal of the mission, who, as such, had been pitched upon for escorting father Tamaral from St. Joseph. Here the giddy disposition of the Indians was such, that they, who in the morning had joined in devotions with the father, now shared all the rancour and fury of the others against him : and thus whilst some heaped wood together for burning him, others dragged towards the pile his bloody and disfigured body, in which still remained some signs of life. Here they stripped him not so much for the sake of his cloaths, as by their execrable insults to revenge the freedom with which he had reproved their beastialities. The several shocking enormities they practised on his breathless corps, together with their abominable scurrilities before they committed it to the flames, are best passed over in silence ! only observing that their barbarity and brutal insults evidently shewed, that the great

object

object of their rage and malignity was the doctrine newly introduced by the father; especially as it required chastity and moderation. Thus amidst shouts, outrages, and execrations, the bodies of Lorenzo Carranco and his little servant were thrown into the fire. After which they proceeded to pillage the house and church, keeping the cloaths and such furniture as could be of use, the rest they burnt: crucifixes, pictures, statues of saints, the altar, chalice, missal, and other sacred things were thrown into the fire, as a sure sign of their hatred of religion. The bodies and furniture of the church were burning amidst the wild exultations of the Indians, when the two domesticks of the father came in sight, bringing with them the two beasts which they had gone out to fetch, but with no other arms than their knives. The Indians immediately getting about them bid them alight and kill the beasts, tho' this was more than they durst do, there was no time for objections: but they had no sooner performed this office than the Indians let fly at them a shower of arrows, and while they continued in the agonies of death, threw them into the same fire.

After perpetrating these cruelties at St. Jago, the murderers went to the mission of St. Joseph del Cabo de San Lucas. But were now accompanied by a much greater number of
people

The Martyrdom of Father Tamaral.

people than at St. Jago, the affault there being before the time appointed ; whereas now, befides thofe who joined them at St. Jago, which was the far greater number of the miffion, others flocked to them from all parts. This infernal company came to the father's houfe at eight in the morning on Sunday the third of October, being the feftival of the rofary of our lady. He was fitting quietly in his appartment without any apprehenfion of fuch violent defigns, when a party of the feditious Californians, confifting of the very Indians of his miffion broke in upon him, all calling out for fomething, that if he denied them, they might have an occafion of quarreling with him. The father from their diforder, and feeing them all armed, immediately knew their execrable intentions. However he mildly anfwered, " ftay children ; there is enough in the houfe to content you all." Seeing themfelves difappointed of their pretence for refentment, without ftaying to contrive any further artifice, the Indians, who at St. Jago had firft laid hands on father Carranco, now knocked down father Tamaral; then dragged him by the feet out of his houfe, where fome arrows were fhot at him ; but all coming up they thought it better to cut his throat with one of the knives which he himfelf ufed to diftribute to them for their neceffities.

fities. Thus, they who a little before had not courage to kill two harmlefs beafts, now, inflamed by the fanguinary fpirit of cruelty, murdered their paftor, who, by innumerable benefits, endeavoured to bring them to a life of purity; when dying, he recommended himfelf and his flock to the good fhepherd of the human race, whofe name he continued invoking with his laft breath. This cruel action was followed by thofe abominable infults on his body, which they had practifed at St. Jago: but at St. Jofeph the feftivity was greater and lafted longer; for here were prefent multitudes of people of all ages: and befides, being now free from any apprehenfions of the two fathers, they could celebrate their villainies in all the brutifh licentioufnefs, with which in the time of their infidelity they ufed to folemnize their victories.

To this delay however was owing the life of father Sigifmund Taraval, miffionary of Santa Rofa now affifting at the village of Todos Santos. At the time they were killing and burning father Carranco and his boy, a lad of this village happened to be at St. Jago, and on feeing what paffed returned to Todos Santos, whilft the rebels went to St. Jofeph. At this place the boy gave an account of all he had feen to an honeft old man, who immediately

taking

taking the boy with him, found out father Taraval; and having made him tell the story, added, " take care, father, for they'll be presently here to kill you; it is out of our power to defend you: but if you are willing, we will carry you over to that island where you'll be safe." Soon after came some other Indians from Santa Rosa, who had been present at the death of father Tamaral at St. Joseph: and had hastened to acquaint their missionary, that they had already sent messengers to their adherents at La Paz, who had murdered Romero the soldier, that they should proceed to dispatch father Taraval and his servant. This message was owing to the cowardice of the insurgents, who, from the dread of the fire arms, were desirous of leaving the assault to others. On this father Taraval, thought it his duty to make provision for saving his own life, and that of his guards: accordingly, he took the furniture of the altar, and on the night of the 4th of October, retired to La Paz bay unperceived by the enemy; and taking also from thence the ornaments and confecrated utensils of that mission, he went on board the boat which the father visitor Guillen had sent pursuant to the intelligence he received from father Carranco, and in it he sailed to the island del Spiritu Santo; where soon after another boat arrived with men

and

and provisions from Loretto: and with these
succours father Taraval was enabled to set out
immediately for the mission of Dolores, for
preventing their intentions against this settle-
ment; and at the same time to concert measures
for restoring tranquility to the missions in the
southern parts. The weather proving fine, father
Taraval with all his company happily arrived
at Dolores, where he found father Guillen over-
whelmed with grief at these shocking cruelties.
He had heard only of the death of father Carranco; but his grief knew no bounds when he
was informed of the murder of father Tamaral
and the utter ruin of all the four missions of St.
Jago, St. Joseph, Santa Rosa and el Pilar de la
Paz. Their discourses chiefly related to the most
proper measures to be taken in this dismal
state of affairs: but during these conferences the
Pericues and Coras had posted from St. Joseph
del Cabo to the village of Todos Santos in quest
of father Taraval, as those of La Paz had not
engaged in the rebellion. But on hearing that
he had made his escape, they turned their rage
against the neighbouring Indians, and falling
on them unawares, killed twenty seven christians, the rest escaping by flight. These violences were succeeded by quarrels among themselves, which broke out into petty wars, the
ranche-

rancherias attacking each other with all the treachery and fury, practised before their conversion to christianity.

SECT. XX.

All the missionaries, from a mistrust of the northern Indians, retire to Loretto. A remarkable instance of fidelity of the Yaquis. Measures taken by the fathers for pacifying the southern Indians. Misfortune which attended the Philippine galleon. The governor of Cinaloa goes to CALIFORNIA. Death of father Julian de Mayorga. The Pericues are quieted, and a new garrison settled at San Lucas.

On the first advice of these shocking transactions, father Guillen, as superior of California, wrote to the other superiors of the society, and likewise to the viceroy don Juan Antonio Bizarron ; that the ruin which threatened the other missions, if the northern Indians should follow the example of the southern, might be prevented; measures taken to supply the damages already sustained, and a stop put to the ravages of the rebel Pericues. But his excellency did not think that the infurrection of the Indians, the murder of the miffionaries and foldiers, the ruin of the four miffions, and the imminent danger of the other fettlements foldiers and miffionaries, were fufficient to warrant any extraordinary expences in behalf of California. And on the 8th of December of the fame year 1734, he fent for anfwer to the father vifitor Guillen, " That, fenfible of the dangers to which thofe miffions were expofed, and of their great importance to religion and the king, he would with pleafure concur with the fathers in any report or account they fhould judge convenient, and would ufe his utmoft intereft with his majefty, that all thofe meafures might be purfued which tended to promote fuch ufeful undertakings: adding, that if he could obtain a warrant from his majefty, he would endeavour to execute it in its full extent." The good difpofitions which appeared in this letter, afforded no manner of relief in the prefent exigency. In the mean time the rebellion increafed, and fome figns of difturbances broke out in the territory of the miffion of Dolores. The captain on the firft account repaired thither with fome foldiers from the fouthern miffions, where he found father Taraval, by whom he was informed of the above mentioned difafters, the ruin of the miffions,

fions, and the infolence of the Indians. As it was not prudent to venture a handful of men againft fuch numbers flufhed with fuccefs, efpecially as the Californians were fo little to be relied on, he thought proper to ftop at the miffion of Dolores, to keep the Indians of that diftrict in order, and there face the rebels in order to cut off their communication with other nations, that the fire might not fpread among the northern miffions, till the affiftance they vainly expected, fhould arrive from the government of Mexico.

But by degrees the knowledge of what had paffed in the fouth, reached the furtheft extent of the conquefts; and the news paffing from one rancheria to another, though of different languages, the Indians of San Ignacio underftood what had happened at cape San Lucas, though at the diftance of above two hundred leagues. This inflamed the vicious paffions of many, who, difgufted at the new manner of living, fecretly fpread malicious reports againft the fathers, who had abolifhed their old cuftoms: adding, that if the Indians of the fouth had been able to deftroy them, they, as more numerous and a braver people, fhould find it an eafy tafk to do the like. Thefe feditious murmurs were likewife heard in other miffions; and though they did not infect the principal Indians, who

on

on the contrary faithfully gave notice to the missionaries of what was intended; but, at the same time desired that a large guard might be sent them against any emergency, their soldiers being very much dispirited. They were indeed greatly intimidated by their comerades being killed by the Pericues, and the opinion that prevailed at Loretto, that the whole nation of California was going to rise. And the father visitor Guillen, not being able to assist them with a sufficient guard, wrote in the beginning of the year 1735, to all the missionaries requiring them by virtue of his authority, to quit the missions and all repair to Loretto; that by the protection of the garrison they might save their lives. Their compliance with this order was at first not perceived by the Indians, as they successively withdrew according to the time of receiving the letters. It must be acknowledged that this command of the superior saved the lives of the missionaries: for the flame of rebellion spread with such rapidity among those unthinking barbarians, tho' of better intellects and dispositions than the Pericues, that had not the removal been made so very seasonably, all California would probably have been lost for ever.

The missionaries being now retired to Loretto, and the missions of the north forsaken,

father

father Guillen again fent an account to Mexico of the terrible condition of the miffions of California; and the imminent danger which on all fides furrounded them at the fame time. Father Bravo, the miffionary of Loretto, fent the bark to the river Yaqui with letters to the governour and miffionary jefuits, acquainting them with the general danger, and defiring that they would immediately fend fixty Indian warriors, and fome exercifed perfons with fire-arms, in order to protect their lives, as they were abfolutely unable to quell the Indians, fhould the nations of the north, the middle parts, and the fouth, join in a league. Thefe advices arrived at Mexico on the 13th of April the fame year: and though the provincial of New Spain immediately delivered the letters to the viceroy, and in two memorials urged him to take fuitable meafures on fo important a juncture, nothing was done. This obliged him to have recourfe to his majefty, fending letters to Europe by a fhip then juft ready to fail. Accordingly, father Gafper Rodero formerly provincial of Mexico, and at that time agent general at court for the Indian provinces, laid the affair before his majefty. But the affiftance which might be naturally expected from civilized people, providence provided among favages, who had very lately been gentiles. The Yaqui na-

tion

tion who had always given the nobleft proofs
of their fidelity, maintained their character in
this juncture.   For no fooner was the report
fpread in their country than above five hundred
warriors came down armed from their villages
to the river, in order to embark for the relief of California.   But as the bilander was too
fmall to carry fo many, they picked out among
themfelves fixty, and the others, that they might
not be without fome fhare in the enterprife,
gave them their bows and arrows for arming
the faithful Indians of the peninfula.   The bilander immediately failed, and landed them near
Loretto, and from thence they marched to Dolores, where they found the captain of the garrifon : for at their arrival the tranquillity of the
north, had been reftored by a remarkable action of thofe new chriftians.

As foon as the leading men among them
were informed that the fathers with the inter-
preters and foldiers were miffing, and had carried away with them the ornaments and furni-
tures of the churches, they were fenfible of the
caufe of their retreat : and being greatly affected with it, agreed by reciprocal meffages to
meet and repair to Loretto. Accordingly they
fet out, fome of them carrying on their fhoulders the croffes of the miffions of San Ignacio, Nueftra Sennora de Guadalupe, and Santa
Rofalia :

Rofalia: and thus in a regular proceffion entered the garrifon, intreating the fathers with floods of tears, that as they had baptized and inftructed them in the chriftian religion, they would not now leave them to perifh and return to their former crimes, their fincere defire being to live and die chriftians: adding that it was unjuft for the whole nation to fuffer for the faults of a few; efpecially as they were willing to deliver up to punifhment, all who had either fpoke or acted amifs, and would undertake to protect the fathers, and convey them fafe to the captain of the garrifon: but if the fathers were not inclined to return to their country they would fettle at Loretto; being determined not to live without them. All were moved by thefe arguments, delivered with fuch figns of contrition and fincerity: and the Indians were detained fome days to reft themfelves, and at the fame time to prove whether treachery was not concealed under the cloak of piety. But no fufpicious figns appearing, the fathers returned to their feveral diftricts, where they were received with inexpreffible joy: the moft guilty were flightly punifhed, purely to gratify the others; and four only belonging to San Ignacio banifhed for a certain term, that in fuch a critical juncture there might be no fparks left to rekindle the fire of rebellion.

The

The auxiliaries from Yaqui having now joined the captain, soldiers, and faithful Indians of California, it was ordered, that as this miſſion was now quiet, a ſufficient guard ſhould remain in it; and the others repair to the bay of La Paz, in order to form a camp there, and keep a communication open by ſea for ſtores and proviſions; and from thence make excurſions towards the ſouth. Accordingly preparations were made for tranſporting thither this little army, partly by ſea, with the proviſions, and partly by land, with the beaſts. They who went by ſea, arriving firſt, landed with great regularity, poſted themſelves advantageouſly, and ſtrictly obſerved military diſcipline, which indeed proved very neceſſary; the Indians, with unuſual courage and ſhouts, attacking them ſeveral nights, ſo that ſome were wounded on both ſides. But the appearance of the more numerous body, which came by land, part of which were horſe, ſo intimidated the rebels, that they did not appear either by night or day. Some Indians alſo came in a peaceable manner, proteſting that they had always been faithful; and as ſuch had ſuffered from the conſpirators. They added, that the inſolence of the rebels was augmented by a misfortune which a little before had happened to the Philippine galleon, and was as follows.

Don

Don Geronimo Montero arriving at Manila, in his return from Acapulco, before the galleon which was to fail had put to fea, gave an account of the reception, he had met with at cape San Lucas; upon which orders were given to the galleon to touch at the faid cape, obferving the fignals agreed on with the miffionary. The galleon happily arrived at the cape, tho' many of her crew were ill of the fcurvy; but not perceiving either the fignals expected, nor any people on the fhore, the pinnace was hoifted out, and thirteen feamen fent to acquaint the father of the neighbouring miffion, with their arrival. When they came near the fhore, they were furprifed at feeing no perfon to receive them; but tho' they naturally might have fufpected fome mifchief, they landed without the leaft care; and leaving a few to take care of the pinnace, went up the country, in queft of the village, which they knew to be at a fmall diftance; but by the way the Indians fallied out from an ambufh, and letting fly a fhower of arrows, killed every man; then running towards the boat, where the feamen were as little on their guard as the others had been, difpatched them in the fame manner. The captain, furprized at this delay of the pinnace, tho' not without fome apprehenfion of mifchief, fent his long boat manned

and

and armed; but on coming within fight of the pinnace, they found her furrounded by a fwarm of Indians, who were pulling her to pieces for the iron-work. Incenfed at this, and much more at the dead bodies, the mariners and foldiers leaped afhore, engaged the Indians, wounded fome, killed one or two, and took four prifoners, whom they carried on board the fhip, where their grief was now greater than their late joy at difcovering the cape. The captain committed the prifoners to the care of the mafter at arms, in order to their being examined before the viceroy; and without taking in any refrefhments or water, tho' in great want of both, weighed anchor, and failed for Acapulco; where, as at Mexico, this deplorable misfortune was allowed to be a fufficient proof of the neceffity, even fetting afide all motives of humanity, for retrieving and fupporting the ruined miffions of California.

Accordingly the viceroy took fome meafures towards fupporting that tottering conqueft; fendnig orders to the governor of Cinaloa, that he fhould go over to California with a body of men, punifh the ringleaders of this rebellion, and intimidate others from engaging in a future; but at the fame time added, that tho' he was occafionally to act in concert with the

captain

captain and foldiers of the garrifon, he was by no means to be fubordinate to him, much lefs under the direction of the fathers. The governor accordingly fent advice of his orders to Loretto, that the miffion's bilander might be fent to him at Cinaloa, adding that they were to abftain from further hoftilities at La Paz. In the mean time, the foldiers and confederate Indians had made fome incurfions into the country, but with little fuccefs, meeting with fcarce any people to engage; the Indians flying and hiding themfelves in caverns, and among the rocks. But now father Guillen fent directions to the captain to repair to the miffion of Dolores, and there continue on the defenfive; and, at the fame time, difpatched the bilander for tranfporting the governor of Cinaloa, and his men. On his arrival at Loretto, he was received with fuitable diftinctions and honours, and likewife with great joy and politenefs, by the fathers. But the governor foon fignified, that he came with an intent to act againft the Californians, according to the prejudices which then prevailed at Mexico; and that he was little difpofed to liften to the advice of the fathers, tho' fo long acquainted with the country, and the nature of the inhabitants. Accordingly he attempted the reduction, by fuch meafures as he judged.

most

moſt proper; but after ſpending two years in
it, with various ſucceſs, he was obliged to own,
to his extreme mortification, that the effects of
his meaſures little anſwered his expectations.
In the mean time died, on the 10th of November 1736, the aged father Julian de Mayorga, who having in 1707 laid the foundation
of the miſſion of St. Joſeph de Comondu, and
governed it in peace, to the great improvement of his Indians, for above twenty-nine
years; it was therefore no wonder that they,
together with all the fathers and ſoldiers, ſhould
entertain a moſt cordial affection for him, on
account of his extraordinary abilities and virtues.

Soon after the death of this father, the governor altered his conduct, and began to execute what the fathers had at firſt adviſed,
namely, to ſtrike a terror into the Indians, by
attempting ſome ſignal action, after which
they would conſider his will as a law. They
added, that leſs damage would attend this
method, than if at firſt he made uſe of gentle
methods, or purſued them by parties; and
that after being thoroughly intimidated, they
would court his clemency, and acknowledge
it with a more laſting gratitude. Accordingly
he went in queſt of the Indians, and had the
good fortune to bring them to a general action,

in

in which they were scandalously defeated.
Their obstinacy and insolence, however, were
grown to such a height, during the two preceding years, that instead of surrendering or
making overtures for peace, they continued the
hostilities by skirmishes, till the governor found
means to force them to a second battle, in
which their behaviour was the same as in the
former; and soon after they surrendered themselves, and in the most submissive manner implored his pardon: but the governor refused
to listen to them, till they offered to discover,
and deliver up the chief promoters of the late
rebellion, and who had the greatest hand in
murdering the fathers and soldiers. Accordingly they were delivered up; but, by an ill-timed
clemency, he only banished them to the coast
of New Spain. Divine justice, however, as
if it disapproved of this clemency, did not suf-
fer the bloody rebellion to go unpunished: for
a few soldiers only being appointed to guard
the banished Indians; the latter attempted to
make themselves masters of the bark; so that
the soldiers were under a necessity of firing on
them, by which means the greatest part of them
were killed. Among the few that escaped,
were the two hardened wretches who first laid
hands on the venerable fathers; " but, adds
father Taraval, they both came to a very mise-

rable

rable end; one being killed in the firſt year of his baniſhment; and the other having climbed a palm-tree, fell from the top of it among the rocks, by which means his body was horribly mangled, and he expired in all the malice of his apoſtacy."

In the mean time, our gracious ſovereign Philip V. on the repreſentation and petition of father Pedro Ignacio Altamiſano and Bernardo Lozano, agents for the province of New Spain, ordered another warrant to the viceroy, with poſitive orders for erecting a new garriſon in the ſouthern part of California, agreeably to the inſtructions ſent ſome years before to the marquis de Caſa Fuerte, that under its protection, the loſt miſſions might be re-eſtabliſhed, and chriſtianity be for the future ſupported; authorizing him, at the ſame time, to take all ſuch meaſures as might contribute to the advancement of the conqueſt. By virtue of this warrant, the governor of Cinaloa was ordered to erect the new garriſon in the bay of La Paz; but afterwards, on conſidering the importance of a proper harbour for the Philippine ſhips to put in at, cape San Lucas was judged a more convenient ſituation. It was likewiſe ordered, that neither the captain, nor the ſoldiers of this garriſon, ſhould be appointed by the

the fathers, nor, in any manner, depend on them; nor be subordinate to the captain of the garrison of Loretto, but subject only to the orders of the viceroy. The person whom the governor nominated for captain, was don Bernardo Rodrigues Lorenzo, son to the veteran captain of the garrison of Loretto, don Estevan Rodrigues Lorenzo, who being born and brought up in California, under the eye of his worthy father, was possessed of that piety, prudence, courage, and knowledge of the country, which, at that time, were particularly requisite in a captain of such a garrison. Under him were thirty soldiers, ten of whom at first he posted at the new camp of St. Joseph del Cabo; ten at the mission of La Paz, and ten at that of St. Jago de los Coras: but capt. don Bernardo Rodrigues being thought to shew too much deference to the fathers, was soon displaced; and don Pedro Alvarez de Acevedo appointed to succeed him. The father, agent of California, at Mexico, protested against this independency, as contrary to the royal schedules, in which it was expressed, that no alteration should be made in the government of California. This, however, procured no change in the orders of the viceroy, who had been the author of the late regulation. His excellency, however, made an augmentation of five sol-

diers

diers to the ancient garrison of Loretto; and thus its number became equal to the new garrison of cape San Lucas; but withal directed, that the captain and soldiers should be entirely independent of the fathers; and that, tho' in case of necessity, they were to escort them, yet the superior, or visitor of California, should not have any authority over them, nor should the entrance, discharge, or payment of officers, artificers, soldiers, or seamen, be under their management. Accordingly, the regulation took place, and the fathers, during eighteen months, were eased of that care. But the greatest disorders resulted from this independency, as forsaking the father in their missions, visits, progresses, and expeditions, the neglect of all military duties, oppression of the natives, trading and fishing for pearls, violences committed on the divers, who came to those coasts from New Spain. In fine, such confusions and irregularities were committed in California, that the whole country was on the point of being utterly lost, by the fault of those very garrisons which had been erected for its security: and it was owing to a very singular providence, that the whole inhabitants of California did not again rise on the fathers. These proceedings produced such numbers of complaints, that the viceroy saw himself obliged

liged to alter his opinion; and, agreeably to the plan of his predeceffors, difcharged the captain of the garrifon of San Lucas, who had been appointed by the governor of Cinaloa; and ordered that the faid garrifon fhould be commanded only by a lieutenant, fubordinate to the captain of Loretto; that both, together with their foldiers, fhould, as before, be at the direction of the father vifitor; and their admiffions, difcharges, and payments put on the former footing.

S E C T. XXI.

The foutbern miffion happily reftored. Excellent meafures taken by his majefty Philip V. for promoting the conqueft. His prefent majefty Ferdinand VI. ratifies them in their full extent.

No fooner, by the zeal and courage of the governor of Cinaloa, were the Pericues or Uchities, the Guaycuros and Coras reduced, and the new garrifon of San Lucas eftablifhed, than the fociety appointed new miffionaries for gathering together the difperfed members of their churches; efpecially in thofe parts which had been ftained with the blood of the two faithful miffionaries; founding and regulating

the four miffions of el Pilar in La Paz bay,
Santa Rofa in Palmas bay, St. Jofeph near
cape San Lucas, and St. Jago among the
Coras. Father Antonio Tempis was fent to
the latter, and by his unwearied labours, gathered the difperfed Indians together, and officiated with exemplary fedulity till his death.
He was a perfon of folid, uniform, and fublime
virtue, and a faithful labourer in the vineyard
to his mafter.

The viceroy, by letters of the 23d of April
1735, and of the 10th of April 1737, acquainted his majefty Philip V. of the infurrection of the Indians, with the fubfequent oc-
currences ; and the fociety was under a neceffity of troubling his majefty on the fame fub-
ject, imploring him to fave that miffion which
had been fo much recommended and favoured
by his princely care. And thefe letters had
the moft happy effect.

The reftoration of the ruined miffions required an expence to which the product of their
lands, or the funds for their fupport, were far
from being fufficient. They had alfo been
exhaufted by the extraordinary charges incurred by the infurrections. But notwithftanding
thefe difficulties, the diftreffed affairs of California were brought to a happy conclufion.
The melancholy accounts above mentioned
having

having reached the ears of Philip V. he gave orders that not only a new garrison should be erected, but on the 2d of April 1742, was pleased to sign a warrant that the expences occasioned by the rebellion, should be made good out of the royal treasury : and lastly, that the council of the Indies should lay before him the most effectual means for totally reducing California. The scheme and measures for its execution were zealously espoused by that excellent nobleman don Joseph Carvajal de Lancaster, at that time president of the said council, secretary of state, and knight of the order of the golden fleece, who immediately caused all the preceding transactions, relating to California to be examined ; and his great penetration soon discovered the importance of the conquest, the various difficulties which retarded it, and the most proper measures for carrying it on with success. Nor did he stop here, but procured the royal signature to the most express orders for carrying them into execution. Accordingly, on the 13th of November 1744, a full warrant was dispatched to the count de Fuen Clara, viceroy, with letters to several private persons, requiring fresh informations on various and important heads ; and a very full account was returned by father Christoval de Escobar Llamas, provincial of

Mexico,

Mexico, dated the 30th of November 1745; and arrived in Madrid after the acceffion of his prefent majefty Ferdinand VI. on the ninth of June 1746, who, inheriting all the zeal and magnanimity of his glorious father, on the report of his council ftrongly recommended by the marquis de la Enfenada, at that time fecretary of ftate and of the Indies, ordered another fchedule, much fuller than the former, and directed it to the prefent viceroy of New Spain. I cannot forbear inferting a literal copy of this inftrument, as it is an illuftrious monument of the auguft intentions and ardent zeal of both monarchs; of the forefight, fagacity, and wifdom of his council; of the knowledge, prudence, piety, activity, and grand defigns of his minifters.

The KING.

" Don Juan Francifco de Guemes and Horcafita, lieutenant general of my armies, viceroy, governor and captain general of the provinces of New Spain, and prefident of my royal audience there, refiding in the city of Mexico: on the 13th of November 1734, was difpatched to your predeceffor in thefe employments the count de Fuen-Clara, an order to the following purpofe:

the

The K I N G.

Count de Fuen Clara, coufin, knight of the illuftrious order of the golden fleece, lord of my bed-chamber, viceroy, governor, and captain general of the provinces of my kingdom of New Spain, and prefident of my royal audience there, refiding in my city of Mexico: The archbifhop viceroy your predeceffor in thofe employments having, by a letter of the 23d of April 1735, and of the 10th of the fame month 1737, fent an account of what has paffed in the infurrection of the Indians of the nations called Pericu and Guaycura in the province of California, and of the meafures taken and the expences incurred by reducing them to the fubjection and tranquillity in which by the good conduct of the governor of Cinaloa they then were, and the preceding accounts have been laid before my council of the Indies for their deliberation, together with the origin, progrefs, and prefent ftate of the fpiritual and temporal conqueft of the faid province of California; and I having at the requeft of father Altamirano of the fociety of Jefus, and agent general for its provinces in the Indies, and particularly of the miffions of its order in California, approved of the mea-

fures

fures taken, and the expences employed in the
reduction of them, as I fignified to you in letters of the 2d of April in the foregoing year;
it is judged proper, till the receipt of the accounts and reports relative to thofe letters and
which are daily expected from California, to
deliberate on in my before mentioned council
of the meafures which may be moft effectual
for the entire accomplifhment of the reduction
and conqueft in queftion; which has been attempted ever fince the year 1523, firft by don
Fernando Cortez marquis del Valle and firft
viceroy of thefe provinces; and fince by fome
of his fucceffors, and by particular perfons at
feveral times: and though large fupports were
furnifhed by my royal treafury, yet by misfor-
tunes and infuperable difficulties never took effect, notwithftanding the propofed conqueft
had the incentive of rich pearl fifheries. Befides
the manifeft inclination and docility of the natives, for embracing our holy religion, and
conforming themfelves to a civil life, as among
other jefuit miffionaries is affirmed by the father Juan Maria de Salva-Tierra and Eufe-
bio Francifco Kino in the year 1698; but more
particularly and clearly by father Francifco
Piccolo in the year 1716, when, by the indefatigable zeal of the religious of the fociety of
Jefus, the only perfons who have dedicated
them-

themselves to that commendable service, and likewise by the contributions of the faithful, those missions and conversions were already very far advanced; to which desirable work likewise my royal treasury added an annual subsidy of thirteen thousand dollars, from the year 1703, intended principally to defray the charges of a body of soldiers for the missions, and pay the officers and men belonging to the bark which carries the missionaries from the coast of Cinaloa thither: and my said council of the Indies having, with the greatest diligence and punctuality, revised and examined all the several articles on this head, as likewise the reports from the auditor's office, and from the before mentioned father Pedro Ignacio Altamirano and other judicious persons of his order, and versed in those conversions; and my follicitor's opinion on the whole, has been represented to me in council on the 12th of May of this year, that it is of the highest importance that the most effectual measures should be immediately taken for bringing back the said province of the Californias into the bosom of the church, and under my dominion: which advantageous enterprise, though vigorously supported by the catholick zeal of my glorious predecessors, and the viceroys of those provinces, has so often miscarried,

that

that not a foot of land in that vaſt territory has been ſecured: and for its more perfect and ſpeedy accompliſhment, my council in their repreſentation of the ſame day ſignified to me, that the ſolid and fundamental baſe of it muſt be the converſion of the natives to our holy religion, by means of thoſe particular jeſuit miſſionaries who have made ſuch progreſſes among them, and all the infidel nations they have taken under their charge throughout all America; and conſequently that near all large and ſafe harbours which may be diſcovered in the reduced parts, a ſettlement be made of Spaniards with a fort and garriſon, and that likewiſe in the moſt convenient part towards the center of their province there may alſo be a Spaniſh town as a check to the Indians and refuge to the miſſionaries in caſe of an inſurrection. And as the tranſporting of families from hence to thoſe Spaniſh colonies, would be attended with great trouble and expence, beſides the want of them for other ſettlements, it is thought proper that theſe emigrations ſhould be made from the city of Mexico and the neighbouring provinces; concerning which we expect the reports and informations required, that we then reſolve for the beſt. The council have farther propoſed to me, that in order to the more expeditious reduction of the Indians of the Californias,

lifornias, it would be very proper that the
jesuit missionaries should enter the province on
the side opposite to that by which those at present there entered, that is by the north part
where this province joins and borders on the
continent; it having been discovered and as-
certained, that the province of the Californias is no island as was commonly believed,
but a terra firma bordering in its upper or
northern part on that of New Mexico; for by
this measure its natives will be surrounded, or as
it were insulated without any passage, or inlet
into the territories of other savage Indians ; and
all the missionaries proceeding along their several departments to the center of the province,
the total reduction of it cannot fail of being
very much shortened. But as to the accom-
plishment of this project, it is thought to be
of great consequence, that in the missions of all
the departments of Indians already reduced,
the teachers should be doubled ; but it is absolutely necessary to make a progress in the
parts contiguous to the Indians not yet reduced: as besides the advantages common to all,
one of the missionaries may pass through the
territories of the infidels for converting them, and
those parts already peopled, not be without the
necessary instructions ; and never left without
a proper person to watch every motion that has
the

the leaſt tendency to treachery or revolt, of which there would be the greateſt danger, if theſe people were left to themſelves.

It is alſo proper, that in all the frontier parts already reduced, a guard of ſoldiers be ſtationed for the ſecurity both of the miſſionaries and Indians, and likewiſe for accompanying the miſſionaries into the territories of the infidels, being always under the direction of the religious, nor doing any thing unleſs directed by them: leſt by an indiſcrete chaſtiſement or excurſion they ſhould alarm the Indians: And by theſe methods it is hoped a great progreſs will be made in thoſe parts where the miſſions are eſtabliſhed. It is likewiſe thought proper that for advancing the reduction of this province by miſſions, they ſhould be extended to the ſouthward from the oppoſite part in order to meet thoſe which are carrying on to the northward; and that the meaſures above mentioned may be eaſily practiſed in the miſſions belonging to the ſame order among the highland Pimas in the province of Sonora, by doubling the miſſionaries in every converted diſtrict bordering on the infidel Indians; and allowing to thoſe religious a guard as above. Thus the miſſionaries among the highland Pimas proceeding to reduce the nations of the Cocomaricopas and of the Yumas, which reach to the north

river,

river, called alfo Colorado, near the place where it iffues into the Californian gulf, the jefuits, according to the former accounts, expecting to be well received by thefe nations; and founding a village of reduced Indians on the bank of the fame river Colorado, they may eafily pafs over to the other fhore of California; and by their fuccefs there with the Hoabonomas, or the Bajiopas, a docile and tractable people, they may there found another village for fecuring the paffage on both fides the river, and a communication with the whole terra firma: and proceeding from hence to the fouthward through the country of California to the ancient miffionaries. With refpect to the guard defired in the miffions of the highland Pimas, either the detachment ftationed at Terrenate, or the other on duty at Pitiqui will be fufficient, as it appears by the report of don Auguftin de Vildofola, governor of the province of Cinaloa, that both of them are not neceffary: but for the greater fecurity the detachment at Pitiqui may remove to Terrenate, and that of the latter to the miffions of the highland Pimas: and thus the proper guard both in the new and former miffions of California, may be furnifhed without any additional expence to my royal revenue. It was alfo by the fame council reprefented to me, that though the expence of miffionary

fionaries fhould be increafed, it muft be remembered that by a fchedule of the year 1702,
an order paffed for affifting the miffionaries of
California, with every thing conducive to their
relief, and the accomplifhment of the work in
which they were engaged; and by another of
1723, that the religious then officiating, or
who fhould for the future officiate in California,
fhould be allowed the fame falary as thofe of
their order, and to be paid regularly and punctually, which hitherto has not been done; no
expence having been incurred in thefe miffions;
nor have they received any allowance or falary.
Fifteen miffions, the prefent number in California, having maintained themfelves without the
leaft charge to me; purely by the liberal contributions of private perfons obtained through
the zeal and intereft of the religious of the order; and as the means propofed will be attended
with fo little expence in comparifon of the prodigious advantage, it will be proper that all
thefe orders be put in execution; or any others
that may be approved by the jefuits, who are
beft acquainted with the province, and from
whom I expect farther accounts: and that
from this prefent time they may fpeedily be affifted with all neceffary fums for the work
out of the royal revenue, that the number of
jefuit miffionaries may be augmented, it being

neceffary

neceſſary that two reſide in every reduced diſtrict bordering on the infidel Indians.

Laſtly, for this corroborating ſubordination, the pay of the ſoldiers is to be remitted to the miſſionaries, that they may receive it from their hands : and that if any ſoldier be of a turbulent diſpoſition and behaves amiſs, the miſſionaries may ſend him away and deſire another in his room, as without theſe and other precautions which ſome able miſſionaries have on ſeveral occaſions tranſmitted to me concerning theſe provinces, the guards have by their irregularities greatly impeded the reduction of the Indians, whom it is neceſſary to keep in awe and reſpect, that they may not attempt any treacherous practices, and at the ſame time treating them with kindneſs, to remove their miſtruſt, and reconcile them to the inſtructions of civil polity.

S E C T.

SECT. XXII.

Preparations at Mexico in purſuance of the foregoing royal orders. Endeavours for penetrating into the province of Maqui. Father Sedelmayer repairs to the rivers Gila and Colorado. The coaſt of CALIFORNIA as far as theſe rivers ſurveyed. Father Courſay's expedition againſt the Apates. Laſt accounts of the miſſions of CALIFORNIA, Sonora and Pimeria, till the year 1752.

The foregoing royal orders gave great ſatiſ-faction to many of the inhabitants of Mexico, as they were an authentick teſtimony of the piety, prudence, and magnanimity of the monarch, and his attention to the publick welfare.

We have already obſerved that father Euſe-bio Franciſco Kino ſurveyed the whole northern country betwixt the province of Sonora and the rivers Gila and Colorado, and the weſtern port of the gulf of California, and found the coaſt entirely peopled by Indians, chiefly infidels; that he entered into terms of friendſhip with the ſeveral nations of thoſe vaſt countries

except

except the Apaches; that he reduced them into
villages; built churches; baptized many thousand Indians; brought many more to a difpofition for receiving the faith; and paffionately
folicited a fupply of minifters for reaping that
plentiful harveft which was ripe for the fickle of
the gofpel: that the magnanimous prince don
Philip V. ordered the ufual fuccours and expences for eight miffionaries to be employed
in Pimeria and in thofe parts of it which had
been already reduced by father Kino: but from
the impediments too ufually found at Mexico for difburfements of that nature, only
four affignments took place. By the death of
father Kino in 1710, the great progrefs which
that father, by his indefatigable zeal, had made
towards a compleat reduction of thefe nations,
came to nothing. Father Juan Antonio Balthafar, whofe papers we have before made ufe
of part. III. fect. V. and muft now again have
recourfe to, complained of the want of accounts
in the year fubfequent to the deceafe of father
Kino. All that the father could gather in his
vifitation of the miffions of Sonora and Pimeria
relative to our prefent purpofe is, that father
Auguftin de Campos, miffionary of San Ignacio and companion to father Kino furvived him
twenty five years; during which he imitated
his real labours and benevolence in the care

of

of his miffion. In the year 1720, new miffionaries came to Conception de Caborca and
Tuhutama; and afterwards going to the rancherias of San Edvardo de Baipia, San Louis de
Bacapa and San Marcelo lying far north, they
found a great defection among the Indians; the
little churches built by father Kino in ruins,
and the cultivation of the fertile plains in which
they had been inftructed by that admirable
perfon utterly neglected. Thefe nations now,
though for what reafon is unknown, go by
the name of Papagos. In Guebavi and San
Xavier del Bac the depravation was ftill greater,
having been above twenty years without miffionaries. The bifhop of Durango, don Benito
Crefpo, with extreme fatigue perfonally vifited
his immenfe diocefe; and perceiving the great
want of labourers in Pimeria, and the importance of forwarding its reduction, he requefted
of his majefty to affign three more miffionaries for it, and accordingly the proper orders
were iffued. Conformable to which, in the year
1731, three jefuits retired thither with a very
large quantity of prefents fent by the prelate to
be diftributed among the Indians. Thus in
high Pimeria, were formed feven miffions which
are as follows:

1. Dolores with two villages of vifitation.
2. San Ignacio alfo with two villages.

3. Tibu-

3. Tibutama with nine villages.

4. Caborca with four villages.

5. Suamca with several rancherias.

6. Guebavi with Spanish farms and a considerable number of Indians.

7. San Xavier del Bac has also a great number of Indians.

The marquis de Villa Puente, who died at his return from Rome, in the imperial college of Madrid in February 1739, left by will a sum of money for the foundation of two other missions in Pimeria; yet even in the year 1749, they had not been erected for want of jesuits in the province of Mexico, and the war had hindered a supply being sent from Old Spain.

Such was the state of Pimeria under seven missions actually existing, and two other endowed; when, in the year 1742, a schedule from his majesty Philip V. arrived at Mexico, requiring the viceroy to recommend to the society the reduction of the province of Moqui, and to furnish it with every thing necessary out of the treasury. The superiors of the society, however desirous of paying obedience to the orders of his majesty, were now under an impossibility of complying for want of labourers, especially in an enterprise so remote and arduous. The province of Moqui joins to the north west part of the kingdom of New Mexico; its inhabitants had been wholly converted and reduced by the zeal of the Franciscans ; but in 1680, they apostatized ; and after massacring the persons who instructed them, revolted, together with the other Indians of New Mexico. The fathers however, after inexpressible labours, restored tranquillity and religion in that kingdom : but all their diligence could not overcome the obduracy of the Moquinos, who for many years opposed all offers of their coming among them. But from the flattering hopes of entirely reducing them, and the great importance of securing New Mexico from invasions on that side, a schedule was sent in the year 1723, to the viceroy, the marquis de Casa Fuerté enjoining him to endeavour the reduction of Moqui. The viceroy concerted with the bishop of Durango, who was of opinion that this difficult enterprize should be put into the hands of the society.

The bishop had not hitherto performed his visitation, and therefore was not well acquainted with the country. The Franciscans could enter Moqui from New Mexico on its western side, without any other impediment than the ignorance and brutality of the Indians. But the only places from whence the jesuits could enter it were Sonora, and upper Pimeria. Moqui indeed lies to the northward of the missions of Tibutama, Guebavi, and others of Pimeria :

but

but the diſtance between Tbutama and the river Gila is not leſs than eighty leagues, and all inhabited by Indians, with whom indeed a friendſhip has been concluded, but the far greateſt part of them are declared infidels. Next to theſe are the ſavage Apaches, implacable enemies to the Spaniards, and all Indians con-nected with them. Beyond theſe the Moqui inhabit an extenſive, but mountainous country. Conſequently there was no direct way for the jeſuits to penetrate into this province; and there-fore the attempt could only be made either through the country of the Sobaypuris, or Pimas now called Papagos, extending along the river Gila to the country of the Cocomari-copas, who were profeſſed infidels, and perpe-tually at war with the Nijoras, Cocomaricopas ſelling their Nijoran priſoners to the Pimas; and theſe to the Spaniards. It muſt alſo be remembered, that beſides the great number of miſſions already under the care of the jeſuits, and moſt of them on the frontiers of the infi-dels, the Marquis de Valero the viceroy had five years before, namely in 1718, charged them with the reduction of Nayarith, a pro-vince incloſed within the Sierra Madre, and only two hundred leagues from the capital of Mexico. And their labours were attended with ſuch ſucceſs, that the chief of that nation came

to

to do homage to the viceroy; adorned with the mantle, thali, bracelets, collar, crown of feathers, and other ornaments ufed by the ancient Chichimeca kings. Such an important reduction was not therefore to be deferred, left they might alter their minds and rebel. It is true the Franeifcans were alfo employed in the miffions of Junta de los Rios, two hundred and fifty leagues north eaft of New Mexico, lately founded and vigoroufly carried on by the zeal of the duke de Linares, viceroy of Mexico. Thefe were of equal importance as lying near the French poffeffions of Miffifippi and Louifiana. From thefe and other obftacles, all defigns on Moqui were fufpended. But the new order in 1742, ftrictly recommending the reduction of that country to the fociety, father Ignacio Keler miffionary of Santa Maria Suamca was ordered to make the firft attempt. This father in the preceding years, had been feveral times as far as the river Gila, both to vifit his neophytes and to keep up a friendship with the Indians who were enemies to the Apaches. But in September 1743, he fet out from his miffion with a very fmall guard, a Spanifh juftice, whofe difpleafure he had incurred by protecting his Indians, not allowing him to take any more: and to this the mifcarriage of the enterprife was entirely owing.

The

The father came to the river Gila, and continued his journey some days further to the northward, till he came among rancherias of a different language, and the people quite unknown. The Indians had not the courage to insult the strangers in the day-time, but in the night they attacked them for the sake of plunder; and it was with great difficulty that some horses were saved to facilitate their return; one of the soldiers also was killed by an arrow. The father however was for continuing his march; but his Indian attendants beginning to leave him, he found himself under a necessity of returning to his mission. The following year 1744, orders were sent to father Jacob Sedelmayer missionary of Tubutama that being less exposed to the barbarians, he should proceed on this discovery: he was directed to take guides, send messages to the Moqui, and, in case he found any Franciscan missionaries settled there, he should exhort the inhabitants of the country to love and obey them; and then withdraw: if he met with none, he was to take a careful survey of these parts, draw up an account of his journey, and delineate a map of the country; but not to involve himself in any known danger.

Accordingly, in October, the father set out from his mission, and after travelling eighty

N 3   leagues,

leagues, reached the river Gila, where he found
fix thoufand Papagos, and near the fame number
of Pimas and Cocomaricopas dwelling in different
rancherias. Here he was well received, having
before contracted a friendfhip with them. A-
mong thefe, as before, he met with feveral axes
and knives, diftributed among them by father
Kino: he informed them of his defign of going to Moqui, and at firft they voluntarily offered to direct him in the way and accompany
him; but foon after began to fhew their diflike of the enterprife, and at laft abfolutely
refufed to embark in it. The true caufe of
this change in their behaviour, was partly owing
to the Tibutamas in his company, who being a
people void of courage had very unwillingly
attended him in fo long a journey; and partly
to the Cocomaricopas, who grudged the little
prefents they carried to be diftributed among
the Nijoras and Moquis. But there was alfo
another reafon for their change of behaviour,
namely, a fear left the Spaniards fhould enter
into friendfhip with thefe two nations; when,
in cafe of a war, they would be utterly defencelefs, being fituated between them, and
the Cocomaricopas were always at variance with
the Nijoras; the Moquis likewife fhewed themfelves fometimes on their frontiers in an hoftile
method, though at other times they vifited
them

them in a peaceable manner. This precaution may perhaps appear too rational and provident for such savage nations. But we muft acknowledge that there is no community without its political myfteries and reafons of ftate: and that in all parts mankind are well or ill governed, in proportion to the culture of the mind. However this be, the father tried every method to purfue his march, but found on all fides unfurmountable difficulties, unlefs he would have opened a way by force, which was contrary to the orders he had received, and incompatible with his profeffion.

But that the expedition might not be entirely fruitlefs, he with the free confent of the Cocomaricopas, took a view of the whole territory they inhabited on each fide of the Gila, went into the inward parts of their country, and returned from thence to the river Colorado, and the country of the Yumas, who were enemies of the Cocomaricopas, though in all appearance a branch of their nation: for the interpreter who accompanied the fathers, fufficiently underftood the language of the Yumas. The original narrative of father Sedelmayer's journey, and the map which was to be annexed to it, have never come to my hands; both I own would have been of great ufe to me in compofing the map at the front of this little work;

but

but the subftance of it is to be found in the New-
Theatro Americano, and in the abovementioned
papers of father Balthafar, which agree in fub-
ftance as being written by thofe who had before
them the fame memoirs, and of which they have
made a very faithful ufe.   What is certain from
both is, that the banks near the fource of the
Gila are inhabited by the Apaches; at fome
diftance below which that river is joined by
the Azul, which is thought to iffue from the
mountains, and waters the pleafant and fruitful
country of the Nijoras, till its influx into the
Gila.   Afterwards on both fides of this river,
there is an uninhabited tract of about twenty
leagues, at the end of which are three large rancherias of Pimas, the greateft of which called
Judac, occupies fourteen leagues of a pleafant
fertile country, well watered by means of trenches
which, the country being level, are eafily carried from the Gila.   Twelve leagues farther
towards the north eaft, is the new difcovered
river of de la Affumption, compofed of two
rivers, namely, el Salado and el Verde; which
in their way to the Gila run through a very
pleafant level country of arable land, inhabited
by the Cocomaricopas who are feparated from
the Pimas by a defert, though united to them
in confanguinity.   Their kingdom is bounded
on the weft, by a defert and mountainous country,

try, extending to the rancherias of the Yumas, who live along the river Colorado, but below its junction with the Gila. Over this defert, the Cocomaricopas pafs to the river Colorado, though there is a much fhorter way by the conflux of the two rivers.

Acrofs this defert they led father Sedelmayer, who it feems did not vifit the abovementioned junction of the rivers, which father Kino faw, and gave it the name of San Dionyfio; nor did he know any thing of the Achedomas, who according to Kino inhabit its eaftern fhore northward from its junction with the Colorado. The Yumas though their idiom differs very little from that of the Gila Cocomaricopas, are inveterate enemies to them : but on the weftern fide of the Colorado, there are likewife rancherias of Cocomaricopas allied to thofe of Gila; and living in a valley thirty fix leagues in length, and for the fpace of nine leagues remarkably fertile and pleafant, cultivated for kidney-beans, calabafhes, melons, and other efculent vegetables; and by their induftry well watered. Here they faw fome Indians crofs the river with their families and provifions in batteaus, and found in them all that courteous and liberal difpofition for which father Kino commends them, though at firft the Yumas fhewed fome aftonifhment at the vifit, being the only one fince the

time

time of that friendly miffionary. From thefe accounts, it was apprehended, that by means of feven or eight miffions along the Gila, two among the Colorado Cocomaricopas, an additional one among the Sobaypuris, and another in San Ambrofio del Bufanic, together with thofe already founded in high Pimeria, the entire reduction of the nations of the Pimicas and Papabotas or Papagos might be accomplifhed.

It was alfo the unanimous opinion of the fathers, that this reduction fhould be vigoroufly attempted, as opening a paffage to the Moqui, and being an effectual barrier againft the continual hoftilities of the Apaches : and in order to this they thought it would be proper, that father Sedelmayer, who had lately taken that fatiguing furvey fhould repair to Mexico. Accordingly, that indefatigable father again chearfully fet out on a journey of five hundred leagues to the capital, where he had the pleafure of finding the provincial engaged in drawing up the report which had been required by his majefty, concerning the miffions of Pimeria and California. He had befides the pleafure of feeing that the fentiments and fchemes of the provincial, abfolutely agreed with his own, even before he had been heard, but much more when he came to fhew the folidity of his propofals,

pofals, by a narrative of his recent difcoveries.
The provincial, from the accounts which had
been communicated to him concerning California, and thefe new lights he now received,
relating to Pimeria, drew up his report with all
poffible perfpicuity, and with the candour due
to the munificent intention of fuch a monarch.
As the report, or memorial, expatiates on
many particulars, of which we have already
taken fufficient notice, we fhall only add the
following abftract of it.

The provincial begins with obferving, that no
fettlement of Spaniards can be made in California
along the coaft, nor up the country ; nor have
the fathers been able to accomplifh any fuch
thing, during the fpace of fifty years, by reafon of the extreme barrennefs of the country,
the qualities of which he defcribes, there being
a neceffity of maintaining the greateft part of
the natives, whereby not only the products of
their lands, but likewife the contributions of
the miffions, on the other fide, and that fent
by the four rivers of Cinaloa are confumed.
That tho' in Monte Rey, and Cabo Mondocino,
the foil is more fertile, it would be very difficult to profecute the reduction on the north
fide, both on account of its barrennefs, and
the want of labourers. And for thefe reafons,
the

the fifteenth miffion from that of San Ignacio,
which till then had bordered on the infidels,
had no fixed ftation. Befides, the miffions
could not be at a great diftance from the garrifon, and extend themfelves along the weftern
coaft of the fea, as they could not there receive
any fuccours without previoufly reducing the
nations on the eaftern coaft of the gulf: and
in order to this, it was neceffary firft to fecure
the conveyance of provifions from the oppofite
coaft of Caborca, on the continent of New
Spain, which had as yet been but fuperficially
furveyed, and the creeks and harbours never
founded.   The coaft alfo is fteep, and the
greateft part of it without water; befides, being inhabited by Seris and Tepocas, but very
imperfectly reduced; and the town of Caborca
lying 22 leagues up the country, a fecond new
bark was neceffary; the firft being employed
in bringing from Matanchel and Yaqui to
Loretto and La Paz, the appointments and
neceffaries for the miffion, and the products of
Cinaloa; and there was no poffibility that fhe
could likewife ferve as a tranfport in the more
inward and tempeftuous, part of the gulf.
Thirdly, it was neceffary to augment the garrifon of Loretto, thirty foldiers not being fufficient for guards and fettlements fo remote,
as the firft new miffion was to be near 50
leagues

leagues N. of San Ignacio; that every thing was possible to the king, but the charge would be great. For these reasons, without forgetting previously to assist California, he proposed the conquest of the highland Pimeria, as a country of easy access, level, well peopled, and, about the Gila and Colorado, very fertile. For as lower California could not subsist without Cinaloa, so upper California could not subsist without Pimeria. This conquest would facilitate that of Moqui, in case it should not succeed, by the way of New Mexico; and would be a check upon the Apaches, or at least forward the reduction of them. In order to this, all that was required, with regard to the society, was that the dismission which it had made of twenty-two missions, in the diocese of Durango, the Indians of them being perfectly converted, and reduced into villages, might be allowed; and that the number of jesuits should be greatly increased, both to act in the remaining missions, and to double the missionaries in the frontiers: that the father general should grant his licence to great numbers of persons in Europe, who were passionately desirous of being employed in such worthy functions; that he should cause the gulf to be again surveyed by the jesuits for ascertaining whether California was united to the continent of New Spain; this

being

being doubted of at Mexico, tho' not in Europe.

The father obferved, that the allowance of three hundred dollars to miffions fettled, near 600 leagues diftant from Mexico, was too little, efpecially at the beginning, the carriage of neceffaries amounting to half the fum: that the garrifon of Pitquin could not at prefent be fpared for an expedition to the river Colorado; for tho' the Yaqui and Maya nations were now quiet, yet as the meafures taken to pacify them were difagreeable, they might poffibly on the removal of the garrifon break out into a fecond revolt. This garrifon is on the fouth bounded by the Yaquis; northward it joins to the Seris and Tepocas, who are either infidels, or imperfectly reduced; and tho' father Salva Tierra civilized them, and the miffionaries have baptized many, they ftill retain fuch a love for their liberty and cuftoms, as all the labours of the miffionaries have not been able tò obliterate; fo that it is impoffible to incorporate them with the miffions by mildnefs. On the other hand, the barrennefs and want of water, in moft parts of the country, will not admit of any miffion being fettled amongft them: his majefty therefore may order his minifters to draw them by prefents to the villages, or a miffion to which they may
all

all repair, may be founded in some fertile spot. But whether the one or the other can be done without the protection of a garrison, is impossible to be known. The removal of the garrison of Terrenate appeared still more inconvenient. For if notwithstanding this garrison, which had been erected by the viceroy, as duke of the conquest, the insolence of the Apaches, those invaders of Sonora, was at such an height, what might not be apprehended, if the province was left defenceless from Colorado, to the garrison of Coro de Guachi de Fronteras? For this reason it appeared, that the garrison, which hitherto had been ambulatory, and without any fixed post, might be constantly stationed among the Sobaypuris, in the mission of Santa Maria de Suamca : as thus its numerous Indians may be instructed, and led against the Apaches ; and, to the same purpose, a detachment of twelve or fifteen soldiers may be sent to do duty as guards in the mission of San Xavier del Bac. Lastly, it seemed most adviseable to the provincial, that a new garrison should be erected on the banks of the river Gila, within the territories of the Apaches : and, instead of fifty, to consist of one hundred soldiers ; for being in their country, and not on our frontiers, a greater number was required ; that, at the same time, some might attend to
military

military duties, and the cultivation of the ground, and others march into the enemy's country, bring them to peaceable terms, or disperse them. Thus all the countries, under the dominion of the king, would be inclosed as in a circle; by the concurrence of the garrisons, the ferocity of the Apaches would be quelled; the reduction of the territories of the Moqui be facilitated, and all the intermediate country being likewise brought to terms, the conquest would be extended to New Mexico; the peaceable nations, along the Gila and Colorado, the Sobaypuris, Pimas, Papagos, Cocomaricopas, and Yumas would be sheltered; a door would be opened for propagating christianity, on the other side of these two rivers; and, what is not of the least consequence, a passage opened to California by land. The erection of such a garrison at first, would be more expensive than the present measures; but, all things considered, it would be the cheapest; as in a small space of time the greatest part of those chargeable garrisons, now subsisting, would be rendered useless, and, consequently, might be spared. For this garrison alone, would accomplish that which experience has convinced us is impossible to be done by all the others.

These

These were the principal heads of the father's report; and those which the prudent zeal of the king recommended to the examination of his viceroy, with orders to enter upon the execution of what he should think most proper, without any further warrant. It will doubtless seem strange to some, that in this report, nothing is proposed particularly in favour of California; but the establishment of a new mission on the coast of the gulf, in the nearest part possible to the Colorado, if properly seconded, on the opposite coast of Caborca, would have greatly facilitated the desired communication by land between the missions of both coasts : besides, the commerce of the mission, with the coast of Caborca, in order to obtain supplies, and the communication of one with the other side of the gulf, would have tended greatly to contract an acquaintance between the inhabitants of both shores; at the same time, the several channels, islands, rocks, sand banks, shoals, and the dangerous passages of Sal-si-puedes, and most of the Seris and Tepocas would have been frequented by sea; and the inhabitants civilized, and inclined to renew their faith, by means of this transitory intercourse from California; and, consequently, have submitted to the mild yoke of the gospel, if, instead of being violently forced from their

coaſt, a regular trade were carried on with
them, according to the earneſt deſire of the
father Salva-Tierra, part III. ſect. IX. Beſides, the miſſionaries in the north of California, by being aſſiſted by a bark or two more,
a greater number of ſoldiers, and the opportunity of receiving their proviſions directly from
the other coaſt, without waiting for the ſlow
ſupplies from Loretto, which, after a long
voyage, are ſubject to a very chargeable
land carriage, might have penetrated thro'
the whole country, to the river Colorado, on
one ſide, and to the famous Puerto de Monte
Rey, on the other. After which, when the
country behind them was intirely reduced, what
difficulty would attend the forming at Monte
Rey, from the Philippines, or New Spain, a
large and ſplendid colony, or garriſon? With
how much greater eaſe might the miſſionaries,
ſoldiers, or inhabitants of the colony, go from
thence to the river Colorado, or the Gila, to
the country of the Apaches, the Maqui, or
new Mexico? But the provincial contented
himſelf with only propoſing the conqueſt of
Pimeria, as the moſt eaſy and leaſt expenſive;
tho' the whole conqueſt would not have been
attended with ſuch valuable conſequences as
the ſingle colony at Monte Rey, and the garriſon of a hundred ſoldiers on the Gila, in the
territory

territory of the Apaches. And this was the opinion of the illustrious don Martin Elizacoechea, bishop of Mechoacan, who, while he filled the fee of Durango, visited, with infinite labour, the whole diocese. Father Juan Antonio Balthasar, who, as visitor of the missions, had seen the whole country, adds, that by this measure, besides the abovementioned conveniencies, the desires of fathers Kino and Sedelmayer of building a city in those remote countries, might have been fulfilled, which would have firmly cemented these conquests with his majesty's other dominions in those parts: for the country is so fertile, and at the same time has so many rich mines, that a garrison here would soon have increased into a populous town, every inhabitant of which might have been instructed in the duties of a soldier. Besides, why should not the Apaches, at seeing the several advantages of settlements made in their countries, be disposed to peace, as was the case with the Chichimicas, once so brutal and outrageous, especially if treated with mildness and humanity. And to this may be added, the example of a virtuous life in the Spaniards; which doubtless would follow from the reflection of individuals, the institution of magistracy, and his majesty's royal proclamation against immorality of every kind.

Whilst

Whilst these reports were sending to Madrid, and his majesty's final resolution expected at Mexico, the father provincial Escobar sent circular letters by father Juan Antonio Balthasar, visitor general of the missions, directing every missionary to send a short account of his mission, its beginning, progress, and present condition, in order to lay before his majesty. He also directed, that a fresh survey should be taken by sea of the coasts of the gulf of California; and likewise that the new entrances should be attempted towards the Gila. The missionaries of California accordingly drew up their narratives, and of them we have made use in the compilation of our work. Besides what has been already inserted, I shall add that in the year 1745, the missions, visitation-towns, and missionaries in California were as follows:

I. Nuestra Senora de Loretto, in 25° 30 min. also the royal garrison, and the place where the barks deliver their lading. The missionary father Gaspar de Truxillo.

II. San Xavier.——Father Miguel del Barco.—— Its villages or towns are

   1. San Xavier, in 25°. 30 min.

   2. Santa Rosalia, 7 leagues W.

   3. S. Miguel, 8 leagues N.

   4. S. Augustine, 10 leagues S. E.

   5. Dolores, 2 leagues E.

6. San Pablo, 8 leagues N. W.

III. Nueftra Senora de los Dolores del Sur, formerly San Juan Baptifta Malibat, or Ligui.—Father Clemente Guillen.—Villages—

1. Nueftra Senora de los Dolores, 24°. 30 min.

2. La Concepcion de Nueftra Senora.

3. La Incarnacion de el Verbo.

4. La Santiffima Trinidad.

5. La Redempcion.

6. La Refurrecion.

IV. San Luis Gonfaga.—Father Lamberto Hotel.—Villages—

1. San Luis Gonfaga, in 25°.

2. San Juan Nepomuceno.

3. Santa Maria Magdalena, in the bay of its name.

V. San Jofeph de Commondu—without a miffionary, on account of the death of father Francifco Xavier Wagner, on the 12th of October 1744, in the interim, ferved by father Druet.—Villages—

1. San Jofeph, in 26°.

2. Another village, 1 league W.

3. Another, 7 leagues N.

4. Another, 10 leagues E. on the fhore.

VI. Santa Rofalia Mulege.—Father Pedro Maria Nafcimben.—Villages—

1. Santa Rofalia, in 26°. 50 min.

2.

2. Santiſſima Trinidad, 6 leagues S. S. E.

3. S. Marcos, 8 leagues N.

VII. La Puriſſima Concepcion. — Father Jacobo Druet —Village—

La Puriſſima Concepcion, in 26°.

It has ſix other villages, within 8 leagues round Cabecera, or metropolis of the miſſion, the names of which are not enumerated.

VIII. Nueſtra Senora de Guadalupe. — Father Joſeph Ctaſteige.—Villages—

1. Nueſtra Senora de Guadalupe in 27°.

2. Concepcion de Nueſtra Senora, 6 leagues S.

3. San Miguel, 6 leagues S. E.

4. San Pedro and San Pablo, 8 leagues E.

5. Santa Maria, 5 leagues N.

IX. San Ignacio.—Father Sebaſtian de Siſtiaga.—Villages—

1. San Ignacio, in 28°.

2. San Borja, 8 leagues.

3. S. Joachin, 3 leagues.

4. S. Sabas, 3 leagues.

5. San Athanaſio, 5 leagues.

6. Santa Monica, 7 leagues.

7. Santa Martha, 11 leagues.

8. Santa Lucia, 10 leagues.

9. Santa Nynfa, 5 leagues.

X. Nueſtra Senora de los Dolores del Noite.—Father Fernando Conſag.

This

This miffion was joined with that of San Ignacio, and cultivated by the fathers Siftiaga and Confag : within its diftrict, which lies 30 leagues from S. Ignacio, and in the latitude of 29ᵒ. were already five hundred and forty-eight baptized Indians.

XI. Santa Maria Magdalena, begun in the N. by the fame father Confag, who wrote concerning it to the father provincial Jofeph Barba, yet no convenient place for its feat was to be found, tho' the converted Indians were as well difpofed, and as regular as thofe of San Ignacio.

XII. San Jago del Sur.—Father Antonio Tempis.—Villages—

1. San Jago, in 33ᵒ.

2. The anchoring-place of Santa Maria de La Luz.

3. The anchoring-place of San Borja.

XIII. Nueftra Senora del Pilar de la Paz. Of this miffion no account came to Mexico, nor of the others which had been reftored in the S. which are,

XIV. Santa Rofa, in Palmas bay.

XV. San Jofeph del Cabo de S. Lucas, the ftation of the new royal garrifon.

XVI. San Juan Baptifta, begun in the N. and at the fame time it was ardently defired that another new miffion might be founded in the

N.

N. at the village of San Juan Baptista; and accordingly several entrances were made, especially by father Consag for preparing the minds of the Indians; but there was neither a fund for endowing it, soldiers for defence, nor missionaries.

Whilst father Consag was thus employed, he received an order to prepare himself for taking a survey of the coasts of the gulf. This service he had been particularly selected for, being in a very eminent manner possessed of all the talents necessary for such an enterprise. The difficulties were very great; as he wanted every thing necessary towards the execution of it. But, as that father observes, " the importance and consequence of this necessary service surmounted them all." The missions, considering this work to be equally advantageous to the service of christianity, and his majesty, tho' labouring under great difficulties themselves, contributed to defray the necessary expences of boats, seamen, provisions, and every other requisite suggested, by those who knew the dangers of sailing on seas, and visiting coasts unknown, and inhabited only by savages. They also put on board a certain number of christian Cochini, furnishing them with cloathing and arms. Every thing being thus in readiness, father Consag left Loretto, accompanied

panied by don Bernardo Rodrigues la Larrea, a fon of the worthy capt. don Eftevan Rodrigues Lorenzo, often mentioned in this hiftory; and arriving at the fhore of San Carlos in the lat. of 28º. he embarked with his men in four boats, on the 9th of June, 1746. The captain did not accompany the father in this voyage; but he procured him a canoe, and took the moft effectual meafures for fuccefs. Within a few days, the melancholy news arrived, that the Indian favages of the coaft had murdered the father, foldiers, feamen, and Indians, and pulled the boats to pieces. The captain, at hearing this fhocking account, was for going immediately in a canoe, with an armed force, to San Carlos; but the fathers oppofed it till the news fhould be confirmed, fufpecting it was only a fiction of the Indians, as it afterwards proved to be.

Father Confag, with his body of men, took an accurate furvey as far as the river Colorado, as may be feen in the father's original journal, at the end of this work, for the fatiffaction of the reader, and to animate others to undertake the like laborious tafks, by fhewing that thofe who employ their talents for the benefit of fociety, will not fail of receiving the honours they deferve. In the new Theatro Americano may alfo be feen a curious extract

of

of this journal. All that we shall at present observe, or rather repeat is, that in this voyage, it was evident, beyond all possibility of doubt, that California is a peninsula, joining to the continent of New Spain; and that the extremity of the gulf, is the river Colorado, which divides the former from the latter.

Whilst the society, in obedience to the royal orders, were employed in these difficult attempts, other measures were likewise taken by the viceroy. The resignation of the twenty-two missions, in the diocese of Durango, was admitted, as now they were only a weight on the society, furnishing no opportunity for that labour which exerts itself in extending the doctrines of christianity. The flying garrison of Terenate was fixed at San Phelipe de Jesu Guevavi, according to the Theatro Americano, in which an account of it is given under that name; and supposes it to have been erected there before the year 1748, when that work was printed at Mexico. Guevavi is situated among the Sobaypures in a fine well watered plain, abounding in wood and pastures, tho' not remarkable for its plenty of other products; at a small distance from the territories of the Apaches, and within a few leagues of the mission of Suamca, the place where father Escovar proposed it should be established.

This

This garrison consists of a captain, lieutenant, ensign, serjeant, and forty-seven soldiers. What contributed to hasten this undertaking was the universal complaint of the whole province of Sonora, which was under continual alarms, on account of the depredations of the Apaches; and these, since the year 1740, were so frequent and open, that the name of Apache is now commonly given to every infidel or apostate who acts as a declared enemy. The Apaches, here intended are those within the circular tract of ground extending from the river Chigagua, by the garrison of Janos Fronteras, Anterenate, or Guevavi, to the Gila. It is bounded on the north, by the country of the Moqui and New Mexico; on the east, by the garrison of Passo; and on the south, by the garrison of Chigagua. Within this circuit of three hundred leagues the Apaches reside in their small rancherias, erected in the valleys and the breaches of mountains. Their country is also of very difficult access, from the cragginess of the mountains, and the scarcity of water. According to some prisoners who have been ransomed, they are extremely savage and brutal; they have very little cultivated land, nor does their country supply them with any plenty of spontaneous productions. They are cruel to those who have

the

the misfortune to fall into their hands; and among them are feveral apoftates. They go entirely naked, but make their incurfions on horfes of great fwiftnefs, which they have ftolen from other parts, a fkin ferving them for a faddle. Of the fame fkins they make little boots or fhoes of one piece; and by thefe they are traced in their flight. They begin the attack with fhouts, at a great diftance, to ftrike the enemy with terror. They have not naturally any great fhare of courage; but the little they can boaft of, is extravagantly increafed on any good fuccefs. In war they rather depend on artifice than valour; and on any defeat fubmit to the moft ignominious terms, but keep their treaties no longer than fuits their conveniency. His majefty has ordered, that if they require peace, it fhould be granted; and even offered to them before they are attacked. But this generofity they conftrue to proceed from fear. Their arms are the common bows and arrows of the country. The intention of their incurfions is plunder, efpecially horfes, which they ufe both for riding and eating; the flefh of thefe creatures being one of their greateft dainties.

Thefe people, during eighty years paft, have been the dread of Sonora, no part of which was fecure from their violences. Our

people

people have occafionally obtained fome advantages over them ; but the actions were not general, and confequently not decifive. Of late years the infolence of thefe favages has been carried to the moft audacious height, from the fuccefs of fome of their ftratagems, principally owing to the variances and indolence of the Spaniards. In one of thefe, capt. Efcalante, who had ferved in that quality in California, loft his life. The like unhappy fate attended the laft captain of the garrifon at Coro de Guache de Fronteras, don Juan Baptifta de Aufa, tho' famous for his valour and conduct, and with him fell a great many private men. The Apaches penetrate into the province by difficult paffes ; and after loading themfelves with booty will travel in one night fifteen, eighteen, or twenty leagues. To purfue them over the mountains, is equally dangerous and difficult; and in the levels they follow no paths. On any entrance into their country, they give notice to one another by fmokes or fires : and at this fignal they all hide themfelves. The damages they have done, efpecially fince the death of the brave capt. Aufa, in the villages, fettlements, farms, roads, paftures, woods, and mines, are beyond defcription ; and many of the latter, tho' very rich, have been forfaken. Out of the twenty-

four

four missions of jesuits in Sonora and Pimeria, twenty are exposed to the incursions of the Apaches, which is likewise the fate of the parish of Nacosari, and part of the garrison of San Juan Baptista, the capital of the province, the only two where secular priests officiate. Hence arises the difficulty of communicating the necessary instructions to the Indians; as there is no continuing for any time at the rancherias, nor can they, without great danger, come to the seats of the mission : and this occasions a necessity of bearing with many of their irregularities; and the unhappy consequence is the impossibility of bringing the new christian communities to a life of devotion and polity as in other parts.

In the year 1747, the viceroy having consulted with the marquis de Altamira, secretary at war, determined to give the Apaches such a blow as should not soon be forgotten. Accordingly strict orders were issued that each of the garrisons of New Biscay, Passo, New Mexico, Janos, Fronteras, and Terrenate or Guevavi, should send thirty soldiers; and that this corps should be augmented by the Spanish militia, and as many armed Indians as could be procured; and all at one time enter the country of the Apaches, and seek them in their secret retreats. The jesuits of Sonora not only encouraged

3

encouraged the Indians of the miffions to join in the expedition, but contributed horfes, provifions, and money. However, at the time appointed, the governor of New Mexico did not arrive, being fuddenly obliged to turn his arms againft fome neighbouring Indians, who were fortunately difcovered, when on the point of executing a fanguinary defign. Thofe at a greater diftance tho' unwilling feparately to enter an enemy's country, joined, and penetrated a great way into it, without meeting fo much as a fingle Indian. For the Apaches being informed of the intended expedition, kept fo good a watch, that they withdrew as our troops approached; and whilft the loyalifts were roving about the country to no purpofe, they fell on Sonora, now quite defencelefs, killing, plundering, ravaging, and deftroying every thing they met with. Nor was this all; the Indians endeavoured to penetrate as far as Moqui; but were obliged to abandon the attempt, for want of provifions.

Thus the expedition, which was intended to reduce the Apaches proved abortive; the expences were loft, the contributions of Sonora diverted to foreign views, itfelf left more expofed, and lefs capable of defence, the enemy daring by their fuccefs, and our people alienated from fuch expeditions for the future.

However,

However, in the year 1748, preparatives were made for a new campaign; and to the soldiers and Spanish militia, were added three hundred Apatas, and the like number of Pirnas, whom the fathers had again fitted out to the best of their power. Their rendezvous was at Coro de Guachi de Fronteras, where they were incommoded by the rains which fall in November and December, the time appointed for their march. They visited the mountains of Chigagua, the usual retreat of the savages; but were so far from finding any Apaches, that they could not even discover any vestiges of their having been there, the melting of the snows having obliterated their tracks. In their retreat they met with a rancheria, where they killed a few of the enemy, and made ten prisoners. Such was the whole result of an expedition which had made so much noise in America. Providence, however, thought proper to bring about an event, which human address had attempted in vain. For some of the Apaches, terrified at the extraordinary preparations of the Spaniards, came to the garrison of Janos petitioning for peace, and the liberty of settling near the mission. At the same time another troop came with the same intention to Fronteras, adding a request, that the father would please to instruct them:

and,

and, tho' they were but few in number, and their pretenfions little to be depended on, they were readily admitted, that thefe might prevail on others to follow their example.

A month before the laft expedition, namely, in October 1748, father Sedelmayer made another progrefs to the river Gila, in which he again travelled thro' the territories of the Papagos, and vifited the Pimas of Gila; from thence he continued his journey among the Cocomaricopas, and afterwards to the Yumas their enemies, who inhabited the weftern banks of the river Colorado; returning on the left or E. fide, till within a few days journey of it's difcharge into the gulf, where he faw other rancherias of Yumas. Thefe Indians feemed amazed at the fight of the father and his guards, not having the leaft remembrance of father Kino, who vifited that country about forty years before. They fhewed a ftrong inclination for pilfering fome trifles; but were afraid to attempt it. The father expreffed a defire of paffing the river, but as the other, or weftern, fide was inhabited by the Quiquimas, who were enemies to the Yumas, the latter were difpleafed at his intention of vifiting their enemy's country; and refufed to affift him. Thefe and other difficulties the father met with, from a great part of his efcorte, laid

him

him under a neceffity of returning to the miffion of Tubutama.

In February the following year 1749, the father intended to make another progrefs ; and in order to execute it with the greater fecurity, waited the arrival of the governor of Sonora, that he might make the moft effectual provifions for it : but whether it was attended with fuccefs or not, I am not able to fay, no account of it having been fent to Europe.

About the fame time the infidel Seris and Tepocas, who lived in the mountains along the coaft of the gulf, animated by the example of the Apaches, renewed their hoftilities in that province with an extraordinary boldnefs, which obliged his excellency the viceroy to haften the meafures for removing them from their barren fhores, and incorporating them with the former miffions. This was under deliberation in the beginning of the fame year 1749 : for in May father Balthafar fent his papers to Europe ; and in them he fays, that from the meafures taken by the viceroy for their emigration, there were great hopes of civilizing and reducing them into communities. Thofe orders were doubtlefs dictated by the greateft forefight and wifdom ; but the effect it feems was not anfwerable, as father Sigifmund Taraval, in a letter written at Guadalaxara,

laxara, in the year 1751, fays, that the Seris had that fame year, in the laft miffion of Caborca, murdered the fathers Thomas Tello, and Henry Rohen; tho' even then the circumftance of the revolt of the Seris, nor of thofe murders were known at Guadalaxara. Father Thomas Tello, a native of the town of Almagro, arrived from Mexico at the miffion, in the preceding year 1750; and purfuant to the royal orders, appointing two minifters in every frontier miffion, was nominated collegue to father Rohen at Caborca. Father Juan Antonio Balthafar, in a letter of the 27th of February 1752, fays, that by the fame opportunity he fends to Europe an account of the tranfactions of the two laft years in Pimeria; and another of a new entrance made into California in the year 1751; but never having come to my hands, I am deprived of the fatiffaction of communicating thofe accounts to the publick. In the mean time it becomes us to hope that the blood of the minifters of the gofpel, which has been fpilt in California will cry powerfully to heaven for the complete reduction of thefe unhappy favages, now involved in the fhadow of death; and that it will infallibly fix the eftablifhment, propagation, and fecurity of the chriftian religion in thofe extreme parts of the globe.

On

On both fides, in Pimeria and California, a door is now opened for fpeeding the gofpel. On the north fide of both are vaft countries, inhabited by infidel nations, who never have heard of chriftianity, and the glad tidings of falvation it offers to the human race. And, furely; it is an undertaking highly conformable both to the dictates of humanity, and the precepts of the gofpel, to convert fuch multitudes of the human fpecies, from their brutal and enormous vices to the paths of virtue and religion,

A

A
NATURAL and CIVIL
HISTORY
OF
CALIFORNIA.

✦✦

PART IV.

APPENDICES to the account of CALIFORNIA.

INTRODUCTION,

THAT the account of California, which I now submit to the publick, may be as complete and useful to the Spanish nation as possible; I have added to what is said in the beginning of the first part of its geographical situation, the most authentick accounts hitherto known concerning its eastern and western coasts, and junction with the continent, the subject of such long contests; and

likewise

likewife the accounts we have of the adjacent iflands, land, and feas, thefe having a natural and political connection with California. The reafon of this is fufficiently evident: California, confidered in itfelf, is the moft difagreeable, barren, and wretched country in the world. But notwithftanding thefe difagreeable particulars, the conqueft of it from the firft difcovery of the new world in Cortes's time, has been attempted with very great expences to the crown of Spain : and at length this defired reduction has been accomplifhed by the jefuits: and our fovereign has lately taken the moft effectual meafures towards the completing of what may be wanting in this enterprife ; as we have already related in the preceding parts. But it may be afked on what account is California of fuch importance to the crown of Spain, and the Spanifh jefuits its fubjects? whence this mighty concern about it ? wherefore is its conqueft preferred to that of many other countries of both Americas, like it inhabited by infidel favages ; countries in a milder climate, rich and fertile ; countries which might be reduced and held at a much lefs expence; and in which a much greater number of fouls might be brought within the bofom of the church ?

It

It is my duty to give all possible satisfaction to these reasonable questions: and this is indeed the principal intention of the 4th part. I answer the first in general: It is the advantageous situation of California which renders it so valuable. This makes the conquest of it preferable to that of any other country in America. Though so wretched and poor, its situation alone renders it more important than all these, both with regard to the propagation of religion, and the good of the state. Add to this, that if the expensive endeavours and repeated attempts of the Spanish nation for the conquest of California in the two last centuries were just and prudent, the nation has at present much more powerful and weighty motives for this enterprise than the former, which however still subsist.

The proof of these assertions may be partly collected from several passages in the former parts of this work ; and partly from what we shall offer in this 4th part. California has an essential connection with the provinces contiguous to it, and belonging to the continent of New Spain. The American coasts on the South sea, from cape de Corientes, and even from Acapulco itself northwards, are not safe, whilst California remains in the hands of savages, and under no subjection to the Spanish crown. The

inha-

inhabitants of thefe coafts cannot follow the rich pearl-fifhery in the gulf of California, nor can the provinces from Acapulco to the river Colorado carry on any maritime commerce. The mean canoes of the Californians are not indeed much to be dreaded, but California has feveral times been a fhelter for privateers and pirates, who have from thence fcoured all thofe feas, taken a great many Spanifh fhips, difturbed the whole commerce of the Pacifick ocean, and filled thofe remote provinces with alarms. What would be the confequence fhould any European power fettle colonies, and build forts on the coaft of California. Admiral Anfon according to the account of his voyage, was of opinion, that if he could have made himfelf mafter of Baldivia on the coaft of Chili, he fhould have been able, with that advantage, to have made the vaft empire of Peru tremble. Though this be the only conjecture, it cannot be denied but that if any foreign power fhould find means of building fortifications in California and maintain its fuperiority there, the empire of Mexico would be in the utmoft danger.

California is alfo of equal importance for enlarging the king's dominions in North America. We have feen that the jefuit miffions have not only reduced the rich provinces of Culiacan, Cinaloa Oftimuri, Yaqui, and Sonora;

but

but hav likewife penetrated to the bay and upper Pimeria, even to the great rivers of Gila and Colorado, and taken a furvey of the Moqui provinces adjacent to new Mexico. What remains is to reduce the Papagos, Guaimas Tepocas, and Seris, who inhabit the extreme coaft of new Spain on the gulf of California, and, as we have related, not long fince revolted, murdered their miffionaries and joined with the lawlefs Apaches. The reduction of thefe Indians will always be very difficult, if the entrance among them be made on the land fide, but very eafy by paffing from California to their coafts, as father Salva-Tierra has fufficiently proved.

If the miffions and Spanifh fettlements are intended to be carried on towards the north of America with fafety and regularity, they muft not only be joined to the reft with New Mexico; but extended from the latter beyond the rivers Gila and Colorado to the furtheft known coafts of California on the South fea; that is to Puerto San Diego, Puerto de Monte-rey, the fnowy mountains, cape Mendocino, cape Blanco, San Sebaftian, and the river difcovered by the marquis de Aquillar in forty three degrees. With what expedition might this conqueft be carried on, were the miffionaries to go at one time along each fide of the gulf of California, reducing the interjacent nations till they all met

on

on the banks of the river Colorado; and proceed jointly from thence till they arrived at the abovementioned coasts, harbours, capes, and rivers on the South sea? How much more, if, at the same time, the northern Californian missions on the South sea were extended from the coast of San Xavier and the islands of los Dolores in 28 deg. lately surveyed by father Taraval, to the aforesaid harbours of S. Diego de Monte Rey, and the others where the missionaries of California and Pimeria, who had joined at the rivers Colorado and Gila, were to conclude their progress?

The immense distances from Mexico of these two rivers and the provinces they water, and especially of the countries near Monte Rey and Mendozino, render it impossible to supply, by land, the missionaries and the other Spaniards with cloaths, utensils, and necessaries. It is therefore requisite to open a maritime communication, by erecting forts near all the harbours on the coast of the South sea, between the lattitude of 30 and 40 degrees: and also in the gulf of California to the mouth of the river Colorado at the 33d degree of lat. Without such provisions for a maritime communication, the missions in these remote provinces can be by no means maintained; much less Spanish colonies, towns, villages, and farms be erected. But if

Cali-

California and the reduction of it be relinquished, how can these improvements be made? How can harbours be discovered, and entrances made either on the gulf of California, or the coasts of the South-sea? and were these improvements made by entering only on the side of Pimeria and Sonora, into the provinces lying on the west side of the river Colorado, how could they be able to maintain themselves for any considerable time, while the whole peninsula of California was inhabited by infidel and savage Indians? Thus California, by its situation, has been, and still is, of the highest importance for the preservation and advancement of the christian religion, and the augmentation of the Spanish sovereignty in America.

It may perhaps, to some seem a very indifferent affair, whether his majesty's dominions be extended to the river Colorado and cape Mendocino, and the reasons for making and maintaining such a conquest may possibly appear extravagant. But with regard to the first, in all great undertakings, the general plan is to be formed immediately, though the execution of it may prove a work of time. A nation acting without a plan, in pursuit of any end, is seldom known to reap the advantages which would necessarily in time flow from it.

Secondly,

Secondly, experience has shewn, that within the space of a hundred years, the jesuit missions and his majesty's dominions in North America are extended from Cinaloa in 20 degrees to the rivers Colorado and Gila in 35. The Sierra or mountains of Topaia and Tarahumara, together with Nayarith have already been reduced. The ancient missions of the Parral, Parras Tepehuanes, Cinaloa, &c. And a tract of 300 leagues of California, from cape San Lucas to near the 30th degree of lat. have likewise been subdued: and all this has been performed since the middle of the last century; and with very little assistance from the government in any of these enterprises.

But if the conquest and preservation of California, has been, and is essential to the advancement and security of the catholick religion, and the Spanish dominions in the other provinces of America, it is equally advantagious to the Philippine islands and their commerce with new Spain. It is not necessary to form so many political schemes for the navigation and commerce of the South sea, as cardinal Alberoni seems to imagine. One single galeon performing annually one voyage from Manilla and Acapulco, and back again, is found to be sufficient; but without this commerce, those rich,

rich, populous, and commodious iſlands could not be preſerved, though they are far from being improved to the greateſt advantage. We have ſeen that this ſhip is under a neceſſity of putting into ſome port in her voyage; that this can only be done in California; that for want of ſuch a port great numbers of Spaniards have periſhed by the length of the voyage, even in time of the moſt profound peace: laſtly that this galeon has been ſeveral times taken by the enemy, who have ſheltered themſelves in California, within ſight of which ſhe muſt neceſſarily paſs. If therefore the Philippine iſlands be worth keeping, can the utility of reducing and ſettling California be any longer queſtioned? But beſides theſe motives there are others of equal ſtrength, and equally intereſting to religion and the ſtate. The Ruſſians, or Muſcovites, whoſe vaſt empire extends to the northern extremities of Aſia, and even near to the South ſea, are not only endeavouring to civilize the natives of thoſe countries, but are actually erecting forts and planting colonies; and have already made docks and arſenals in ſeveral parts, where they have built ſhips, fitted and mann'd them; taken ſurveys of their own coaſts, ſailed as far as the iſlands of Japan, and, croſſing the South ſea, landed in ſeveral parts of Spaniſh America.

In

In one voyage made in 1741, the Ruffians landed on this very coaft in the latitude of 55 degrees 36 minutes, not above 12 degrees from cape Blanco, the moft northern part of California hitherto known. And is it not natural to think that the Ruffians in future voyages, will come down as low as cape Blanco: and if California be abandoned by the Spaniards even as far as cape San Lucas? and we may well fuppofe that they who to-day take a view of the coafts and country, may to-morrow determine to plant colonies there. The laft Spanifh garrifon on the Northern American coafts of the South-fea, is that of cape San Lucas at the fouthern point of California, and to the fouthward of the tropick of Cancer: and even this is but weak and lately fettled. But along the immenfe extent of the coaft northward, Spain has not one fingle fortification. How fhall we hinder the Ruffians from making fettlements there, unlefs we be beforehand with them? would it be proper that the Mufcovites fhould become our neighbours and rivals, and eftablifh the Greek church in California?

The repeated attempts of the Englifh for finding a paffage to the South-fea by the north of America and Hudfon's bay, are known to all the world. The laft was undertaken in the spring of the year 1753. If they should one day succeed in this, why may not the English come down through their conquests, and even make themselves masters of the provinces of New Mexico, Moqui, the rivers Gila and Colorado, Pimeria, Papagos, and Apaches; and lastly of the northern part of California itself, which borders on our missions and garrisons in the north of America. The publick papers have informed us that the English had a design of crossing the South-sea from the East Indies, erecting fortifications, and making settlements on the coast of America above California towards Hudson's bay; that is, in those very parts which the Russians have visited. Whoever is acquainted with the present disposition of the English nation, and has heard with what zeal and ardour the project for a North-west passage has been espoused by many considerable persons, will be convinced that the scheme is not romantick; and it would not be surprising if the execution of it should one day come under deliberation. If this should ever happen, I would ask, what would be the condition of our possessions? would the faith of treaties be a sufficient protection? Jamaica, Georgia, Carolina, Virginia, New York, Pensylvania, Newfoundland, and the other provinces of that nation in America were discovered

vered by Spaniards; and for a long time made part of our dominions: yet at present they are in the hands of the English; and with equal ease may they settle on the coasts on the north of California, unless we prevent them by attempting the reduction of it, without delay. I therefore beg leave to repeat it that in all times, but especially at present, the conquest of the poor and barren province of California has been considered as of the utmost importance to religion and the state; and more desirable than that of many happier countries in America.

It should be remembered that we have already shewn the situation of California itself, of Sonora, Pimeria, and other provinces contiguous to it, and the continent of New Spain. All that remains therefore to be done is to add the most authentick memoirs existing both ancient and modern, relating to the two coasts of this peninsula: and this is the intention of the first appendix in this fourth part, which contains a short description of Gomara; the voyage of captain Sebastian Vizcaino in the year 1603; the last survey of the gulf of California, to its furthest extremity the river Colorado in 1746, by father Fernando Consag: and lastly the short description of the famous English navigator capt. Woods Rogers. Next to these

is

is the account given of California in the voyage of the Englifh commander George Anfon, efq; fince raifed to the peerage; and wherein he mentions the commerce of the Philippines, and of that which he fuppofes thefe iflands carry on with California: this will give us an opportunity of correcting feveral pernicious miftakes; and of forming in the reader's mind the moft falutary ideas for the good of religion and the ftate, without any regard to the temporal intereft of the fociety.

APPENDIX I.

A fhort defcription of the outward coaft of CALIFORNIA by Gomara.

IN order to fhew what was moft certainly known concerning the outward coaft of California, before captain Vizcaino's furvey, I fhall lay before the reader the fuccinct account given by Francifco Lopez de Gomara, a careful writer, and whofe geography Antonio de Herrera has chiefly followed, as an author of the beft judgment and intelligence, obferving only that what he calls Punta de Balenas is the point of California or cape San Lucas, but was then, both in books and maps called, by that name.

Extract from the XIIth chapter of the
history of the Indies by Francisco Lopez
de Gomara.

From Mira Florez bay to the Punta de Balenas, by the way of Puerto Escondido, Belen, Puerto de Fuegos, and La Bahia de Canoas and
Pearl island is above two hundred and twenty
leagues. Punta de Balenas is under the tropick, and eighty leagues from cape Corrientes,
and between these capes runs the sea of
Cortes, which resembles the Adriatick, and is of
a reddish colour. From the Punta de Balenas
to Bahia del Abad, is one hundred leagues along
the coast, and from the latter to cape del Enganno, which lies in about 30 deg. 30 min.
lat. is one hundred more, though some make
the distance greater.

From cape del Enganno to Cabo de Cruz,
is about fifty leagues : from Cabo de Cruz to
Puerto de Sardinas in 36 deg. is about one hundred and ten leagues. Along this coast are
the Ancon de San Miguel, Bahia de los Fuegos
and Costa blanca. From Sardinas to the Sierra
Nivadas or snowy mountains, is one hundred
and fifty leagues; by the way of Puerto de
Todos Santos, Cabo de Galera, Cabo Nevado,
Bahia de los Pinos. The Sierras Nevados or
the

the fnowy mountains lie in 40 deg. and is the furtheft country on this fide inferted in the maps. Yet the coaft runs northward five hundred and ten leagues further to us, to include within this vaft ifland both Labrador and Groenland.

APPENDIX II.

Narrative of the voyage of captain Sebaftian Vizcaino in the year 1602, for furveying the outward or weftern coaft CALIFORNIA on the South-fea.

The three volumes of the Monarchia Indiana, by father Juan de Torquemada, a learned Francifcan, having been publifhed at Seville in the year 1615, and a new edition at Madrid in 1725, it may be thought fufficient to have referred the reader to thofe books, without fwelling the prefent work by a narrative of captain Vizcaino's voyage: but the copies of the firft impreffion are extremely fcarce, the greateft part of them having been loft at fea: and when that illuftrious patron of literature Don Andrez Gonzalez de Barcia, privy counfellor, and one of the board of treafury, was defirous of having that valuable work reprinted, after all his diligent fearch, could meet with only three copies of it

in

in Madrid; and the impreſſion was made from that in the library of the imperial college of jeſuits, father Martin de Raxas having gene-rouſly parted with it for that purpoſe. How-ever ſince this ſecond impreſſion the books of the Monarchia Indiana are become ſcarce, and captain Vizcaino's narrative is eſſentially ne-ceſſary towards an exact account of California: and though ſome readers will find here what they have already ſeen in father Torquemada's volumes, yet I ought not to deprive a much greater number, who have not that work, from the pleaſure of the peruſal, and who will be glad to have every thing relating to California collected here, eſpecially as this work is not intended only for European readers, but like-wiſe for thoſe in America, who trade in theſe re-mote ſeas and countries where other books are not ſo eaſily procured.

I was extremely deſirous of finding captain Sebaſtian Vizcaino's narrative and the repre-ſentations of the council to his majeſty Philip III. eſpecially the maps, plans, charts of his voyage and diſcoveries, in order to communi-cate the whole to the publick. Accordingly at my requeſt ſearch was made in the ſecre-tary's office of the council of the Indies. But in this intention of being ſerviceable to the pub-lick I have been diſappointed.

Extract

Extract from Lib. V. of the Monarchia Indiana, by father Juan de Torquemada.

In the reign of Philip III. and during the viceroyship in New Spain of Don Antonio de Mendoza, when the navigation to the isles of Luzon, by us called the Philippines, was first discovered by some ships built at La Navidad, a town of New Spain on the coast of the South-sea; these ships in their return near the lat. of 42 deg. perceived a point of land which they called Cabo Mendozino in honour of the viceroy, by whom they had been sent; and keeping pretty near the shore, it appeared that from thence to La Navidad, was one continued Terra Firma. On their arrival at New Spain, they laid this discovery before the viceroy, who was desirous that the whole coast as far as cape Mendozino should be carefully surveyed at his own expence. But the person appointed to conduct it, could reach no farther than the harbour called San Jago, now La Magdalena in 25 deg. the continual N. W. winds rendering it impossible to continue his course any farther. His majesty also was informed that other viceroys by his father's orders had attempted the same discovery, and had also failed, as will be related hereafter. His majesty also found among other

Q 3 papers

papers a narrative delivered by fome foreigners
to his father, giving an account of many remarkable particulars, which they faw in that
country, when driven thither by ftrefs of weather, from the coaft of Newfoundland; adding that they had paffed from the N. fea to
the S. by the ftreight of Anian, which lies
beyond cape Mendozino; and that they had
arrived at a populous and opulent city, walled
and well fortified, the inhabitants living under
a regular polity, and were a fenfible and courteous people; with many other particulars well
worth a further enquiry. On the other hand,
he was alfo informed that the fhips in their return from China to New Spain, were in great
danger; and that they met with very bad weather about cape Mendozino, and therefore for
the fafety of the fhips, it would be highly proper
to furvey the coaft from thence to Acapulco, in
order to provide a place on the coaft for them
to put in at, as they ufually belong to his majefty. For thefe and other reafons, he ordered
the count de Monte Rey, viceroy of New
Spain, to caufe the difcovery to be undertaken
with all poffible care and diligence, and at the
royal expence.

Accordingly, count de Monte-Rey, defirous
of accomplifhing what his majefty had fo po-
fitively ordered, had recourfe to perfons, from
whofe

whose knowledge and experience he might expect information, in order to pursue the best measures for this purpose. The method being resolved on, the necessaries were prepared with the utmost care and dispatch; and general Sebastian Vizcaino appointed captain-general for this voyage, as he had before acted in that quality in California. The admiral was captain Toribio Gomez de Corvan, both persons deserving the great confidence reposed in them. For general Sebastian Vizcaino was at that time employed in the pacification and conquest of California: and was of all persons in New Spain the best acquainted with that coast, having as we have already related gone on a discovery there in the year 1594: and was the most concerned that the discovery should be made pursuant to his majesty's orders, as it was carried on at his expence. For the better securing the success of this enterprise, the post of admiral was conferred on captain Toribio Gomez, as a consummate seaman, having served his majesty many years in crusing ships; and in recompence of his fidelity and courage had been made captain of the Pataches, and entrusted with many affairs of consequence, as appears from the papers and certificates which he presented to the viceroy in testimony of his services. He was immediately sent to the pro-

vinces

vinces of Honduras and Guatimala in search
of two ships, having for assistants Sebastian
Melendez, a land-officer, and Antonio Florez
a pilot: the viceroy also sent ensign Juan de
Acevedo Texeda to Acapulco in order to get
every thing ready there for the voyage, and
to superintend the building of a small frigate.
The general was directed to deliver in an account of what he should want for the voyage,
provisions, stores, seamen, and soldiers: and
was completely furnished with every thing.
Three bare-footed Carmelites, namely, father
Andrez de la Assumpfion, father Antonio de
la Afcension, and father Thomas de Aquino,
were ordered to accompany him. And because
as Cicero says, great things are never accom-
plished merely by strength and activity of body,
unless conducted with the wisdom and foresight
of prudent and experienced counsellors, the
viceroy appointed captain Alonfo Estevan Peguero, a person of great valour and long experience, who had served in Flanders, and
also with Magellan; and captain Gaspar de
Alarcon, a native of Bretagne, distinguished
for his prudence and courage; and for sea affairs several pilots and masters of Ships; likewise captain Geronimo Martin, who went as
Cosmographer, in order to make draughts of
the countries discovered, for the greater perspicuity

cuity of the account intended to be tranfmitted to his majefty of the difcoveries and tranf-actions in this voyage. Every thing being thus provided, the count ordered don Francifco de Valverde, agent for the treafury at Mexico and likewife for the king's fhips, to fend to Aca-pulco what ftores and money he had by him, and to pay the foldiers, who were all picked men, and formed one of the moft fightly com-panies ever raifed in New Spain. The enfign was Juan Francifco Suriano and the ferjeant Miguel de Legar.

At the time of their departure, the viceroy called them together; and recommended to them the affair on which they were fent, peace and amity among themfelves, obedience and refpect to fuperiors, and efpecially to the reli-gious, on whom he chiefly founded the hopes that their voyage would prove fuccefsful. On the 7th of March 1601, the religious and cap-tains fet out from Mexico and arrived at Aca-pulco, where they were to embark on the 20th of the fame month.

Every thing being in readinefs for the voyage, the general iffued orders for all to repair on board the fhips to which they had been ap-pointed: this being punctually complied with, the Capitana, Almiranta, and the frigate failed from Acapulco at four in the afternoon on

Sunday

Sunday the 5th of May in the year 1602. They had with them a barco longo for surveying bays and creeks and other services inconvenient to ships of burden. After standing out to sea about two leagues, they took their departure and steered N. W. that being the direction of the western coast. During the whole year a N. W. wind generally prevails all along this coast; and this proved a continual obstacle to the voyage from the time of leaving Acapulco till they reached cape San. Sebastian, which lies beyond cape Mendocino, being continually at sea, during nine months; during which time they underwent the greatest hardships.

The wind being thus contrary, and blowing hard, there was no possibility of making any way unless by tacking, which is a very great fatigue to the men; and if the wind be fresh, and the currents set with the wind, instead of advancing a ship, drives to leeward. But when the wind seemed to render their progress impracticable, it changed in their favour, by which means the squadron reached Puerta de la Navidad, on Sunday the 19th of May at five in the evening. There was a necessity of putting in here, the ships labouring very much for want of ballast; the cargo not being of a weight proportionate to their burden and dimensions. Besides the Capitana had made a

great

great deal of water, and there was a neceffity for ftopping the leak; all which was done with the utmoft difpatch, and at the fame time both fhips fupplied themfelves with wood, water, and a quantity of provifions, in which they met with no manner of difficulty or obftruction, the country being a part of New Spain, and the inhabitants chriftians. In this harbour the fhips, which difcovered the Philippine iflands and cape Mendocino, were built. The galeons from China, before the difcovery of Acapulco, ufed alfo to frequent this port. It is a very good harbour, has plenty of wood, and the neighbouring country pleafant, abounding in all kinds of cattle and other provifions. They however tarried here no longer than was requifite for fupplying themfelves with neceffaries, failing from thence on the 22d, continuing their courfe under the fame difficulties as before, and arrived at cape Corrientes on Whitfunday being the 26th. Here they took a furvey of the country, and then proceeded along fhore; and on the 2d of June about noon, reached the iflands of Mazathan. Thefe are two iflands of a middling fize, lying very near to each other, fo that between them and the continent is a good rode into which a large river from New Galicia empties itfelf. This was the place where the celebrated Englifh navigator

vigator fir Thomas Cavendifh careen'd his
fhip, while he was waiting for the return of the
Chinefe fleet to plunder them.   The Capitana
and Almiranta came to an anchor in this rode to
wait for the frigate, which foon after their leaving
la Navidad had been feparated from them:
but fhe had got before them into the river.
The general and admiral together with the religious and captains, went afhore on one of
thefe iflands, where they found an infinite number of fea birds, which breed there, their young
not being then able to fly. They live chiefly on
pilchards, fardines, and other fmall fifh. Thefe
birds are nearly of the bignefs of geefe, with
a bill little fhort of half a yard in length; their
legs are long like thofe of a ftork ; their feet
and bill fhaped like thofe of a goofe.   Thefe
fowls have a large crop, in which they keep
their fifh for their young, throwing them out
upon the ground before them.

Here are alfo a great many wild goats and
deer, together with a fruit which was found to
be of great benefit to the fick in their return,
as fhall be related in its proper place.   The
inhabitants of the continent here are chriftians,
and confequently friends : and the country itfelf is called the province of Acaponeta or
Chametha.   Here the gulf of California along
the coaft of New Spain begins ; and betwixt

30 and 40 leagues from these islands towards Cinaloa and Culiacan, the Rio Grande now called the Toluca, discharges itself into the sea, which is there called the river de Rarito.

The ships having found the frigate sailed out that very same day, in order to cross the mouth or arm of the sea, betwixt the said islands and cape San Lucas, which is the extreme point of the continent of California : the distance from side to side, being about 60 leagues ; and on the 9th of June in the evening they made the land of California. As they were standing towards cape San Lucas in quest of an harbour, such a thick fog came on, that for near a day and a half they had no sight of each other ; and the Almiranta was within fifty paces of a reef of rocks, from which she was saved by a sudden clearing of the fog, which I may call providential, as it lasted only long enough to shew the danger they were approaching, This happened about seven in the morning; at nine the sun rarefied the fog so as to give a little light : by which means the Almiranta and Capitana had sight of each other ; and coming within hearing, orders were given to stand in for a bay near the said cape, where to the great joy of all, they found the frigate at an anchor.

The

The fquadron entering this bay on the feaſt of St. Barnabas, it was called after the name of that faint. As they were coming to an anchor near the ſhore and furling the ſails, they obſerved along the coaſt a great number of Indians naked, with bows and arrows in their hands, and ſome armed with ſpears; and who by their ſhoutings and throwing the ſand up in the air, ſeemed to be calling to the men in the ſhips. On this the general ordered the boats to be got ready; and that ſome ſoldiers ſhould take their arms, go aſhore, and get intelligence from the Indians, and alſo endeavour to know the meaning of their ſhouts and throwing about the ſand; accordingly the general, the admiral, the three religious, and ſome officers, went in the boats with twelve ſoldiers armed with their harquabuſes and lighted matches. When the boats were near the ſhore, the Indians ſeeing ſuch a number of armed people, retired in great conſternation to an eminence, in order to ſecure themſelves if the ſtrangers ſhould attempt any thing againſt them. All the people in the boats landed; but as they advanced towards the Indians, they retired; till father Antonion, de la Aſcenſion, in order to allure the Indians to a friendly conference, went up alone towards them; and by his ſigns and geſtures ſo far prevailed, that they

ſtaid

ftaid for him; and coming up to their, he embraced them all in the moft affectionate manner. They laid down their arms on the ground, and intimated to him by figns to fit down with them, and order the others not to advance unlefs they would lay down their arms as they had done. Father Antonio did as they defired, and called to a negro to bring a bafket of bifket to diftribute among them. They feemed greatly pleafed at the fight of the negro; and fignified to him that they lived in friend-fhip and correfpondence with a people of his colour; and that not far from thence there was a negro village. In the mean time the general and admiral laid their arms on the ground; and with the two religious came up to father Antonio. The Indians kept their feats, and accepted of the beads and toys given them, though not without fome apprehenfion of an ill defign; and with thefe little prefents retired to their rancherias very much pleafed. After the Indians were gone, the general with the others walked about the country; where, not far from the fhore, they met with a pond of clear and pleafant water: and the day drawing now towards a clofe, they retired to fome rocks by the fea fide. Here they found a great quan-tity of fardines and pilchards, which, flying from the large fifh to the water's edge, had been

thrown

thrown afhore by the breakers. And thefe
ferved the people of the fquadron that night,
and the following day; when they found on
the fhore heaps of pearl-oyfter-fhells, fo fmooth
and glittering, by the reflection of the fun, as
to render the appearance of the ftrand truly
magnificent: and hence the great advantages
which may be derived from the pearl-fifhery, may
in fome meafure be conceived. Under the
above rocks the general ordered a large tent
to be pitched for the reception of an altar;
where during their ftay, the religious daily
faid mafs.

In this bay the fquadron lay fome days to
wait for the change of the moon; repair the
fhips, and take in wood and water; and as
every fhip carried nets, the boats conftantly
went a fifhing, the bay abounding with great
variety, as foles, lobfters, pearl-oyfters, &c.
The foil is very fruitful, healthy, and in a good
climate; level and capable of fine improvements, abounds with rabbets, hares, deer, lions,
tygers, wood-pigeons, and quails. Among its
trees are the fig, the lentifk, the pitahaya, &c.
an infinite number of plum-trees, which, inftead of refin or gum, copioufly emit a very
fine and fragrant incenfe. As to the plums I
never faw any but what were fmall and green;
and confequently wanted the rich tafte of ours,
                                        though

though they who have been in California highly commend them : but what is more advantageous, falt-works might be erected here ; there being a lake of falt-water formed by the fea in the time of the S. E. winds, and it was then full of a fine clear falt : the Indians came to the tent where mafs was faid, and brought to the general and the foldiers, deer, lion, and tyger fkins, cotton caps and little nets, curioufly formed. Thefe Indians were naked, but faftened in their hair every thing they met with which has a glittering appearance. Some mong them are red-haired. They dawb their bodies with black and white colours; are a cheerful, docile, courteous, and good natured people.

In this bay the Englifh who took the St. Anne in her return from the Philippines fome years ago, put the people afhore, and after taking out of her all the goods, fet her on fire, by which means fhe was burnt to the water's edge: but the wreck being driven afhore, the Spaniards went on board, and having thrown her ballaft over-board, and erected jury-mafts, fortunately reached Acapulco. Thefe Spaniards it feems carried off by force an Indian woman, which the natives lament to this very day. And this was the true reafon that they did not feem very fond of contracting an intimacy with the people of the fquadron, left another misfortune of that kind fhould happen : this I mention that proper care may be taken not to give offence to thefe people ; as fuch ufage muft naturally alienate them from agreeing to terms of peace, or giving any credit to the Spaniards who preach the gofpel. Here part of the goods carried for the foldiers at the king's expence, was diftributed among them to their great relief and fatisfaction. In the mean time the change of the moon being paft, with the appearance of fair weather, the general ordered every thing to be taken on board, and the fquadron at midnight left the bay to continue their voyage ; but they had not failed above three leagues, when it blew fo hard at N. W. that the frigate not being able to keep the fea, made again for the bay, whither the Capitana and Almiranta followed her, that fhe might not be left alone. Three times the fquadron failed out of the bay, and were often through the violence of the wind and the roughnefs of the fea, obliged to put back. At laft it was refolved to leave the barco longo which the Capitana had in tow at the frefh-water lake in the bay, that fhe might tack and work the more eafily : and the wind being abated, and the fea fomewhat fmoother, they again on the 5th of July fet fail, which was the fourth time ;

and

and by continual tacking made some progress in their voyage, though the frigate could not keep company with the two ships, and was obliged to run in under the land.

In the mean time the Capitana and Almiranta stood off to sea, till they lost sight of California, to try if they could make any way. Thus the frigate was left behind; and the people thought themselves very happy in getting back to the bay. The Capitana and Almiranta supposing that the frigate would continue her voyage under the land, pursued their course by continual tacking; however they determined to make for the shore, to see if they could get sight of the frigate; and coming near it on the 8th of the month, facing some highlands they were becalmed, that in a week they did not gain a single league; and on this account they gave that high land the name of Sierra del enfado or Mount Tedious. This was not however wholly owing to the want of wind; but the currents were so strong, that what was gained by one, was lost by the other: but a particular circumstance was, that when the wind lulled, the current ceased; and when it began to blow, the tides ran with their former rapidity. At last however, a delightful and moderate gale sprung up, which carried the ships near to the harbour de la Magdalena, otherwise called

St.

St. Jago, where such a thick fog arose, that one man could not see another at the distance of six paces. The Capitana stood in for the land in order to take a view of that harbour, concluding that the Almiranta followed her; and finding it convenient, entered it on the 20th of the said month. The Almiranta, to avoid running on any shoal or rock during the fog, stood from the land, that when it became light, the Capitana was not to be seen, nor was there any appearance of an harbour thereabouts: at last concluding that she was ahead, the Almiranta continued her voyage: and thus they lost each other, till they fortunately met again at the island of Cerros.

The Capitana as we already observed, stood into Magdalena harbour, supposing that the Almiranta would follow her. The very next day the general ordered some soldiers to ascend a high mountain which commanded an extensive view over the sea, in order to look out for the Almiranta, and in case they saw her to make a smoke. Accordingly, they kept a large smoke all the day, the ship being all the time in sight; but imagining the smoke to be made by the Indians, as they had done all along the coast, on seeing any ships, that the people might come ashore, the Almiranta kept her course in quest of the Capitana; looking into every bay, island,

I   or

or harbour, to fee if they could find the Capitana which now was a great way behind.   The general ufed many other endeavours for finding her out, but to no effect.   The Capitana being thus alone on St. Magdalen's day, the father commiffary and father Thomas faid mafs afhore : and on account of this feftival the bay was called la Magdalena; it is very fpacious with feveral fafe creeks, and anchoring places; has two entrances, and through it a wide arm of the fea runs up into the country.   Within this bay they found a weyer half a league in length, of large pieces of timber, which the Indians had made for their fifheries.   In the country round the bay were great numbers of Indians naked, and armed· with bows and arrows; they were well made, and very fociable. On their approaching the Spaniards,   they offered them their bows and arrows in token of peace;   they likewife brought frankincenfe, their country abounding with trees which produce it, being a fort of plumtree.   Within this bay is a fmaller, abounding with excellent mufcles.   But they could get no intelligence of any water, except in a cavity among the rocks; and what they had there was exceffively bad : fome cafks were however filled; but under extreme dejection on account of the Almiranta and the frigate.

We

We have already obferved that the frigate had returned to St. Barnabas bay, without knowing any thing of the Capitana and Almiranta ; but the wind being abated, fhe failed a fecond time in queft of them ; and coming near the land they faw a large bay, which they entered, hoping to find them there. This was one of the entrances which we have mentioned belonging to this bay : and here they met with great numbers of Indians peaceably difpofed, and as a fign of it offered their bows and arrows to fome of her people who went afhore. But not meeting here with the fhips they fought, they returned the fame way they came in, and called the bay Eugan017a, i. e. deceitful, on account of their difappointment. This bay is now called el Puerto del Marques or San Jago. They kept coafting farther on ; and meeting with the other part of Magdalena bay, failed up it and there found the Capitana. The general having the frigate now with him, gave orders for leaving the place and going in fearch of the Almiranta being certain that fhe had proceeded on her voyage. Accordingly the Capitana and the frigate failed out of the bay on Sunday morning the 28th of July; and that the frigate might keep company, orders were given that the Capitana fhould take her in tow,

About

About five leagues beyond Magdalen bay, a hard gale came on at N. W. which gave them a great deal of trouble: for ftanding in towards a bay, the entrance appeared to be very dangerous, as they plainly faw breaches on both fides, fo that inftead of entering it, they again ftood off to fea in queft of the Almiranta. The whole coaft beyond this place is level and pleafant, and has only a few mountains in the inland country. On the 30th of July, they had fight of a bay, which feemed to be formed there by the iffue of a river. The general in order to have a certain account, fent in the frigate to furvey it. But here again they were difappointed by the breakers at the entrance, that on calling a council, it was determined to return and make a report of the obftacle to the general. This fpot or bay which is called San Chriftoval, had been before furveyed by the Almiranta; which came to an anchor two leagues from it, and captain Peguero going in the fhip's boat to view it, faw that it was a river, and that thefe breakers were occafioned by the collifion of the current of the frefh water with the flood of the fea. For at thofe breakers in the entrance there was above fix fathoms water; and the Capitana would have gone in, had not the night been coming on apace. He therefore returned on board,

not

not knowing what might happen before the morning, and made the above report. The bay was called San Chriftoval from its being furveyed on the anniverfary of that faint, and the fame night they continued their voyage, till they came to the bay called las Balenas, from whence the Capitana and frigate continued their voyage in fearch of the Almiranta and alfo of frefh water, of which they both were now in great want. At a confiderable diftance they faw a large bay, into which the general fent the frigate, in hopes it might fuit their circumftances : but on approaching, it was found to be as it were intercepted by fhoals : and accordingly making a fignal to the Capitana not to come nearer, they jointly profecuted their voyage.

This bay alfo had been already furveyed by the Almiranta, who gave it the name of Bahia de Balenas or Whale bay, on account of the multitudes of that large fifh they faw there, being drawn hither by the abundance of feveral kinds of fifh. The vaft flights of birds and fowls are alfo fo great that they cannot be feen without aftonifhment both for their number and variety; and like the whales all prey on the fmall fifh. The country along the bay is pretty populous, and the inhabitants affable and friendly to the higheft degree. They

are

are also well-made and of a fairer complexion than any hitherto seen along the coast. The Indians presented them with pearl-oysters in nets of a very fine thread and curiously wrought; and were very desirous of going to the ship: but the water was so rough, that they durst not venture to swim off, nor the Almiranta's people to come ashore, their boat being very small. However ensign Acevedo and another soldier jumped over board, and swam ashore to see the country. When they were landed, the Indians reached to them the nets with the oysters on long poles, for they looked on the Spaniards as so many gods, and therefore did not presume to touch them. The Indians gave them to understand that there was wood and water in the neighbourhood; and that the country was very large and populous with a great many towns: that several things might be purchased here for trading with the inland people, for they seemed to be fishermen, and carried their fish for sale to the towns in the neighbourhood.

The Almiranta continued here two days, in hopes of better weather, that some armed men might be sent ashore for taking in water and wood, which they greatly wanted; and, during the whole time, the Indians kept continually on the shore, calling out to the people on board: but the agitation of the sea not abating, the Almiranta sailed away in quest of some other place, where they might find relief in their present necessity. This was on the last day of July, and, prosecuting their voyage, came to the island of San Roque, about eight or ten leagues from the former bay. In the middle is a high ridge of mountains called de los Siete Infantes, i. e. of the seven children, there being seven different mountains in a chain.

The Capitana and tender prosecuting their voyage from the bay of Balenas, had on the 8th of August sight of a bay which seemed favourable to their wishes; accordingly they sailed up it, and came to an anchor; but some soldiers being sent ashore, in search of wood and water, they found the country every where extremely barren, and therefore returned on board. Being disappointed here, they continued their voyage, and, on the eve of the assumption, came to an island near the land, where the Almiranta had before anchored, and her people ranged the coast. But the Capitana seeing another island, two leagues further, stood towards it, without bringing to at the first, which was called La Assumpcion, and where the admiral arrived on the 5th of August. This island is of a middling size;

the

the foil fandy and gravelly, and covered with fea-gulls. In fome creeks are an infinite number of fea-wolves, as large as calves; and multitudes of different kinds of fifh, that in an hour's time only with lines, two foldiers caught as many as the boat would carry, all wholefome and palatable. The fardines were particularly large and good. Here father Antonio celebrated mafs on the day of the transfiguration of our Saviour. After the fervice was over, ferjeant Miguel de Legar, with fome of the foldiers, went in fearch of water and wood, and facing the ifland where the Capitana had put in, they found a lake full of very good falt, and near it fome pits or wells made in the fand, fome of which had frefh water, but that in others was brackifh. The admiral, with his council, confidering the great diftance, and confequently the difficulty, of watering there, it was refolved to continue their courfe, in queft of the ifland of Cerros, and the Capitana. Accordingly, on the 9th of Auguft, the Almiranta failed from this ifland, father Antonio having previoufly taken a draught of it.

We have already intimated that the Capitana and tender came in fight of the ifland of Affumpcion, but inftead of coming to an anchor there, ftood over to another ifland two

leagues

leagues beyond it, where they came to an anchor on the evening of our lady's assumption, and called it La iflar de San Roque. The day following the general ordered enfign Ferez Alarcon to go afhore with fome foldiers in fearch of water; with him went enfign Martin de Aguilar, who, with indefatigable labour found the wells and the falt-pits, which the Almiranta's people had before met with; and to their great joy, they difcovered fome marks of the Almiranta's people having been there. From thefe wells they, with great difficulty from the great furge of the fea, fupplied themfelves with water. Whilft the Spaniards were there, the Indians flocked down to the fhore, and interchanged prefents with the Spaniards. The Capitana and tender having thus provided themfelves with water, falt, and wood, fet fail for Cerros, concluding her next trip muft have been thither. In the continuance of the voyage, they paffed by a very high mountain, at the diftance of about twelve leagues from the fea; but without approaching it. Here the Almiranta was detained by a ftrong N. W. wind for about a week, from weathering a cape formed by this mountain; and in their tacking, they came every time within a ftone's throw of this head-land and the continent. No kind of herbage or ver-

dure

dure was to be seen on this mountain, it being every where veined with a variety of colours, which exhibited a very beautiful appearance, and some of the soldiers, together with an experienced seaman of Peru, who had all seen mines, and worked in them, affirmed that this stupendous mountain consisted entirely of mines of silver and gold: and would the wind and the shore have permitted the boat to land, the admiral would have sent some persons to examine into the truth of this affirmation. At length the violence of the wind abating, they weathered the point, and made the best of their way for the mountain, or isle of Cerros, going in betwixt the terra firma, and the small island of La Natividad de Nuestra Senora, and on the 19th of August came to an anchor close under the island of Cerros.

The Capitana and tender did not meet with that obstruction from the painted mountain as the Almiranta had; but entered a good harbour which they called San Bartholomew, three leagues on this side the island of Cerros. Here the general sent ashore ensign Alarcon and some soldiers in search of water, but they found none, that country being extremely barren. Along the shore they indeed met with a kind of resin, but being of an ill smell, they did not think it worth their while to take any

of

of it with them. According to their account, it fhould feem to be amber; but whatever it be there is enough to load a fhip.

The admiral was for furveying this port, but night coming on, it was not thought fafe; and as no water was to be found, the general gave orders for continuing their courfe; accordingly they left it the night of the 24th of Auguft. Soon after they paffed by the ifland de la Natividad without feeing it, and the next day found themfelves near the ifland of Cerros; but miftaking it for the main land, they were for coafting along it. It however pleafed him whom the winds and waters obey, that in above nine days they were not able to double a point called Cabo de San Auguftin. At length, tired with continual tacking, the general determined to run clofe in under the land, where, he judged, he fhould be fheltered from the N. W. gale, and there come to an anchor, fending the tender, with the cofmographer, Geronimo Martin, to take a draught of the country, and make a report. Thus, on the laft day of Auguft, he came to an anchor in the fouth part of the ifland of Cerros.

We have already mentioned the Almiranta's coming to an anchor clofe under the ifland of Cerros, on the 19th of Auguft. The next morning, which was the anniverfary of St. Bernard,

Bernard, admiral Toribeo Gomez, father Antonio, and captain Peguero, with some soldiers, went ashore, in search of water and wood; and in their search came to a narrow path, full of the prints of mens feet; and following it up an eminence, they came to a spot overgrown with flags of a very bright green colour; and near them some traces of a rivulet which had lately run that way; and still following the path, along a rugged valley, they found several wells of a brackish water, but such as might be used in case of necessity. They still followed the path which now led up a steep eminence, till they came to the highest part of the island. But desirous of knowing whither the path would lead them, they followed it till they came to the sea-side, near cape San Augustin, which we before observed the Capitana had never been able to weather, and as they saw no signs of water in any other part, they determined to dig wells near the others, which they did with inexpressible labour, and carried the water in casks above half a league. After spending twelve days in this laborious work, the admiral and his council were of opinion, that the best way would be to sail round the island, in search of the Capitana. Accordingly, on the 31st of August, they got under sail with that intent, standing to the southward,

but

but they had scarce sailed a league before one
of the men discovered a ship at anchor, close under the island; and soon after the whole ship's
company perceived that the seamen were furling their sails, as if she had just let go her
anchor. No event ever gave them more pleasure, for they were convinced it was the Capitana: and at the same time father Thomas de
Aquino, who was on board the Capitana, difcovered the Almiranta standing towards them,
which spread a general joy through the whole
ship's company. Nor is it possible to express the
congratulations on board both ships, when they
came near each other. The Almiranta's company being asked in the general's name what
part they were in, answered, that it was the
island of Cerros, that they had been waiting
for them above twelve days, and that they had
just returned from a cruize in search of them.
At this the Capitana's company were astonished,
having always taken the island for the main
land; but their admiration was still greater,
when they turned their thoughts to the methods
which providence had been pleased to take for
bringing them together. On the Capitana's
people declaring their want of wood and water,
both ships returned to the place where the Almiranta had before laid at anchor. And the
general immediately ordered a tent to be pitched

ed on the shore for religious exercise during their stay; but the general, on going to see the wells, from which the Almiranta's crew had fetched him water, it appeared to him to be a work of such infinite labour, that he sent ensign Juan Francisco, and serjeant Miguel de Legar with twelve soldiers to walk over the island, in order, if possible, to find out some spring or rivulet, nearer the shore. After a long search among breaches, the serjeant, at two leagues distance met with a small stream of fresh water, which ran into the sea; on which the general ordered every thing on board, and the ship to stand in for the watering place, discovered by the soldiers; which was accordingly done, and a kind of a church erected for the three religious to officiate in.

Whilst they were taking in water and wood, and the ship's company refreshing themselves, the general ordered the tender to make the circuit of the island, and look into a bay betwixt the main land and the country adjoining to the harbour of San Bartholome; and that father Antonio de la Ascension, and the cosmographer should go in the tender. Accordingly she got under sail, and from their observations it appeared, that the 30 leagues in circuit, and the summits of the highest mountains, covered with woods of pines and cedars,

had a confiderable number of inhabitants, but
of implacable difpofitions; as inftead of an-
fwering the peaceable figns made by the Spaniards, they ran to the mountains, and threatened to attack them with their bows and arrows;
making figns for them to retire, and not pre-
fume to enter their country. The tender afterwards went to take a view of the bay, which
appeared like a large arm of the fea; but running to a great length up the country to the
eaftward. They next furveyed the fmall ifland
of La Natividad, between which and the main
land the Almiranta had paffed; but this ifland
is a mere defert producing only a fort of wild
fennel.

After executing the general's orders, the
tender returned to her former ftation; and
after taking on board water, orders were given
for getting under fail. Accordingly, on the
9th of September, the fquadron left the ifland
to proceed to that of de Lenizas, fteering N.W.
towards the main land; and on the 11th
made the coaft, which on their approach they
found to be level and pleafant; and feeing a
bay, to which they gave the name of San Hyppolito, the fhips came to an anchor in it.
Here the general ordered fome foldiers from the
Almiranta and Capitana, under captain Peguero, and enfign Alarcon to go afhore, and

fee

fee what the country afforded; and to take with them nets, in order to fifh at their return.

They found the country very fertile, and of a delightful appearance, and a broad beaten road, leading from the coaft to the inland parts. They alfo met with a large hut, covered with palm leaves, and capable of holding conveniently fifty perfons.   They alfo brought a-board with them a great quantity of excellent fifh, called pexes reyes, of the fize of the white fifh of Mechoacan, and have the flavour and tafte of a fardin.   The general now gave orders for proceeding in the voyage, and accordingly betwixt eight and nine at night, they got under fail.

Four leagues farther to the N. W. of San Hyppolito bay is another called San Cofme, and Damian, which the Almiranta had furveyed, while fhe was in fearch of the Capitana.   It is defended from the N. W. winds; and not far from the fhore, is a famous frefh-water lake. The country alfo is level, and makes a good appearance.

In the profecution of the voyage, the fquadron now faw all along the coaft very large fires; a fufficient indication that there were a great many Indian rancherias.   The N. W. wind, all along that coaft, is generally attended

with

with fevere weather; and it now blew fo violently, that the fquadron was obliged to run clofe in with the land, under fome lofty black mountains, on the top of which were large plains. Thefe they called Mefas de San Cypriano, or St. Cyprian's tables. S. E. of this fierra, or ridge of mountains, were fome white cliffs; and on them great numbers of Indians. The general therefore ordered the tender to ftand clofe under the fhore, to difcover what kind of people they were, and the cofmographer to take a draught of the country, whilft the other fhips lay to till her return. But the tender, on her coming under the high land, was becalmed. The following day the fhips ftood in near the land; but could get no fight of her: and the N. W. wind beginning to blow with great violence, and the fea of courfe very high, they were obliged to lie to for twenty-four hours; during which the Almiranta was near foundering.

In the morning they continued their voyage, in the beft manner poffible, but at noon the wind increafed, and even blew with greater violence than in the night; and towards evening a thick fog arofe, which in thefe feas is a certain prefage of bad weather. The general feeing that the Almiranta would be in great danger, altered his courfe to difcover a

place

place where they might come to an anchor; but had not the good fortune to find any. However, the next day the weather became fair with a gentle land breeze, by which they recovered what they had loft during the ftorm, and arrived off the Mefas, where the land forms a cape, near which the tender had left them. Here they were again overtaken by a moft violent gale at N. W. attended with a thick fog, that the fhips were obliged to lie to all night under their mainfails; and by the badnefs of the weather and the darknefs of the night, the Capitana and Almiranta again loft fight of each other.

The reafon for the ufual violence of the wind at this cape called el Enganno is, that the air is there contracted, in paffing betwixt the cape and the ifland Ceniza, which lies about eight leagues E. N. E. from the main land of cape Enganno, which is divided in the middle forming two lofty round mountains of an equal height. It was difcovered by the Almiranta, after parting company. But now the thick fog intercepted it from their fight.

The Capitana being again alone, ufed every poffible method for finding them; and even ventured to double cape Enganno; and by keeping as near the fhore as poffible, they found the tender; but having no fight of the Almi-

ranta,

ranta, they were under great apprehenfions that fhe was loft during the continuance of the ftorm; and having on the N. W. of St. Cyprian's tables and cape Enganno found a good harbour, the general ordered the two fhips to ftand in for it. Accordingly, on the 3d of October, they entered the bay, to which they gave the name of Bahia de San Francifco. In a rancheria they found onions and goats horns. The country is level and fruitful, and by the dung and other indications feems to have a great plenty of cattle and deer. The tender's men alfo reported, that a little farther they found a fmall ifland which they called San Geronymo; and the general ordered fome of the failors to go afhore and take a view of it. Here they faw prodigious flights of birds, the ifland being almoft covered with woods; and the fhips plentifully fupplied themfelves with cod and other fifh. A little beyond this ifland there feemed to be a large bay with a very impetuous current both at the ebb and flood: and the general fuppofing there might be a large river at the bottom of it, ftood in with both fhips, in order, if it afforded a good harbour, to wait fome days there for the Almiranta, which, if not loft, muft pafs near the mouth of it. The tender ftood in firft, founding all the way; but at the mouth of the creek found

only

only three fathoms water, fo that the Capitana did not think it advifeable to venture in; but the tender failed over the bar, and found a very good harbour. Enfign Alcoran being ordered afhore with twelve foldiers to look out for water and wood, found near the creek a great number of naked Indians, fifhing in canoes made of thick and pliable flags which grow in the frefh water. The Indians came up to the Spaniards with the greateft marks of friendfhip, gave them fifh, and fhewed them feveral wells of very good water which they themfelves drank of. Thefe wells were in a thick wood of willows and ofiers intermixed, with the flags of which the Indians made their canoes. This report was very acceptable to all on board, and the general ordered a tent to be pitched for the religious to fay mafs; and while they waited for the Almiranta, they took on board wood and water and catched fifh in abundance; though they had little occafion for the latter, the Indians bringing them every morning more than they could ufe; and were fo fond of the Spaniards, that they always kept near them. Nor would they go to the rancherias in the neighbourhood, without firft afking leave of the general and the religious. The Spaniards returned their courtefy with prefents of little value, which the Indians could not

fufficiently

sufficiently admire; and the report spreading through the country, an infinite number of them flocked to the shore: they eat with our people, and pronounced their language as if they had been natives of Spain. Whatever they saw done, they also did, and repeated any words they heard. The women were covered with skins of beasts, behaved very decently, and the greatest part of them had two infants at their breasts.

These Indians carry on a commerce with the people of the inland country; and in return for fish receive mexcalli, or maguey root boiled, and made into an admirable conserve, and purses of network very curiously wrought. Of these particulars the Indians thought they could never give enough to the Spaniards for a few beads and other toys. The Indians also intimated by signs that up the country there were great numbers of people cloathed, who had beards, and that they had also fire arms. Perhaps these were the people attending don Juan de Onnate then on an expedition to New Mexico; for according to the draught of the country and the distance of the meridians, and difference of climates in the maps by father Antonio de la Ascension, the distance from thence to don Juan de Onnate's camp, could not be above

two

two hundred leagues; but if this be not thought probable, the people mentioned by the Indians, muſt be a civilized nation living under a regular polity, and the people which the Indians of New Mexico mentioned as reſiding in thoſe parts.

The Capitana and tender having ſtaied in this bay the time propoſed, the general gave orders for putting to ſea, in order to look out for the Almiranta; accordingly ſhe got under ſail on the 24th of October; but as they were ſtanding out of the bay ſaw the Almiranta, which gave them the greateſt joy, not having ſeen her for twenty eight days, and had now given her over for loſt.

We have already related the manner of the Capitana's parting from the Almiranta off cape Enganno, and what happened to the Capitana from their ſeparation, till they both came into the bay of the eleven thouſand virgins: it will now be proper to give an account alſo of the Almiranta from that time to their junction. The Almiranta ſuppoſing that the Capitana, as had been ſettled between them in caſe of their parting in bad weather, would have continued to leeward, the admiral and his council were of opinion, that they ſhould ſearch for her in the harbours they had paſſed; and accordingly returned on the 24th of September, and running

ning

ning along the coast, looked into the bays of
San Cosme, Damian, and San Hyppolito, and
the island of Cerros, where they supplied themselves with wood and water which they wanted
extremely; but not finding the tender, they
returned to their former station in order to
look for her along the coast, hoping she might
have stood beyond the parallel where they separated: and to avoid being again impeded by
cape Enganno, they steered E. five days successively, when they found themselves about
eight leagues from a large island, which they
supposed to be de Paxaros; but though they
kept working towards it above two days, the
wind baffled all their efforts.

At last, the ship from the violence of the
winds and the extraordinary agitation of the
sea, made a great deal of water, besides what
she shipped in rolling, and it was judged prudent
to stand in for the shore, that in case she should
founder or sink, the people might save their
lives. When they came near the shore, they
saw the island of Ceniza astern; and on coming
into the bay of the eleven thousand virgins,
they saw the Capitana and tender sailing out to
sea. Now the same scene of joy was revived
as at their former meeting; and the general
gave orders to continue their course to the first
harbour they should find. Accordingly they
passed

paſſed near a ſmall iſland near the main land, which they called San Hilario, and ranging along the coaſt they came in ſight of a large bay, which the general ordered the tender to ſound and ſurvey: they found it afforded a very good ſhelter againſt the N. W. wind and on the ſhore appeared great numbers of Indians. Soon after they were overtaken with a ſtrong gale at N. W. which obliged them to put back into the ſaid bay; and it being the anniverſary of St. Simon and St. Jude, they gave that name to the bay. Here the general ordered the Almiranta to take in wood and water.

The next morning the general ſent captain Peguero and enſign Alarcon aſhore on the main land with ſome ſoldiers in the Capitana's and Almiranta's boats to look out for water. Near the ſhore they found a conſiderable number of Indians, who ſeemed very alert and courageous, but did not moleſt the Spaniards, who dug ſeveral wells in a moiſt ſpot of ground overgrown with ſedge and flags, and here they watered. But ſoon after the Indians on ſeeing our men behaved civilly, and offered them little preſents, ſuppoſed their complaiſance proceeded from fear; and this made them ſo inſolent, that they offered to take ſome things from the ſoldiers; and put their bows over their head by way of contempt; they were alſo for taking one

of

of the boats from the boys who were left to keep her; and when the Spaniards put off, the Indians kept throwing ftones at the people in the boats, till a foldier to terrify them fired his piece in the air: but the Indians feeing it did not hurt them, the day following, when captain Peguero came again for water with fix foldiers and landed at fome diftance from thofe who came with enfign Alarcon, came down to the fhore, and encouraged by the fmallnefs of the number, began to behave in the fame imperious manner as before, on which three of the foldiers who had their matches lighted, ordered them by figns to keep at a diftance; but inftead of complying, they attempted to throw their bows over their heads, and actually did fo to one of the foldiers. On which the pilot Antonio Florez drew his fabre, and at one ftroke cut both bow and ftring: which fo incenfed the Indians, that they drew up in form, and began to place their arrows for fhooting; but it was thought advifeable to prevent them, and accordingly the foldiers who had their matches ready, were ordered to fire, and the firft volley with partridge fhot and balls, fix of the Indians fell; but their countrymen took them on their backs and carried them to a little eminence in the neighbourhood, and immediately gave notice to their neighbours of what

had

had happened: about an hour after two hundred Indians painted with different colours and wearing large plumes of feathers on their heads, came down in a regular body with their bows and arrows to attack the Spaniards who had landed with enfign Alarcon, who on feeing them ordered his men to make ready. The arquebufes however kept the Indians at a diftance; and at length they fent an Indian with a little dog as a token of peace; and the Spaniards went up to them. The Indians kept their eye continually on the arquebufes; and told our men by figns that four of them were dead, and others were dying by the wounds they had received from them. At the fame time they expreffed a diflike of their rudenefs: giving at the fame time, in token of fincere friendfhip abundance of little prefents to our people, and retired. After taking in water, the general gave orders for departing; which was done on Wednefday the firft of November.

The fquadron having left the bay of St. Simon and St. Jude, and continuing their voyage under the former difficulties, they came before a very large bay inclofed within lofty mountains on every fide except the entrance: and by the breaking of the fea near the harbour, it appeared that it was the mouth of a river. In the weft part of the bay are two iflands, which

which they called Todos Santos. The tender being ordered in, the Almiranta followed her; but the Capitana, as night was coming on, stood off to sea; and the others that they might not be separated from her, also put back: this happened on the 5th of November, and the next morning it was agreed to stand again into the bay and take a plainer view of it: but a favourable breeze springing up, and the general thinking it most adviseable to take advantage of it, and refer the survey of the bay till their return, they continued their course. After sailing a few leagues, the wind again shifted to the N. W. but they kept coasting along the shore, and were amused with the smokes and fires made by the Indians all along the strand, as an invitation to the ships to send their people ashore. At the distance of six leagues from the main land, they fell in with four islands, to which they gave the name of los Coronados; the two smaller appeared like sugar loaves, the other something larger. To the north of these islands on the main land, is a famous harbour called San Diego, which the squadron entered at seven in the evening, on the 10th of December; and the day following the general ordered several persons to survey a forest lying on the N. W. side of the bay. This expedition was undertaken by ensign Alarcon,

Abarcon, captain Peguero, father Antonio de la Afcenfion, and eight foldiers. In this foreft they found tall and ftrait oaks, and other trees; fome fhrubs refembling rofemary, and a great variety of fragrant and wholefome plants: the high grounds commanded a view of the whole harbour which appeared fpacious, convenient, and well fheltered. The foreft borders on the harbour towards the N. W. and is about three leagues in length, and a half a league in breadth. And to the N. W. of this wood is another good harbour. On their return with this report to the general, he ordered a tent to be pitched for religious worfhip: and that the fhips fhould be cleaned and tallowed, the people in the mean time being employed in wooding and keeping guard. They had their water from a little ifland of fand, where they dug deep trenches, in which, during the flood the water was frefh and good; but on the ebb falt. One day a centinel pofted in the wood, gave notice that he faw a great number of Indians coming along the fhore, naked, and their fkins daubed with black and white colours, and armed with bows and arrows. On this the general defired father Antonio to go and offer them peace. He was attended by enfign Juan Francifco and fix foldiers. On coming up to the Indians, having made figns of peace with a bit of white

linen;

linen, and throwing the earth up with their hands, the savages immediately delivered their bows and arrows to the soldiers. Father Antonio embraced them, gave them bread and necklaces, with which they were greatly pleased; but on coming to the general's quarters, the Indians, at the sight of such a number of people, drew back to a little eminence; from whence they sent two women, who approaching the general's tent, with a timid air, the religious and others made them presents of beads, biskets, and strings of bugles, and thus dismissed them to give their countrymen an account of the usage they had met with from the strangers. Their report was doubtless very favourable; for soon after they all came with them to see the Spaniards. Most of them were painted or besmeared with black and white; and their heads loaded with feathers. The general and others received them with extreme courtesy; distributed among them several things and a great deal of fish which had been caught with the net in their presence. The kind of paint they used looked like a mixture of silver and blue colour: and on asking them by signs what it was, they gave them a piece of metallic ore, from whence they made it: and signified by signs that a certain people up the country who had beards and were cloathed like the Spani-

niards,

ards, made from this mineral very fine ribbons; resembling the laces on the soldiers buff-coats: and some like that on a purple velvet doublet, in which the general was then dressed; adding that these men, by their dress, complexions, and customs seemed to be of the same country with themselves. The Indians were quite transported with the good treatment shewn them, and every third day came for bisket and fish: bringing with them skins of several kinds of beasts, as sables, wild cats, and the nets with which they catch them.

In this harbour is a great variety of fish, as oysters, muscles, lobsters, soles, &c. and in some of the rocks up the country were found geese, ducks, and quails; rabbits and hares were also here in great numbers. The general and father Antonio being desirous of viewing the country, took with them some soldiers, and walked a considerable distance from the coast, and were highly delighted with the mildness of the climate and goodness of the soil.

Every thing being completed according to the general's orders, they left this place on the 20th of November, but many of the soldiers were sickly, and some very valuable persons had died while they continued in this harbour. They had no sooner left San Diego, than they met with their common difficulty, a strong N. W. wind. The ships, however, came in fight of a bay, where the neighbouring country made a pleasant appearance. On every side of it they also saw the smoke of large fires which the Indians had kindled, that the ships might put in there. But on approaching the coast, found no shelter for the N. W. wind; they therefore continued their course, and a few leagues further discovered in St. Catherine bay, a large island about twelve leagues from the land, and from the day of its discovery, they called it the island of St. Catherine. On the 28th of November the ships came close in with it, and from thence had fight of a much larger lying off St. Catherine. They however thought proper not to survey it till their return. At their approaching the island of St. Catharine, the inhabitants made fires in all parts: and when they saw the ships near the strand, the women, children, and old men, began to shout, and with great rejoicings came down from some heights to the shore. The general ordered the admiral Toribio Gomez to go ashore with father Antonio de la Ascension, captain Peguero, and ensign Alarcon, and twenty four soldiers, to know what the people wanted, and take a view of the island. The men with the admiral were no sooner landed, than they were met by great numbers of Indians of both sexes, who behaved

with

with that candour and courtefy, as feemed to indicate that this was not the firft time they had feen Spaniards. On being afked for water, they brought a veffel made of rufhes, and fhaped like a bottle. The water was very good; but they were obliged to fetch it a confiderable diftance, from a little fpring furrounded with favins and briars, with which this ifland is over-run. This report having been made to the general, he ordered a tent to be pitched for the fathers Andrew and Antonio to fay mafs in, father Thomas being ill; and all the people came afhore to affift at divine worfhip. On this occafion alfo, a great many Indians, robuft and well made, came to the tent, who the day before had been fifhing in a kind of veffel made of planks well put together, but of a very odd conftruction. Some of thefe veffels conveniently hold twenty men, though generally three perfons only, namely two men and a boy go in each.

The manner of fifhing among the Indians is very ingenious, eafy, and pleafant. They carry in their boats long and thin poles, and to one of thefe fix a harpoon made of fifh bones, faftening to the harpoon a long rope. When they perceive at the bottom near the rocks a fea wolf or any other fifh worth catching, they ftrike it with the harpoon; then vere out the

rope,

rope, till the fish being spent, they draw it ashore if large; and if small into the boat. Thus they catch as many fish as they please. The sea wolves serve them both for food and cloathing. The Indian women are well shaped, have fine eyes, and beautiful features; they have a decent behaviour and real modesty: both boys and girls have a fine mixture of white and red, and are generally very good natured. These Indians live in large huts, and their utensils are in general made of rushes, so closely wrought as to hold water. The island abounds with roots like small potatoes, and the Indians drive on a great trade by carrying them for sale to the continent. This island like most of those adjacent is very populous; and the inhabitants live together in rancherias. Here was also a temple for sacrifices. It was a large inclosure entirely level; and near the altar an ample circle surrounded with the feathers of different kinds of birds, possibly of such as had been sacrificed to the idols. Within the circle was a figure painted with a variety of colours; and resembling the image by which the Indians of New Spain represent the devil: in its hand it held the figures of the sun and the moon. It happened that when the soldiers went to see this temple, there was within the circle two crowns of a very uncommon size: and at the

3   approach

approach of the Spaniards they flew away: but alighted on a neighbouring rock, and the foldiers feeing them fo remarkably large, fhot them both; at which an Indian, who came with the Spaniards as a guide made the moft vehement lamentations, and expreffed great horror, at the action. This ifland has feveral good harbours, abundance of fine fifh, efpecially fardins; and in the country are found partridges and quails, rabbits, hares, and deer. The people themfelves are very ingenious, particularly in pilfering and concealing, fome fpecimens of which artifice they gave the Spaniards.

After taking a furvey of feveral parts of this ifland, the fquadron left it on the 25th of December, in order to take a view of others near it; and then to ftand in for the main land. Beyond St. Catherines there is a regular row of iflands, five or fix leagues diftant from each other. Some are larger than others, but all populous, and the inhabitants trade with each other and with thofe of the continent. Thefe iflands take up near a fpace of one hundred leagues; and follow each other in the fame direction as the main land: and their number, largenefs, and proximity often occafion the Philippine fhips in their return to New Spain, to miftake them for the continent; and thus to keep

at

at a diftance from them. They are however very populous, and have a fafe paffage betwixt them and the main land, in fome parts twelve, in others ten, and the narroweft eight leagues broad, called el Canal de Santa Barbara, and lies eaft and weft. The fhips being arrived near the continent, at the mouth of this channel, a boat came off with four oars, bringing an Indian, who was the lord of the coaft. The canoe made for the Capitana, and with furprifing celerity rowed three times round the fhip, whilft all who were in it joined in a chorus as the Indians in New Spain fing Almatote. And afterwards without the leaft apprehenfion came along fide; and the Indian king, or cacique of the country, entered the fhip. He firft took two or three turns round the quarter deck, finging in the fame manner as before; and then addreffed himfelf in his own language to the governor and others. When he had finifhed his fpeech he gave them to underftand by figns, that the people of the ifland of St. Catherine had fent him notice by canoes four different ways, that fhips had been upon their coaft, and that the men belonging to them had beards and were cloathed; adding that they were alfo very brave, generous, and friendly, and had made many prefents to to thofe who came to fee them. This report

he

he informed them had induced him to come on board to offer them his country and all it afforded, requesting that the ships might come near the land, where he would furnish them with every thing they wanted. And seeing no woman in the ship, he asked for them; but the general answered that they never carried women, nor did they want any. At this the Indian was more urgent with the general to come a-shore with his people, promising to give to every man in the ship ten women; which made all the Spaniards smile. The Indian supposing that this was sarcastically intended as promising more than he could perform, said, that if one of the soldiers would go on shore, he would soon be convinced of the truth of what he had promised, and in the mean time, he and his son would remain as hostages, till the soldier returned: but night coming on, it was thought proper to defer the experiment till next morning, when, if the weather would permit, the ship should go in. Accordingly they dismissed the Indian with some presents; and he went away, charmed with the liberality of the Spaniards, and determined to make the best preparations for the entertainment of his new guests. Within an hour after the Indian was gone, a S. E. wind sprung up, and was the only gale from that quarter they had felt during

their

their voyage. And it being directly fair, the general thought proper to defer his visit to the Indian, till his return. Accordingly they set all their sails, and as the gale lasted from seven in the evening on the 3d of December, till eight the day following, the ships had nearly reached the last cluster of islands in the channel, which are six in number, and at two leagues distance from each other. The channel is about twenty four leagues in length, and the coast of the continent very pleasantly interspersed with woods, and a great number of Indian villages.

In the following night, the wind shifted to the N. W. which caused a great consternation, it being dark, and the ships among islands and in a channel where the sea ran very high. This gale lasted all that night and the two following days; on the third it abated; but they lost sight of the tender among the islands. This fair weather enabled the ships to get out of this Archipelago; and standing in for the continent to take a draught of the coast, they found it extremely high and mountainous, but with some well-sheltered bays, from one of which four rush canoes, each containing two naked Indians, rowed directly for the ships, and coming aboard, very liberally distributed the fish they had, especially salted sardins and other

smaller

smaller fish which they brought for bait. These Indians, as if sensible that they could not be understood, did not speak a word, but expressed their thoughts by signs. They are taller, better made, and more robust than any they had yet seen, and covered themselves with goat skins when they came on board. The Spaniards gave them some provisions and cloaths, so that they departed extremely well satisfied. These Indians appeared to be of good dispositions, not at all addicted to theft or riot. The following day other Indians came aboard, whose visit passed like that of the former. They were very pressing that the ships would come to their country, offering plenty of fish and acorns, which is their common subsistence. These also received presents of victuals, cloathing, beads, and bugles; with which they returned to their island, very well pleased. Here the tender came up with the ships, and related, that the Indians of those islands had presented them with fish and acorns. On the coming up of the tender, the general ordered the ships to stand nearer the shore, to see if there was any harbour, the coast being hid by a thick fog. Here they had a favourable gale which lasted till the 14th of December; and the weather clearing up, the ships found themselves near a very high and white ridge of mountains; but

reddish

reddiſh towards the ſkirts, and covered with woods. This they call Sierra de Santa Lucia; it is the uſual land mark for the China ſhips. Four leagues farther a river falls into the ſea among rocks, after a precipitate courſe from ſome high and white mountains; the banks of it are covered with black and white poplars, willows, and other trees and ſhrubs known in Spain. This river is called del Carmelo. Two leagues farther is a noble harbour, there being betwixt it and the ſaid river a wood of pine trees two leagues in breadth, and at the entrance of the harbour the land forms a cape called Punta de Pinos. Here on the 16th of December the ſquadron came to an anchor, in order to tranſmit accounts of its proceedings to New Spain.

We have already obſerved, that on the 16th of December the ſquadron put into this port which was called Monte-rey, in honour of the count de Monte-rey, viceroy of New Spain; by whom they had been ſent on this diſcovery, purſuant to his majeſty's orders. The next day the general directed preparations to be made, that the fathers Andrew de la Aſſumpcion and Antonio de la Aſcenſion, might ſay maſs during their ſtay there. The church was erected under a large oak cloſe to the ſea ſide, and within twenty

twenty paces of it were some wells affording plenty of excellent water.

After mass it was moved in the council to consider of the means for transmitting an account to the viceroy of New Spain of their discoveries and proceedings. And as all the ships companies were remarkably sickly, that scarce one was in perfect health, and very few able to do duty; the master of the Almiranta and his mate were not able to stir themselves in their beds; and the master and mate of the Capitana could hardly stand on the deck, a great many of the soldiers, sailors, and boys were very ill, and sixteen had died before their arrival at this port; it was resolved that the Almiranta should be sent as an advice-boat under the admiral Toribio Gomez de Corvan and the two pilots Pasqual and Balthazar; that the sick should be sent in her to New Spain with a number of sailors sufficient to carry her to Acapulco; and that the remainder should be turned over to the Capitana and tender; likewise that what provisions were on board the Almiranta, besides, a plentiful allowance for their voyage, should also be put on board these two ships.

These resolutions being taken, the general ordered them to be executed with the utmost dispatch : and every particular which had been disco-

discovered, inserted in a chart to be sent with a letter to the viceroy, and a reinforcement requested, in order to make a perfect discovery and survey of the entrance of California; the Capitana and tender being to wait for this reinforcement, till the middle of May following; they also drew up a catalogue of the stores necessary for completing the discovery of the whole coast of California. Accordingly the sick, together with father Thomas de Aquino, were put on board the Almiranta; and every thing being ready for her departure, the seamen were ordered on board; and on the 29th of December the Almiranta sailed out of the harbour. It will not be foreign to the purpose to mention here the sickness wich raged among the squadron, being the same, which in these parts generally seizes on those who are coming from China to New Spain, and is so deleterious as to sweep off half the ship's company. In this latitude the air is very sharp and cold, which pierces those of weak constitutions, and perhaps of a pestilential nature; unless we suppose that its great subtilty is sufficient to cause such a disease in bodies attenuated by fatigues. Its first symptom is an universal pain all over the body; which now becomes so tender as not to bear the least touch; and sometimes this will extort tears and cries from the most reso-

lute

lute men. After this the body, especially the lower parts, is covered with purple spots, larger and more prominent than grains of mustard seed : the next symptom is wheals of the same colour two fingers broad. They appear first under the hams, and spread from the middle of the thigh to the flexure of the knee, rendering the parts so rigid, that the legs resemble petrifactions, it being impossible to move them in the least from that posture in which this symptom seized them. The patients swell so prodigiously, that they cannot be moved from one side to the other without extreme torture : and these blains extend themselves so that the calf of the leg and thigh becomes wholly livid; and thus the morbid humour pervades the whole body, and seizes the shoulders in particular more than any other part, causing at the same time, excruciating pains in the loins and kidneys. Nor is the least ease to be expected from change of place, as the slightest motion is attended with such severe pains, that they must be very fond of life, who would not willingly lay it down on the first appearance of so terrible a distemper. This virulent humour makes such ravages in the body, that it is entirely covered with ulcers ; and the poor patients are unable to bear the least pressure, even the very cloaths laid on them

deprives

deprives them of life. Thus they lay groaning and incapable of any relief. For the greateft affiftance poffible to be given them, if I may be allowed the expreffion, is not to touch them, nor even the bed cloaths. Thefe effects however melancholy, are not the only produced by this peftilential humour. In many the gums, both of the upper and lower jaw, are preffed both within and without to fuch a degree, that the teeth cannot touch one another: and withal fo loofe and bare that they fhake with the leaft motion of the head; and fome of the patients fpit their teeth out with the faliva. Thus they were unable to receive any food but liquid, as gruel, broth, milk of almonds and the like. This gradually brought on fo great a weaknefs, that they died whilft talking with their friends.

Such was the diftemper with which all were afflicted; which removed numbers from this world to the manfions of eternity.

But to return to the harbour of Monte-rey, where the Capitana and tender remained to take in wood and water. This is an excellent harbour and fecure againft all winds. Near the fhore are an infinite number of very large pines, ftrait and fmooth, fit for mafts and yards; likewife oaks of a prodigious fize proper for building fhips. Here likewife are rofe-trees, white thorns, firs, willows, and poplars; large

clear

clear lakes, fine paftures, and arable lands. Wild beafts, particularly bears of an uncommon fize are found here, and a fpecies of horned cattle refembling buffaloes, and about the fame fize; others as large as wolves, and fhaped like a ftag, with a fkin refembling that of the pelican; a long neck, and horns on the head as large as thofe of a ftag, their tail is a yard in length, and half a yard in breadth, and their hoof cloven like that of an ox. The country alfo abounds in deer, rabbets, hares, and wild cats, buftards, geefe, ducks, pigeons, partridges, thrufhes, fparrows, goldfinches; cranes and vultures are alfo found here, together with another kind of bird of the bignefs of a turkey; and the largeft feen during the whole voyage, being feventeen fpans from the tip of one wing to that of the other. Along the coaft are great numbers of gulls, cormorants, crows, and other fea-fowl. In the rocks are a great many cavities, fome like the matrices of a large fhell-fifh with conques equal to the fineft mother of pearl. The fea abounds with oyfters, lobfters, crabs, &c. Alfo huge fea wolves and whales. This harbour is furrounded with rancherias of Indians, a well-looking affable people, and very ready to part with every thing they have. They are alfo under fome form of government. Their arms are bows and arrows.

They

They expressed a great deal of concern when they perceived the Spaniards were going to leave them, which happened on the 3d of Jan. 1603, when the Capitana and tender sailed out of this harbour.

The Capitana and tender had no sooner left the harbour of Monte-rey, than they had a favourable wind, which lasting till twelfth day, carried them beyond port St. Francisco. But the day after, which was the 7th of January, the wind shifted to the N. W. but blowing an easy gale, still made some way; and the tender concluding that there was no necessity for standing in for the shore continued her voyage; and the Capitana thinking that they went in company did not shew any light; by which means in the morning they had no sight of each other, and the general in the Capitana returned to port St. Francisco to wait for the tender, which he supposed was making all the sail possible after him; but the first account they had of the tender, was not till after the Capitana's return from the voyage: Another reason which induced the Capitana to put into Puerto Francisco was to take a survey of it, and see if any thing was to be found of the San Augustin, which in the year 1595, had by order of his majesty and the viceroy, been sent from the Philippines by the governor to survey the coast of California, under

under the direction of Sebaftian Rodriguez Cer-
mennon a pilot of known abilities; but was
driven afhore in this harbour by the violence
of the wind.   Among others on board the
San Auguftine, was the pilot Francifco Vola-
nos, who was alfo chief pilot of this fquadron.
He was acquainted with the country, and affirmed that they had left afhore a great quantity
of wax and feveral chefts of filk; and the general was defirous of putting in here to fee
if there remained any veftiges of the fhip and
cargo. The Capitana came to an anchor behind
a point of land called La Punta de los Reys:
but no people were fent afhore, that the fhip
might be in readinefs for the tender: and accordingly on the day following the Capitana
failed out in queft of her.   The wind was N.
W. and blew fo eafy a gale, that the Capitana
moved very flowly.   However on Sunday the
12th of January fhe made fome high red mountains: and fourteen leagues further to the
N. W. diftinguifhed a cape running into the
fea, and near it fome fnowy mountains, from
whence the pilots on board judged it to be
cape Mendozino, which lay in the latitude of
41 deg. 30 min.

The day following, namely the 13th of January, they had a very violent gale at S. W.
accompanied with fleet; and fuch a high fea,

that they apprehended the ſhips would founder;
to avoid this danger, as likewiſe a higher latitude, where both the ſtorm and the cold would
be increaſed, it being the depth of winter in
thoſe parts, it was thought proper to lay to
till the wind would admit of their returning
towards Acapulco.

At the arrival of the Capitana in theſe parts
ſhe had not above ſix perſons able to keep the
deck : ſoldiers, ſeamen, and boys were all down
with that terrible diſtemper we have deſcribed;
the religious and ſupernumerary captains were
alſo ill, ſo that the father commiſſary could hardly
confeſs them ; or adminiſter the extreme unction
to thoſe who were dying: beſides as the healthy
men were too few to work ſuch a ſhip, their
calamity was aggravated by a violent conſternation at their danger, being near a terrible
coaſt and without aſſiſtance : and had a ſtorm
come on, they muſt infallibly have been loſt
for want of hands to manage the ſails. The
general in this exigency called his uſual council, where, after deliberating on the beſt meaſures poſſible to be taken, it was reſolved not
to proceed further ; but on the firſt weather to
return and make for the harbour de la Paz in
California, and there wait for the ſuccours which
the Almiranta had been ſent to aſk of the viceroy. This reſolution raiſed the ſpirits of the
people,

people, as they now thought they should live some days longer than if they had proceeded to a higher latitude : and on the 14th of the said month the weather cleared up, and they found by a good obfervation, that they were near cape Mendozino, the currents having carried the ship thither in two days only. But the fun was foon after obfcured by a thick fog intermixed with a cold mizzling rain : and the wind being ftill S. E. the ship lay to till the 19th of January, when the wind came about to the N. W. which diffipated the fog, and the pilots were able to make another obfervation, and found themfelves in the latitude of 42 deg. On the coaft they perceived a white cape extending to high mountains covered with fnow; and from its colour and being firft feen on the eve of St. Sebaftian was called Cabo Blanco de San Sebaftian. This wind animated the fickly to affift the healthy feamen, fo that with extreme fatigue the yards were hoifted, and the ship put before the wind in order to return to Acapulco along fhore in queft of the tender, and likewife for taking a draught of the coaft.

The tender, as I have above obferved, had loft the Capitana, and thinking her to be before, followed in fearch of her : and in the latitude of 41 degrees, the fouth eaft wind brought her to the Capitana, but the ship not

U 2

being

being able to live in the fea, ran before the wind
near the fhore, and came to an anchor under a
huge rock near cape Mendozino: and when
the wind abated, continued her voyage along
fhore. On the 19th of January, Florez the
pilot who was in the tender found himfelf in
the latitude of 43 degrees, and the land forming a cape called Cabo Blanco where the coaft
begins to ftretch, towards the N. W. and near
it a very large river having its banks covered
with afh trees, willows, and other Spanifh trees.
This pleafing appearance rendered them defirous of putting into it, but the currents hindered them *. And foon after enfign Martin
de Aquilar commander of the tender, and the
pilot Florez finding they were in a latitude
beyond that mentioned in the viceroy's inftructions, that there was no appearance of the
Capitana, and that the crew were very fickly,
agreed to return to Acapulco.

This river is fuppofed to be that which runs
up to a large city difcovered by a Dutch fhip,
and that it is the ftreight of Anian, through
which the fhip paffed from the north fea into
the fouth. The city de Quivira is doubtlefs
in thefe parts; and to this country the narra-

* It is worth obferving that what thefe Spaniards fay
was not an entrance, ftreight, or arm of the fea, but a river
that what is added about the ftreight of Anian, is plainly mer
conjecture without any foundation.

tive delivered to his majesty, and which first induced him to order an improvement of those discoveries; and a report to be made to him of the several proceedings, relates.

We have already mentioned the departure of the Capitana from cape San Sebastian, in order to return to Acapulco in New Spain, from whence they first sailed: and they kept along so near the land as plainly to discern, whether any thing worth notice had escaped their first observations. In this latitude the country along the coast made a very verdant appearance, and that on the inland parts, which had all the signs of fertility, was also very populous, there being a great number of fires in all parts. The wind being now at northwest, very favourable, and the weather easy, they had a clear and continual view of every inch of ground along the shore. While the Capitana was thus delightfully sailing along a very pleasant coast, a little distance from St. Barbara's channel, two canoes were seen coming towards the ship, each with three men without any other covering than a kind of goats skins: and after rowing three times round the ship, without any further ceremony came on board, with the same freedom and chearfulness as if coming into their own houses. Bisket and some other trifles were

given

given them and they returned to the shore highly satisfied.

When the Capitana on her return came to this coast, her condition was truly deplorable; all the people on board, the general and three soldiers excepted, labouring under the above-mentioned distemper, and it was with great pain that the father commissary went about admi-nistering the sacrament to the sick. As for father Antonio de la Ascension he was not able to stir; and the sickness was so excruciating that nothing was heard in the ship but cries and lamentations. Some by way of ease made loud complaints, others lamented their sins with the deepest contrition; some died talking; some sleeping; some eating; some whilst sitting up in their beds.

The sight of so many fellow-adventurers lying dead, together with the cries, groans, and la-mentations of the afflicted, would have moved the most obdurate breast, and providence was pleased to inspire hearts which before were strangers to every humane and tender senti-ment, with such fervent benevolence, that those in health attended the sick, and performed all services to them with as much diligence and care, as if every one had only a single patient. The religious, especially father Thomas de Aquino, foreseeing these terrible extremities, had

had at Aquapulco provided themselves with cordials and conserves, which were all reserved for this day of affliction; and doubtless many owed their recovery to the prudence and liberality of the fathers in the distribution of them.

The Indians were no sooner returned on shore, than the Capitana entered the channel of San Barbara, with an intent of viewing the large island which in their first voyage they had seen to the E. of the island of St. Catherine, proposing to stay there some days in expectation of the tender. But the council dissuaded the general from this intention, the ships company not being able to hand the sails nor get up the anchor; the people likewise were dying apace; and if they remained there all would perish, to the great prejudice of his majesty's service, and be a crime against humanity itself. The general immediately acquiesced in these reasons, and without viewing the island or coming to that of St. Catherine, the chief pilot was ordered to steer directly for the island of Cerros: from thence to cape San Lucas; and there in the harbour of La Paz, wait for the succours which had been desired from the viceroy. Accordingly they continued their voyage, passing by the island of St. Catherine at the distance of five or six leagues, when three canoes came off from the island loaded with sea wolves skins

and

and fish, which the Indians exchanged for bead necklaces, scizars, and knives. When the Spaniards had been there before, they perceived them to be very fond of these skins; and thus, like sagacious traders, had laid up a considerable stock of them, and now came to bring them out to a good market: but being accidentally detected in their address at pilfering, they were ordered to repair to their canoes, and the ship continued her course. Here the wind lull'd, that the ship made but little way along shore; however at length she reached the wells in the bay of Todos los Santos, which, as I have already observed, was omitted in order to be surveyed on their return: but there was a necessity of leaving it this time also, the greatest part of the people who had kept their health as far as the channel of St. Barbara, being ill, so that now there were not above three or four who were able to work the ship: and on this account they stood off from the coast to shorten the passage; and all that was done was to observe the courses steered along this coast, that, with his majesty's approbation the China ships might know what course to steer, after making cape Mendozino, in order to reach New Spain. On the 3d of February the Capitana came in sight of the island of San Hilario. Here the north wind

freshened,

freſhened, that the ſhips ſtood farther from the
land, and they had only ſuch a ſight of it as
to diſtinguiſh the ſeveral parts. After paſſing
by the bay of los Virgines, on the 5th of the
ſaid month, they made the iſland of Cenizas,
which, as we have mentioned above, had been
ſurveyed by the Almiranta. Here the N. W.
wind increaſing, the ſhips ſtood in for the iſland
of Cerros, and the day following in the evening, the Capitana came to an anchor at her
former ſtation, in order to take in wood and
water. And here ſome of the ſeamen by the
ſalubrious change of the climate, had recovered
a little ſtrength ; and they encouraged one another to go aſhore and aſſiſt in wooding and watering. Before their departure they left ſignals
and writings, that in caſe the tender ſhould put
in there, ſhe might know where to find the
Capitana. Every thing being completed and
the weather favourable, the ſhip proceeded for
cape San Lucas. On the 9th of the ſaid month,
being Sunday morning, the Capitana ſailed out
among the iſlands, the bay and arm of the
ſea, having been before ſurveyed in the tender by father Anthony: and when the ſhip
was clear of the iſland, the chief pilot availed
himſelf of the fair wind to ſhorten the voyage ;
and ſtood from the land directly for cape San
Lucas, of which he had ſight about noon on
Friday

Friday the 14th. Here it was refolved not to put into the bay of San Barnabas, nor touch at the entrance of the gulf of California, but ftand directly for the iflands of Mazatlan, the inhabitants of them being chriftians, and there wait while an exprefs could be fent to Mexico, to acquaint the viceroy of their arrival, and defire his excellency's farther commands.

Accordingly the Capitana croffed the mouth of the gulf of California; and on Monday the 17th of February happily entered the harbour of the ifland of Mazatlan: and the next day came to an anchor in the place which afforded the moft fecure fhelter, and was alfo very convenient for going afhore.

The Capitana being thus fafely anchored at the ifland of Mazatlan, the general's firft care was to fend advice of their arrival to the inhabitants of the continent; and determined to go himfelf in perfon, together with five of the moft healthy foldiers, and to proceed to the village of San Sebaftian, about eight leagues up the country. Accordingly, on the 19th early in the morning, the general and his five attendants went afhore; but being ignorant on what fide the town lay, there being no road or path, they ftruck into a wood, and travelled two days in extreme hunger and thirft, which, with the great heat, weakened the foldiers to
fuch

such a degree that they were in great danger of perishing in the forest; but wandering about, they at last fell into a broad road which they followed, without knowing whither it would carry them. Whilst they were resting themselves under a tree, they heard the noise of bells. At this they started up and looking round saw a drove of mules going with provisions from Castile to Culiacan. When this caravan came up, they asked the muleteer whither that road led, he answered to Culiacan; and the general enquiring after the town of San Sebastian, and the chief alcaldi of the country, he offered to convey them to the place where he resided; and having relieved their wants, furnished them with mules to carry them to the place the general desired. The chief alcaldi was at a village in the neighbourhood, and proved to be captain Martin Ruiz de Aguirre, an intimate acquaintance of the general's and known to all the military men in the ship. The general related to him their distresses; and desired to be furnished with bread, fowls, kids, calves, and other things for the time they should stay there: likewise to recommend to him a diligent and careful man to go with all possible dispatch to Mexico with letters for the viceroy, acquainting him of their arrival and their extreme distress; the five soldiers with him being

the

the only men belonging to the ship who were in any tolerable state of health. Captain A-guirre with joy complied with every thing that was asked; and without this care in the general and the captain's alacrity, the whole crew must have perished, and the ship been left as a de-solate wreck. Immediately seven or eight mules loaded with bread, fowls, kids, calves, plan-tains, lemons, oranges, &c. were sent to the ship, and the same quantity sent every third day; that the people might not only be plen-tifully supplied during their stay, but likewise provided with a sufficiency till they came to Acapulco, where they would find an afflu-ence of every thing.

From what has been said, some idea may be formed of the condition of the company of the Capitana at their arrival in this harbour; we shall therefore only add, that by the di-stemper above described they were helpless and sick, covered with ulcers, and their gums so swelled that they could neither speak nor eat: and the malignity of the distemper such, that none thought of ever being restored to perfect health. Nothing was heard in the ship at her arrival here, but cries and passionate invocati-ons of heaven. However in nineteen days all of them recovered their health and strength; so that when they departed, the sails were loosed,

the

the ship worked, and every part of the duty performed as in the preceding year, when they visited this harbour on their passage. Such salutary effects had the fresh provisions, fruits, &c. sent on board by the general; the eating of a fruit which abounds in these islands, and by the natives called xocohuilztles, was also of very great service. It resembles an apple; the leaves of the tree are exactly like those of the pine apple; and the fruit grows in clusters, like that of the cypress: it is also nearly of the shape of the cypress nut; the rind or shell is yellow; and the pulp like that of a white tuna, with seeds something larger than those of the tuna. It has a very pleasant taste and a tartish sweetness. This fruit is endued with such virtue, that it cleansed and relieved the gums, fastened the teeth; and, after eating twice of it, the mouth would be closed, so as to eat any other kind of food without pain. The use of this fruit was discovered in the following manner: some soldiers going up the island with the father commissary to a burial, Antonio Luis, the officer, seeing the fruit, from a curiosity of being acquainted with the products of the soil, plucked one and began, though with extreme pain in his teeth and gums, to bite it; and finding it of an exquisite taste he eat the whole; and immediately

mediately voided from his mouth a great quantity of purulent blood. And on putting the other to his mouth, he found that the pain in his teeth was much lefs, and he could chew it with great eafe. On his return to the fhip, he related the happy effects of this fruit: and diftributed fome among his friends, who all found the fame pleafing confequences, which induced them to go afhore and gather a great quantity for the relief of others. So that, on the general's return, he found many whom he defpaired of feeing again able to eat the frefh provifions continually bringing to them. Thefe were the only means by which, within nineteen days, they perfectly recovered from fuch a horrible and fatal diftemper. This fruit is the chief fubfiftence of the Indian warriors of the provinces of Acaponeta and Chametla, which lie within the government of New Galicia: but their general way is to roaft or boil it, as more wholefome and palatable. The general finding his fhip's company thus happily recovered, but being without caulkers, and his fhip leaky, he ordered the anchor to be weighed, and fail for Acapulco to refit the fhip, and procure additional hands and provifions, that if the viceroy pleafed they might return to California; or otherwife put a final period to the perils and diftreffes of fo unpleafant a voyage. Accordingly

ingly, on the 9th of March the ship sailed for these islands with a fair wind, steering for Acapulco; and after passing by cape Corientes and coming within sight of Puerto de la Navidad, kept near the shore till they arrived at Acapulco, where they came to an anchor on the 21st of March in the same year 1603.

On the arrival of the Capitana at Acapulco, the whole city was joyfully surprised, no body expecting to see her any more; especially to find the people on board so healthy, having concluded from the account given by those who arrived in the Almiranta, that all belonging to her, who had visited Puerto de Monte-rey had certainly perished: and doubtless this would have been the case, had not the winds favoured their return, and they fortunately put in at the islands of Mazatlan. But it is now time to relate what befell the Almiranta from their leaving Puerto de Monte-rey till their arrival at Acapulco.

The natural distress and toil of the voyage were aggravated by the general sickness which prevailed among the company; and which proved so fatal, that when she came into the harbour, only three persons were in health on board, all the rest being in a very languishing condition. These three persons were the admiral Torrebio Gomez de Corvan, corporal Francisco

cisco

cifco Vidal, a Galician, and Juan de Marchina,
a foldier; fo that had not the admiral been a
man of great refolution, fpirit, and experience,
in fea affairs, the fhip could never have reached the harbour. Of thofe who came fick to
Açapulco, only fix foldiers recovered. In
fine the Almiranta loft twenty five perfons.
Among thefe were four of the admiral's fervants
and three flaves. And hence it was concluded
that the Capitana would fuffer more than the
Almiranta; the greateft part of her people being fick at her departure; and as they were ftill
to go to the height of 42 degrees, they were
confidered as a forlorn hope, every one never
expecting to hear of them any more. And
hence that pleafing aftonifhment at the arrival,
and the healthy condition of the crew, of the
Capitana.

At the Almiranta's coming into port, notice was immediately fent to the viceroy, who
difpatched orders to the officers of the port of
Acapulco to take all poffible care of the fick,
efpecially of father Thomas de Aquino, who
was alfo to be furnifhed with every neceffary
for bringing him to Mexico, and it muft be
owned that the officers conformed to thefe
orders with the moft cordial diligence. The
general on his landing procured the chief
alcaldi of the town to difpatch a courier to
the

the viceroy with an account of his arrival, and that he waited his farther commands. By the time the courier reached Mexico, the viceroy had been acquainted that the tender alfo was arrived: for Eftevan Lopez the pilot and commander of it had fent advice, that after parting with the Capitana, he went in fearch of her as high as 43 degrees, and had furveyed the countries already mentioned: that according to the judgment of enfign Martin de Aquilar and the mafter Antonio Florez, they had returned towards Acapulco; that before they reached San Diego the Enfign and pilot both died; and the command devolved on him, four perfons only, befides himfelf, being left on board; that he fteered directly for New Spain in fearch of the Capitana; and put in at la Navidad, paffing by the iflands of Mazatlan where the Capitana had anchored. On reaching la Navidad, Lopez fet out exprefs to the viceroy, committing the care of the tender to the four furviving foldiers. He was fent back immediately by his excellency to carry the tender to Acapulco, which was performed within one month after his departure from Mexico. The viceroy on receiving the general's letter fent him from Acapulco, returned an immediate anfwer, directing the king's officers to pay the foldiers all their arrears, and to enter-

tain the religious, who were father Andrez de
la Aſſumcion and father Antonio de la Aſcenſion, and ſupply them with every thing neceſſary for their journey to Mexico, in a manner
becoming their character : all which was done
with the greateſt care and diligence. The
greateſt number of perſons who died on board
this ſquadron in the voyage to California, a-
mounted to 48; among which were enſign
Juan de Acevedo Texada, a Portugueſe; enſign Sebaſtian Melendez, an Andaluzian; enſign
Martin de Aguila, a native of Malaga; Antonio Florez, a native of Aviles, and Balthaſar
de Armas, both pilots; ſerjeant Miguel de Legar, a Biſcayan; Juan del Caſtillan Bueno,
ſhipright, born at Seville; and ſeveral other
brave and valuable men, but of leſs note.

On the 27th of April the religious, the general, the captains Peguero and Alarcon, and
enſign Juan Franciſco, together with the ſoldiers, left Acapulco, and on the 19th arrived
ſafe at Mexico: whence they went in a body
to Chapulte Peque to pay their duty to the
viceroy, who received them with great joy and
affability, complimented them on their ſafety,
praiſed their conduct and reſolution, and pro-
miſed to take notice of them and preſerve
them as opportunity offered. Nor was this the
effect of complaiſance only, his promiſes were
foon

foon performed; all, to their entire fatisfaction, being promoted within a fhort time according to their refpective pretenfions.

This voyage in which nothing has been magnified or added is, I think, an evident proof of Spanifh fortitude and valour, as under fuch fufferings, dangers, and fatigues, our countrymen completed an enterprife, which all had before failed in: and if this affords matter for honour and triumph, how much greater glory belongs to the adventurers in this voyage. Their difcoveries would have been more extenfive, their achievements greater, had not ficknefs obftructed their plan: for had only fourteen perfons been able to have done duty at cape Blanco, the general intended to have entered the ftreight called Anian, faid to be thereabouts; and through which it is fuppofed the foreign fhip paffed into the South fea: and thence if poffible to have reached the North fea, and after vifiting Newfoundland, to fail directly for Old Spain. This would have been making the tour of the world, cape Mendozino being the Antipodes to old Caftile and particularly to the cities of Salamanca, Valadolid, and Burgos; but though they were difappointed in this, envy itfelf muft own they deferved fignal rewards for what they actually performed: they have difcovered a new world in which the chriftian re-

ligion

ligion is now planted, and will produce fruits in such abundance as to fill the mansions of heaven: besides the great advantages to the state; articles which our sovereign has so much at heart. We are all children of Christ and all brethren; and thus besides universal benevolence, by the law of brotherly love, it is incumbent on us all to supplicate the God of mercy in whose hands are the hearts of men, that he will have mercy on these our brethren; and send among them able and exemplary labourers for their conversion, that being thus brought to the possession of our holy faith, they may obtain eternal felicity.

A P P E N D I X III.

Account of the voyage of father Fernando Consag, missionary of CALIFORNIA, performed for surveying the eastern coast of CALIFORNIA to its extremity, the river Colorado, by order of father Christoval de Escobar and Llamas provincial of New Spain in the year 1746.

ON the ninth of June 1746, we departed in four canoes from San Carlos, which lies in 28 deg. north lat. the shallowness of the water in this harbour admitting only of canoes.

noes. The watering places of St. Anne are three leagues from it; being feveral brackifh pits, but the rains wafhing away the nitre greatly mend the water. The harbour, its watering places, and fome hamlets are included within two capes, which advance a great way into the fea: thefe are Las Virgines, and San Gabriel de la Sarmejas or Sal-fi-puedes. Both points are lofty and lie N. E. and S. W. from each other. Having ftaid till it was flood, we departed about eleven, and towards the evening came into the bay of la Santiffima Trinidad, where there is a pearl fifhery. Though this bay be large beyond the firft cape, it affords little fhelter againft a S. E. wind; and beyond the other you are expofed to the N. In the middle of it is an ifland from which a reef of rocks ftretches into the fea, and by the ebb and flood are alternately feen and covered. This ifland has been very fatal to the pearl-divers many of them having perifhed here. The water in a creek of the bay is brackifh; and though the cape where it terminates be S. S. E. the adjacent coaft runs N. E. and is full of rocks; fome above and others under water. At its point and extremity is the bay of San Bernabé, and oppofite to it a low ifland frequented by fea wolves.

10th, We profecuted our voyage againſt the wind ; but ſtormy weather coming on, in the laſt quarter of the moon, we ran under San Bernabé.

11th, We ſet ſail in the morning with a calm ſea for San Juan Baptiſta, which cape lies N. N. W. of the place we left. This cape is only ſuch in regard of the bay of de S. Bernabé, which lies behind it. But beyond is a continued ſhore running alſo N. N. W. It is low, and being clayey, makes a reddiſh appearance. The whole coaſt is very bad, and dangerous from the many rocks and ſtony ſhelves about it. At three in the morning we were obliged to run in between a reef of rocks, and cape San Juan which lies a little further, where we found ſome ſhelter from the hard gales at N, which blew that day and part of the night.

12th, About ſix in the morning after maſs, we proceeded to weather the firſt cape of San Juan. This point and another form a bay, but of no manner of ſhelter unleſs againſt winds blowing from the ſhore. The bay beyond it is pretty large, but ſo far from being land-locked, that any wind makes a terrible ſea there. We croſſed it in a calm ; it terminates at the low cape of San Miguel. This and Punta Gorda form another bay, in which is a pearl fiſhery ; and the ſea in a ſtorm throws up great
quantities

quantities of fhells, on which account the divers call this place la Pepena. It has a fpring near a creek, but the water thick and brackifh. The natives are all chriftians. The bay is entirely open to all winds, except the N. and N. E. under Gorda point, where we anchored being wind-bound.

13th, In this country of San Miguel de la Pepena, numbers of Indians came from feveral parts, to whom a fermon was preached, and many children baptized, their fathers bringing them voluntarily.

14th, About fix in the morning we left San Miguel bay, after founding the places fit for fhelter. Near Gorda point, oppofite to a low gravelly fhore, there is at low water good anchorage, in a fandy bottom with four fathom water: but nearer the point, where a broken rock lies on the fhore, is fix fathom water, and the bottom ftone or fand.

Another anchoring place was difcovered facing a broken rock: hence are alfo feveral other rocks, and the country of a clayey foil overrun with thiftles and broom, and watered by ftreams from the neighbouring heights. The beach confifts of fmall gravel; and at the diftance of a mufket fhot is a good anchoring place in nine fathom at low water, and a fandy bottom. All thefe ftations are fheltered from

X 4

the

the N. and N. E. winds, by the cape which also breaks the violence of the sea. Cape Gorda consists of rocks resembling red marble decorated with yellow and white spots; and is frequented by innumerable flights of birds. The island of Tortuguilla, by the Californians called Serro blanco or the white mountain, lies E. and W. from Gorda point on the other side which is lower; and bears from San Gabriel de las Almajas or Sal-si-puedes, S. S. E. and N. N. W. These capes form a large bay, half of which is surrounded with mountains; the other part is low and sandy. At the end of those mountains is a spring, situated among the rocks, the water of which the Indians of that place make use of in time of ebb. There is also a rancheria of Indians on the low coast behind the last piece of high land, a small spring of brackish water being found here in a kind of bog. The people on seeing the canoes took us for divers, and fled up the country; the outrages and brutality of those men having rendered them equally dreaded and detested by all the natives of California: but on being acquainted by some of their countrymen, who were with me, that a father was come in the canoes, they immediately returned. The great sea which runs here even in fair weather would not allow us to stay: and it was with great difficulty

difficulty we took in a little water. We now attempted to weather the cape of San Gabriel de Sal-fi-puedes fo greatly dreaded by feamen, on account of thofe iflands, feveral contiguous points of land, and many ledges of funken rocks extending a great way from the land. Here the fea is fo agitated by the current, that a gale or a calm makes but little difference. Among the capes oppofite to a yellow cavern and a fhore of white fand, is an anchoring place fheltered from all winds except the E. and a little on this fide of it is a creek, at the mouth of which is three fathom at low water: further up two; and afterwards only half a fathom. On the land or W. fide it is deeper than to the eaftward: the bottom is compofed of fand and fhells. Soon after we had anchored, the Indians before mentioned at the watering place, came to me with their children, defiring they might be baptized. Oppofite to cape San Gabriel, the famous iflands of Sal-fi-puedes begin; which at the middle of the ftreight formed four channels. As we were departing, two new converts came with advice that the Indians further up the country were coming in a warlike manner, with a refolution to kill me and all my company. They gave me feveral bundles of arrows for my men, advifing me to keep a good look out.

15th,

15th, In the afternoon, by the help of a S. E. wind, we went out of this harbour which terminates in a black cape of rocks, on both fides of which are caverns and a ledge of rocks extended all along the fea, as far as the next bay called San Raphael, where are feveral funken rocks and capes; but among them many caves for canoes and a tolerable good harbour; a favourable wind affifted us to weather thofe capes, but I was obliged to leave it in order to take a furvey of the bay. It is moftly level and fandy, efpecially towards the E. fide; partly bordered by rocks and high banks of fand; in fome parts beach. The three ifles near California lying before this bay are, by reafon of their diftance, no defence to it againft the fea. At the clofe of evening we anchored near a part of the fhore fheltered from the S. E. wind.

16th, Though the fea was rough we proceeded to take a furvey of the remaining part of the bay. At the mouth of the Cadacaman we faw fome Indians to whom we fent word, that they fhould forbear any hoftilities againft the divers: their anfwer was that neither they nor any of the inhabitants of the coafts committed any but the mountaineers only. The N. E. wind hindered us from reaching the watering place of San Raphael: but gave us

an

an opportunity of difcovering feveral fprings of hot water, near fome white rocks. At full fea they are covered: but at low water are feen iffuing from the fand, behind fome fragments of rocks. There are alfo others along the fame beach, at the beginning of a fandy bay. At full fea the water for the fpace of half a league is tinged with red mixed with a faint blue. Here we met with fome Indians, who inhabited the coaft, and others who refided among the mountains, and feemed to be of a cheerful, friendly difpofition. They offered all the prefents their poverty would admit of, but we only accepted of a little fifh, and that they were well paid for. On hearing that we were going to the watering place of San Raphael, they accompanied us, and we arrived there at fun fet. Here is but little fhelter for canoes, fo that the fafeft way is to ground them. Not far from the beach is a large pond, and near it a well, which when cleanfed affords good water. Here we found a great number of Indians, who appeared very well pleafed at feeing us, and made us prefents of fifh, though they had the year before killed a diver, being informed by thofe whom we had met, that the canoes did not belong to thofe people; but that a father was coming. This affured them of good treatment; and out of curiofity to fee

him,

him, they all came down together to the shore.
But on seeing some of the natives of the other
coast whom, from their wan complexion, they
call Yaques, they began to whisper to one another, till, no longer able to conceal their aver-
sion, they openly asked their christian countrymen, why the father, as he was coming this
way, would have any Yaques with him. I
have already intimated that these animosities of
the Californians against the Yaques proceeds
from the hostilities committed against them,
and the depredations their rancherias have suffered from them. In the diving time they endeavour to drive them from the country: so
that it is no more than natural, that savages,
whose vindictive temper has not been softened
by instruction, should make little scruple of
killing a Yaque wherever they meet with him.
At our return from the expedition we had a
signal proof of the terror which these excesses
had impressed on their minds, for many whole
families who were come down, being told when
night came on to withdraw with their wives
and children to a place of safety, shewed some
unwillingness; and when I urged them, they
answered, that if they went away, the Yaques
would come in the night to their dwellings.
I bid them not be afraid; for the centinels of
the soldiers and natives would hinder any such
design;

defign; and that if fuch a thing fhould happen, affiftance fhould immediately be fent them. At this they feemed eafy and went away, being firft informed that thofe whom I had with me from the other coaft, I had brought as men who underftood the management of canoes, which their Californian countrymen, from refiding in the mountains, knew nothing of.

17th, I called the Indians together, and talked with them of the injuftice of the action, fhewed them the foulnefs of the crime, and the danger to which they expofed themfelves by a return of the like violences; and reprefented to them the inconveniencies of their wild life, and the indecency of their cuftoms. In the mean time water had been taken on board; and we failed away with a favourable land breeze, which however foon after failed us, and we were obliged to go round the cape by rowing. Between this cape and another formed by the coaft of San Antonio northward of the former, the fhore forms a femicircular bay. A little farther is a dufky mountain which being a peninfula, has on one fide a fhelter for the S. E. winds; and on the other from the N. A little beyond the middle of this coaft, are two other creeks nearly contiguous, but the many funken rocks thereabouts make the entrance very difficult. Through thefe openings you have the

prospect

profpect of a fertile country, but the fhore being very dangerous, a more accurate view could not be taken. Here two Indians from San Raphael called to us from the top of the rocks, telling us that a little farther there was a bay; and that they were going to inform the inhabitants of our coming. After having rowed the greateft part of the day, we in the night obferved an inlet, furrounded with high mountains; but after getting round the cape, we found it had a fhore, where at the foot of the mountains canoes might be fafe from the E. and S. E. winds. We continued our way for fome time in the dark, without well knowing whither we were going, till we had fight of feveral large fires; and thence concluded that we were not far from the fhore, which however we did not reach till midnight. As we were unacquainted with it, and to avoid any hofti-lity from the Indians, among whom it is a ftratagem to fet fire to their cottages, and lurk in fome adjacent place, in order to fur-prife and fall upon any that come thither, we lay at an anchor till day came on.

18th, The preceding night was very trou-blefome on account of the continual rowlings of the canoes. In the morning finding ourfelves near a ftony fhore, we weighed anchor and went further into the bay, where three iflands
form

form a bafon, where any veffel may lie fecure from all winds, with a fufficient depth of water, and a fandy bottom. It has three creeks, one at each extremity, and one in the middle, which is the fhalloweft; and at the end of it, is the watering place. Here we landed on a very convenient and fafe fhore, to which we were directed by one of the Indians who had followed us. We called the bay Purgatory, in commemoration of our having amidft the darknefs of the night fortunately efcaped from the multitude of rocks in it. The diftance from the bottom of the bay to the point is about three leagues: not far from this point and the middle of the entrance, is another ifland, the land of which is remarkably broken and craggy. The inhabitants of the country came to pay me their compliments; and befides fome agreeable prefents for the comfort of their bodies, I did not difmifs them without difcourfing on the falvation of their fouls in a manner beft fuited to their capacities. The neighbouring country, confidering it is a part of California, is not defpicable.

19th, The canoes which had anchored in a fufficient depth of water, in the morning were grounded; the water having ebbed away more than a fathom. We took in water, and were preparing to fail, when an Indian came as

an

an exprefs that the mountaineers had the night
before intended to give us a morning vifit:
but as all who had been concerned in this purpofe were not come, they referred paying it
till they arrived at the watering place: at laft
we were obliged to put to fea with a contrary
wind, which increafing, hindered us from weathering the cape; and all we could do was to
run in fhore near the northern extremity of the
bay, which, though furrounded with mountains,
has a good fhore of fand; but with fome
rocky fpots.

20th, We weathered cape Las Ánimas,
which is every where bordered with rocks above
and under water. The two points lie S. W.
and N. E. from each other. North of this
cape is a low ifland which, with the rocks that
run from it to a great diftance into the fea, appears triangular. It is only the haunt of fea
wolves and fowls. A little farther are feveral
convenient inlets affording fhelter from the S. E.
and N. winds, which are moft to be feared in
this ftreight. Not far from hence is alfo another cape in the form of a trident with reefs
of funken rocks running into the fea near half
a league. Here is generally a great agitation of the water. Beyond this cape veffels,
at leaft fmall craft, may lie fecure from the
S. E. winds: this is followed by a bay called

De

De Los Angeles. Along its entrance runs a chain of islands which contribute to its security; their number is so great that we could not count them either in going or returning. Most of them are lofty, but of no great circumference. The bay is large and affords anchorage for all kinds of vessels. The water extends to the foot of an eminence which makes a part of the high and craggy serrania or ridge of mountains : for going directly to the spring the land-mark on the starboard side is a black rock, beyond which are some others white. On the larboard side is a sand a league in length, projecting from the low land. Besides these marks the verdure of the herbs growing near the spring shew the watering-place. The water is good, and being on an eminence may be easily taken on board. It is sufficient for watering ships, but not for the lands, there being no great quantity of it. The Indians here were an assemblage of different rancherias; they were all well armed, very haughty, and had quivers full of arrows contrary to the custom of the country. Besides the precaution given us at Los Animas, their gestures and cries gave us to understand they had no good design. We however endeavoured by all manner of presents and signs of affection to make them easy, but to no purpose, continuing with con-

fused

fufed cries and fhewing their bows to challenge us to an engagement. This induced us to make preparations againft any night affault; their courage never failing to call in the aids of treachery, and they watch the time of the night as the fitteft for a furprife. They approach with all the caution and filence imaginable, difcharge their arrows, then give a fhout and fly. Thefe Indians in their affault on us had divided themfelves, fome being pofted on the N. at a little diftance from our camp; others fouthward and nearer, in order to have us, as it were, between two fires and utterly cut off our retreat. The natives of the bay of Los Angeles, elevated with the murders they had committed on the divers, looked upon themfelves as invincible, efpecially as they were joined by auxiliaries from all the rancherias with whom they were in friendfhip; fo that poffibly fuch a number of them was never before feen together; but by the favour of the Almighty this formidable army was difperfed only by a fally of five foldiers, and thirty chriftian Indians; who about three in the afternoon marched out againft the largeft body, who was encamped on the north fide. Thefe arrogant cowards at the fight of our men, without ftanding one fire, fled in the utmoft confufion, leaving behind them even their

wives

wives and children; nor did they stop till they had reached the very summit of the rocks, where concluding they were safe, they skipped, shouted, and made many threatening postures which we did not think worth regarding. We examined all their caverns and retreats, but finding only the women and children, which had unnaturally been left behind, we treated them with all possible marks of tenderness, assuring them that no harm should happen to them; but all our promises were not sufficient to hinder them from running away, and leaving their children. These were taken care of with the few women that remained, whilst others went after the fugitives to endeavour to bring them back; but it being now sun-set, and the mountain extremely difficult, they returned: some muskets were fired to terrify them which it did to such a degree that though the remaining part of the mountain above them was remarkably steep, it is incredible with what agility they gained the utmost peak, and the next morning not one of them was to be seen; the other body who lay to the southward continued without making any motion: and tho' we concluded that either of themselves by spies, or by some of the northern fugitives, they would hear of the fate of their confederates, to prevent their attacking us in the night; yet the

centinel

centinel at that quarter was ordered to fire from time to time. We enquired of the women left behind what was the reason of such a concourse of people, and they ingenuously confessed they belonged to the rancherias of the north, some of which had failed coming; that the time appointed for the general meeting had been that night; that an Indian, father of some girls then present was the chief of the northern rebels, who fomented a hatred against all those who came in canoes; they added of their own accord, that the design of dividing themselves into two parties was to hem us in on every side, that we might not escape. On their asking for water, we gave them also something to eat, and the children we pleased with sweet-meats, then directed them to go to sleep without any fear, that the centinel would take care of them. One thing raised our admiration, namely, the total nakedness of the girls. The Californians of the Cochimy nation, tho' extremely poor, and have no cloathing, yet decency and modesty have taught them to make a kind of apron of the filaments of sedge strung on threads of miscal, which reach from the belly to the knee; and this, I think, shews a great regard to that virtue which constitutes female excellence; and a woman who is pregnant, in case the child should prove of her

own

own fex, provides it with a little apron of this fort; but we faw nothing of that commendable practice in the territory of this bay. Let us hope that by the favour of heaven, it will be foon introduced, and that by the light of the faith they will come to fee the turpitude of fuch nudity.

21ft, The Indians were fent away with their children and effects; but leave was hardly given before they, like the former, left their children, and in fhort, all their effects. They were foon brought back again, and frefh arguments ufed with them not to be in the leaft afraid, and to acquaint their hufbands and the reft of the people, that they alfo might be perfectly eafy and return to the weft, and the watering-place; and that if they had been purfued the day before, it was not with an intent of hurting them, but that as they had provoked the chriftians by an unbecoming defign of falling on them by night, it was neceffary to fhew them notwithftanding their great numbers, we were not in the leaft afraid of them : that had we been enemies, we fhould have killed their wives and children ; that they might be affured of a fincere peace ; that we were chriftians, and as fuch made war on no nation, but endeavoured every where to promote tranquility and benevolence; that thefe

Y 3   canoes

canoes and the people in them were under the
direction of a father who had a great love for
the Indians. This difcourfe made them perfectly eafy, fo that they took up their children
and utenfils and retired to their countrymen ;
afterwards fome of our people, having fight of
a fpy coming from the fouthern party, ran
after him, but he was too nimble for them ;
however in the purfuit they met with a woman
who informed them of another watering-place.
The people had all difperfed, and in the place
fhe mentioned we found a great deal of frefh
fedge lately cut. In the mean time fome of
the northern party appeared, poffibly moved
by the report of their wives, or the fight of
their children and effects, which they had left
behind, or compelled by thirft, there being no
water within a great diftance, except at the
place where we were encamped. In the evening when the great heats were abated, three
foldiers with the Indians who came in the canoes, went to take a view of the coaft towards the fouth : in their way they faw fome
Indians on a mountain, but our men making
towards them, they with an activity feldom
feen in Europeans, climbed up the peak. They
did not reach the watering-place, as the fun
was juft fetting, but returned to the boats. The
land-wind here blew fo frefh, that in the
morning

morning it tore away the tent in which mafs was faid. At night its violence increafed, fo that one of the canoes broke from her anchor, and was not recovered till near the iflands which defend the entrance of the bay of Los Angeles.

22d, We continued our voyage with a favourable wind, which for fome hours was fucceeded by a hard gale from the land, that we were obliged to make for fhore. On the beach we faw feveral Indians armed with bows and arrows, but on our approach, they fled as ufual. We purfued them till late, and not knowing whether we could weather the cape, and there find fhelter for our canoes; we ran into the northern elbow of the bay, which is large enough to contain a great number of fhips, and terminates in a fhallow creek where the current of the ebb is extremely violent.

23d, We got round the point of Los Angeles, which in refpect of the other lies N. N. E. and S. S. W. The N. N. E. point is formed by three craggy eminences, at the foot of which are a great many rocks, fome funken and others appearing above water. In it are two ports affording fhelter in bad weather; but it muft be noted, that oppofite an ifland, above the cordelera of the ifland of Los Angeles is a cape bordered with a multitude of rocks.

The

The coaſt as far as Los Remedios is alſo rocky and gravelly. The bay of Nueſtra Senora de Los Remedios begins at a ſmall iſland, and near a white ſhore. In this bay is ſhelter from the S. E. winds, and ſome black eminences ſecure it from the N. Here is a pearl fiſhery.

24th. Being now wind-bound, ſome went to take a view of the mountains; but found nothing remarkable. They imagined to have diſcovered a bay; but it was the coaſt, which, with regard to the large iſland del Angel de la Guarda, has the appearance of a bay. This iſland begins a little beyond cape San Raphael, and terminates a little on this ſide of San Juan and San Pablo. This iſland, which is very mountainous, has ſeveral bays and capes: its extremity on the S. E. part is narrow, but northwards ſomething broader. The channel betwixt this iſland and the coaſt is ſo full of whales, that it is called Daranal de Balenas. Whilſt ſome were taking a view of the country, we made an experiment of diving for pearls: and the ſhells near the ſhore were found better than thoſe in the offing.

25th, We were for ſailing out with a land-gale, but the violent ſqualls with which it was accompanied, detered us from venturing: at length it ceaſed: and during the remainder of the day we proceeded, it being ſometimes calm,

calm, and fometimes the wind contrary. We kept along the coaft which is very mountainous, and the fea fo full of funken rocks, that the canoes often ftruck againft them: that in which I was ftruck twice, and thereby damaged her rudder. A light canoe was fent before in order to get every thing ready for taking in water. The Indians of the country perceived us, and running to their arms, fet up thofe fhouts and outcries which are cuftomary among them before an action. Thefe were intermixed with leapings and ridiculous gefticulation. But when they faw that our people put the canoe afhore and leaped on the beach, well armed, they betook themfelves to their ufual refuge the fummits of the mountains. Here they ftopped; and our men called out to them. But fuch was their fear, that inftead of entering into a conference, they turned about and fled. At fun fet we came to a level gravelly fhore; but unfafe: however the want of water, and being unacquainted with the coaft beyond it, obliged us to ftay here, though with fome danger.

26th, Some people were fent up a pretty large creek, to fee if there was any watering place thereabouts: which was conjectured from fome frefh palm branches, and flags which had been left there by the Indians; but were certainly

tainly brought from other parts, as our people
found neither tree nor flag in all their fearches.
Others who had followed the tract of the Indians in their flight found a pond at a few leagues
diftance. In order to find the watering place,
the following marks, in coming from the fea,
fhould be obferved. The fhore is narrow and
of a white fand, terminating at a hill of a red-
difh colour. This place was dedicated to St.
John and St. Paul, the day we vifited it being
the feftival of thofe martyrs.

27th, We departed with a land breeze; and
after failing by fome low hills along the coaft,
we faw on a neighbouring mountain two Indians, who called to us, but we were too
far below them to underftand what they faid.
However from their being in an inacceffible
place, and their infulting geftures, we fuppofed
they challenged us to an action. Perceiving
we took no notice of them, they brandifhed
their bows and arrows with loud acclamations,
leaping at the fame time with great agility.
One efpecially diftinguifhed himfelf in thefe feats
of activity, either by way of parade, or as
more enraged againft us; his motions were
furprifingly quick, fometimes dancing, fometimes turning round on one foot, till at laft
forgetting himfelf in the conceit of his dexterity, and not attending to the danger of the
rocks,

rocks, his foot flipped and he rolled down the precipice like a stone : but to our astonishment he received no harm, climbing up again; though not with his usual celerity, and even his companions came to assist him. This occasioned a great deal of diversion to our people, but the Indians were so ashamed, that they made off, and we had no farther sight of them. At noon we opened a bay, which has a deceitful appearance of safety, the only sheltering place being behind the first point : and this is rocky, with a narrow beach, which at spring tides, is entirely under water. The mountains surrounding this bay, have the appearance of rich mines. We took a view of the remaining part of the bay, whilst others went to view the coast; and having found the whole of it to be full of rocks, and the sun being near setting, we came to an anchor.

28th, We set sail with a land wind, but a squall from between the mountains carried away one of our masts, which in its fall hurt one seaman and was near killing two others. We passed by some rugged eminences, which project a considerable distance into the sea. On weathering a white cape surrounded by rocks; some above and others under water, we entered a bay, not very spacious and shaped like a G. In the part betwixt a huge rock on the land

2   and

and the cape, is good anchoring ground ; and facing the rock a veſſel lies ſheltered from the S. E. wind. At low water indeed a great many rocks appear above the ſea. The other point would afford good ſhelter from the N. wind, were it not for the rocky bottom and the very extraordinary fall of the ebb. About a quarter of a league from an inlet is a pond ; but the water turbid and impalatable. We called the bay St. Peter and St. Paul, for our entering it on the anniverſary of thoſe great apoſtles.

29th, It being calm, we rowed out of the bay ; and when we had got round the white-cape, opened another bay running weſt and ſouth weſt. It is of a conſiderable extent ; has ſeveral iſlands, and includes the leſſer bay of San Luis Gonzaga. On this ſide of it the ſhore forms ſome elbows, but ſhallow ; and in one of them we ſaw a kind of ſhells, which though of naker, were very beautiful and re-ſembled the ſhell of the genuine white pearls. We did not take a view of it ; referring it till we reached the other ſide, but the weather did not favour us till our return, when on a ſur-vey we found the bay to be capable of receiv-ing any number of ſhipping. It is ſeparated by a narrow channel from another harbour ; and both are ſecure from all winds and ſeas. It

has

has feveral creeks which abound with fifh: and this caufes a great refort here of the neighbouring rancherias. But amongft thefe advantages it wants the greateft: for the water in it is too falt for ufe. Indeed fix leagues up the country, it is perfectly good, but very fcarce. To fee if fuch good harbours did not alfo afford frefh water, we dug wells nine feet deep, but to no purpofe.

After three days our extreme want of water, drove us out of the bay to fearch for it in another place. Thefe harbours are formed by an ifland of fuch a length, that from the fea it appears to be main land. Beyond this bay, in the white fhore forming a crefcent betwixt two black mountains, called San Sebaftian, we found a river of brackifh water, but beyond in the contiguous ferrania the Indians informed us there was better and many palm trees, which we found true; but made little advantage of them. We paffed three other capes, and in the evening came to a little creek, where the canoes lay fafe from the S. E. wind, but it is full of funken rocks. Here we found a balza, but no traces of any people belonging to it.

30th, Before break of day came on, we faw a light moving along the fhore; from whence we inferred that there was a watering place

in

in the neighbourhood: accordingly some people were sent early in queſt of it; and having found it, returned with an old man bringing an earthen pitcher, which they are very ingenious in making; a piece of induſtry unknown to the northern Indians, and alſo to the chriſtians who lived beyond them in the ſame direction, till they were taught it by the inhabitants of the other ſide of the bay. Having this intelligence of the water and a good ſhore, at eleven o'clock we proceeded with the wind at S. E. but blowing freſh and oppoſite the current, cauſed ſuch a ſea, as greatly retarded our arrival at the intended port, though at no great diſtance. Here we found a great number of Indians, from ſeveral rancherias; and whoſe dialect could hardly be underſtood. Their deportment had all the ſigns of ſullenneſs and ferocity, and one of them was making ready his bow in order clandeſtinely to diſcharge an arrow at me: but I prevented him by taking no notice of his deſign, and changing my place. We treated them with all poſſible courteſy, and beſides victuals, diſtributed among them ſeveral toys and trifles with which they were highly pleaſed; and made us returns in feathers with which they adorn their heads. Theſe they would have us accept of as tokens of their good will: though this was no more than a feint,

for

for they fufficiently fhewed their quarrelfome
intentions by licking their arrows, which among
them is a kind of preparative for an engagement. We now came down from an eminence
we had afcended to enjoy the frefhnefs of the
wind, the heat being unfupportable near the
fhore ; when the Indians again challenged us
by their leapings and fhouts. A chriftian boy
of a fprightly difpofition taking a rag in his
hand mocked the ridiculous geftures of the
favages. This farcafm provoked them fo, that
they fent one among them whom we had beft
underftood with a formal challenge, but he
added they were many in number and had
prepared an ambufh. We readily conceived
that this information did not proceed from ignorance, but was a ftudied fineffe to intimidate us. The anfwer was that we would very
readily give them fatisfaction. The word
was no fooner given, than fix foldiers and
twenty fix Indian archers marched out. The
alacrity with which they afcended the eminence,
together with the courage and agility of a chriftian in taking away and breaking the arrow
of an Indian, who was going to difcharge it at
him, ftruck fuch a terror into the favages, that
they immediately retired. But one party came
up with fome, with whom the foldiers and
chriftian Indians returned except two, who had
rafhly

rafhly continued the purfuit. I had no fooner
feen their temerity, than I fent away the people
who had remained with me and the canoes.
They were foon out of fight and came to a
place, where feveral rancherias had joined together againft us; and our two men feeing the
danger they had plunged themfelves into, one
of them called out, with a refolute compofure,
as if he had a body of men behind him, and
pointing feveral ways with great eagernefs faid,
let fome go on that fide, others on this; haften
fome yonder, and form a circle that we may
fall on thefe favage mountaineers, before they
can make their efcape. The Indians were
drawn up in a line with their weapons in their
hands, but ftruck with what they heard, did
not proceed to any act of hoftility; whilft they
were in this fufpenfe, thofe who had been fent
to affift our two defperadoes came in fight, and
the Indians concluding the imaginary affault
was now going to be made on them, betook
themfelves to flight, leaving their wives, children and neceffaries: all were taken care of
with that punctuality and tendernefs which chriftianity enjoins; particularly in cafes where the
confequences may be very detrimental or advantageous to its propagation. Several of the
men who were taken prifoners being infidels and
unacquainted with the chriftian cuftoms, made

an

an offer of their wives and their neceffaries for
a ranfom. Night coming on a guard was ordered to take care of the prifoners whilft they
flept. In this rancheria our men faw a dog,
which was the only one feen among the Californians before the father miffionaries came a-
mong them.

July 1. We releafed the prifoners, after advifing them, that if any canoes came to their
coaft, they fhould forbear all infults and hoftilities. Two we kept to fhew us the way to
the watering place. It was late before we got
under way, having been obliged to wait for a
canoe, which had gone further up, though
the coaft is very unfafe as being flat and rocky:
yet the fqualls which fly all round the com-
pafs obliged us to run the canoes afhore, having been informed that further on there was
ftill water. The diftance of the canoes from
the watering place, hindered us from taking in
our full quantity, that we might look out for
a fafer ftation. Some went afhore to trace the
coaft: but hearing the fhouts of a troop of
gentiles on the mountains; and fearing to be
intercepted by them, returned, fignifying to
them by geftures that they would foon be with
them. But the Indians renewing their fhouts
and pointing to the water, fled. In this brook
we faw fome palm trees which had been carried

away by the floods. The marks for finding this watering place of San Eftaniflao are a reddish rock near the ferrania; and along the coaft fome red walls in the low part of the fhore: before coming to thefe walls there is an eafy road to the watering place, where having continued till noon we went further, but the wind blowing very hard, and a great furf continally breaking in on the canoes, it was midnight before we could reach the place we had in view.

2d, We entered the bay of la Vifitation, in one extremity of which is good fhelter though not very large. We here again faw Indians, who upon feeing us, behaved like the reft of their countrymen. But one belonging to San Eftaniflao fhewed us a watering place, fituated at a very convenient diftance, fo that it was thought better to fend a canoe back to San Eftaniflao, to take in water, while one of them which leaked very much was refitting. Here the bay which begins at San Luis Gonzaga terminates. The neighbourhood of San Eftaniflao and la Vifitation affords great quantities of nakre fhells. In our return we came here at midnight, and by the many fires which we faw, concluded the place to be well inhabited; and confequently that there was water nearer than that which the Indians had fhewn us. On this we endeavoured to fpeak with fome of the natives,

natives, that we might enquire about the water: early in the morning several families came down to us, but they gave us the same account as the former. The women here were totally naked, having not so much as the slender covering, used by the sex in the more southern parts, as an indication of their modesty. Here the series of islands which lie within the bay terminates; cape Visitation, bearing from the bay where we anchored, almost due north. On this side of the cape, after passing a low gravelly point of land, is a small cove proper for canoes. On the larboard side lie a great many rocks, and most of them under water; on the starboard side is a low cape. And betwixt these head lands are two other coves or small harbours.

3d, The canoe returned with the water: all damages were repaired, and every thing got ready for sailing.

4th, Made sail with a land wind, which shifted to the S. E. Weathered cape la Visitation; the shore low, and level; the soil clayey, and rocky. We continued our course till the afternoon, when the wind being contrary, we anchored near a bed of shells newly thrown a-shore. In the evening we were for removing from our first anchoring place, the canoes beating against the rocks, which were under water when we entered the bay, but dry at low water.

The

The three canoes by the fwiftnefs of the ebb were grounded, fo that we could not effect our defign.

5th, We continued our voyage with oars the wind being contrary, and faw a great number of wild goats, and Californian fheep. Several of our people went afhore with a defign of bringing off fome of thefe creatures, and meeting with a rancheria of Indians, enquired for a watering place. They pointed to fome flats on the fhore, which were covered at high water, and then immediately made off. This water is fo hot that it emits a fmoke and has a fulphureous fmell. Thofe who followed the goats took a view of the fhore, and found a deep well of brackifh water, whither we came about fun fet. Some who walked up the country met with two families, and one of the Indians immediately afked if they were enemies: and on the chriftians replying that they were friends to them and all mankind, they accompanied them to the canoes, and thefe were the laft Indians with whom we converfed: and even this was with great difficulty, on account of their ftrange deviation from the Cochime idiom, of which they retain only a few words. This place I am inclined to think is the furtheft limits of the pearl beds, having feen none beyond it.

6th

6th, Fifteen men went afhore to view the country and endeavour to find better water. We lay in a bay on the fouth fide, and eaft of us was a ftony point running a confiderable diftance into the fea. Northward is a fand bank projecting from a low point, and feen at low-water to run above a league into the fea. One of our canoes ftruck on it: and as it has feveral branches, we were fometimes obliged to return a confiderable diftance. The low cape of this long and wide bank with another of rocks northward of it forms a bay, but fhallow and unfafe. Having with difficulty got round the ftony point, we had notice that the people would continue furveying the country and return to this fpot. We put afhore in queft of the watering place which is the brook juft mentioned; and almoft at the water's edge; the neighbouring parts being in fpring tides wafhed by the fea. Here the canoes had the good fortune to fill all their veffels: at the approach of night our fcouts returned with intelligence that the country was barren and uncultivated; adding, that fome leagues further there was good water, but little of it.

7th, A canoe being light and under no apprehenfion of the Indians remained here, but the others put to fea. They were however foon obliged by a very high fea to make for the

fhore.

fhore. The fea continued in the fame agitation the whole day and night, fo that no provifions could be fent to thofe who were gone
afhore.

8th, We fteered to another part better land-
locked and called San Fermin, lying betwixt
two fand-banks. Three canoes got fafely in;
but the fourth run aground, and lay till the
flood. In the mean time the loading of one
was put afhore, fhe being fo leaky that the
provifions were very much damaged. The
water here is good; but large veffels cannot
without great difficulty make ufe of the watering places beyond la Vifitation. This part of
San Fermin has two very long fand-banks on
the N. and S. that at low water they are dry
for two leagues, as we faw at our return.

9th, It being flood we went out at three in
the afternoon, but in going over the bar all
were obliged to go forward. We next came to
the bay of San Phelipe de Jefus; the capes of
which lie N. and S. from one another. That
of the N. terminates in fome black mountains,
but being unwilling to lofe the opportunity of
a fair wind, we continued our courfe, leaving
the furvey of it till our return, and then found
it to afford fhelter againft the N. wind, even
for large veffels; but it is at a great diftance
from the fhore, which is fo lined with fand-

banks

banks that there is no landing but at high-water. The fhore is fandy, and on the N. fide is a creek, which at full and change of the moon has a depth of water fufficient for boats, but at other times is dry. At the foot of a flat eminence it affords plenty of water, but thick, difagreeable, of an ill fmell, and noxious in its quality. Its effects on thofe who drink it refembling the fymptoms of the fcurvy. At our return we ftayed fome days near this watering-place, but faw not a fingle Indian: and our people being fickly and fpent coming from the Rio Colorado, no excurfions could be made into the country. All along the low country from la Vifitation to this harbour are fheep and wild goats: we went round the N. point, which although at full fea, it appears to have feveral fmall inlets fafe from the S. and S. E. winds ; yet in reality has only one little fheltering place running fouthward, and this not proper for any thing larger than ca-noes. Indeed at fpring tides, and with good cables, a larger veffel may put into it in cafe of a hard gale at S. and S. E. but not at neap-tides, there being no depth of water nearer than a league and a half from the fhore. From this place at the rifing and fetting of the fun, we faw the land on the other fide ; and from the N. point of San Phelipe we had fight of

Z 4

another

another cape on this fide, which appeared to form a large bay, but it was no more than appearance, there being no fuch bay ; the point of the hill lying within the mouth of the river Colorado up the country. From this corner the fhore is entirely level, marfhy in feveral parts at fpring tides ; and in hard weather overflowed.   All the way from San Phelipe to the river Colorado there is neither bay nor watering-place.

10th, We made little progrefs this day, a ftrong N. E. wind blowing from the fhore, which was contrary to us : the points in that part running N. E. and N. N. E. the ftreight clofing here.   At noon we got afhore with great difficulty, the water being fhallow and a great fea running along this coaft, which is extremely barren.   The ferrania or ridge of · mountains is three or four leagues diftant from the fea, and in fome parts more.   At night we came into a better fhore, though with a high fea.   The bottom here we found to be mixed with mud.

11th, Made but little way, and came to fome red marfhes, whence we concluded we were near the mouth of the river Colorado or red river.   We however continued our courfe till the evening, having endeavoured to land in feveral places; but to no purpofe, the fens not
only

only hindering the boats from coming afhore, but likewife would not bear thofe who endeavoured to crofs them. Under this difficulty we came to an anchor facing an ifland, which forms a creek at the end of the ftreight in the form of a bow: the water even here differs from that of the fea, being of fuch a malignant quality as to carry off the fkin wherever it touches, and all were wet with it except myfelf; and were accordingly afflicted with very painful inflammations in the moft fenfible parts of the body, and which continued till the end of the expedition. In fome the firft fymptoms only of the fcurvy appeared ; but in others it was arrived at fuch a height, that during the whole return they were unable to ftir.

12th, Had a hard gale at S. which feparated the canoes. One endeavoured feveral times, but without effect, to weather, by tacking, the point of the fen, at which the ifland mentioned yefterday terminates. This canoe was very near foundering, the fea running very high : another canoe was obliged to throw the greateft part of her lading overboard ; but the other two, though the lading and people were wet, had the good fortune after weathering the cape to find a fafe fhore, being now beyond the fens.

13th,

13th, The canoe which had put afhore on the other coaft, after making way the greateft part of the night, betwixt feven and eight in the morning, arrived at San Buenaventura, where the lading was taken out and expofed to the air, and the canoe grounded. Some people from the others came in fearch of her, but were hindered by a creek.

14th, Whilft the provifions, cloaths, and other things were drying, a party went to take a view of the neighbouring country, and found a great many prints of men and beafts. Thofe at San Buenaventura ufed all poffible endeavours to find out a watering-place, but with no fuccefs, though they were a day and a half about it. The fmalleft canoe came and joined them in that part, and brought intelligence, that all the people and the canoes were fafe in the fame outlet of the river Colorado. Some drinkable water was found which iffued from the river Colorado.

15 and 16th, The fmaller canoe having affifted the other in taking in water : on the 17th they removed to the ftation where the other was.

18th, Went up the entrance of the river Colorado, and within it lies the before-mentioned ifland, which is triangular, and divides its ftream into two arms ; one in California running

running northward, and the other of the oppofite fide running N. W. The people went afhore in the ifland, and found themfelves betwixt two rapid currents. One of the river's ebb, and the other in the fea was flowing in with no lefs impetuofity, that they had a very narrow efcape; but loft only fome of their lading. The canoes removed to the coaft of California as more fecure, where in the night time they faw fires; but in the day time none of the Indians fhew'd themfelves.

19th, Continued the difcovery of the river, but the currents here became fo rapid that the canoes could not ftem it with rowing, that they were obliged to have recourfe to towing by which they made a little way; but as one canoe could not be towed for want of ropes, it altered its courfe and ftood for the other fide which was one of the three iflands difcovered by our people on this occafion. On the 18th day they faw the firft, which divides the river into two parts; the fecond, like the firft, lies in the river's bed, and faces it at a little diftance: the third lies on the fide of the other two; the river dividing itfelf on the fide of this lateral ifland towards the other fhore, forms an arm, but fo fmall that at low-water it is almoft dry. This fide of California, lying low, is overflowed by the Colorado, that all along to

the

the foot of the mountains one fees pieces of trees, weeds, and the like, left there by its water. Our people alfo faw here a kind of threfhing floors, where the natives threfh a kind of feed like wheat, but as fmall as annifeed.

20th, The canoes continued grounded, and the flood was attended with fuch rapidity, and at the fame time a very high fea, that the canoe which had parted from the others, was in the greateft danger; and the fmalleft which was now coming in, immediately made for it, in order to fave the people: and it pleafed God and his moft holy mother that it came in time for that purpofe, but the provifions and effects of all on board were loft, and the canoe was burnt to fave the iron-work.

21ft, The canoes were fent to look out if any thing of the wreck had been thrown afhore, and on the continent they found two cafks of water.

22d, The canoes were hindered from going out by the appearance of tempeftuous weather. In the mean time the people took a view of the country, and at the diftance of five leagues faw Cauzal and Sauceda.

23d and 24th, During thefe days, though we endeavoured to go forward, the wind and the current obliged us always to put back to the place whence we had come. This was an
elbow

elbow near a great wall running eaftward. The canoes were not able to make way. They who had been fent on the furvey reported that the river took its courfe along the ferrania on the fide of California.

25th, The furvey of the gulph, or fea of California being carried to its utmoft limit, we fteered not directly to the harbour, from whence we had failed; but to take a view of fome harbours, which, by reafon of circumftances, had been omitted in our coming. Fifteen men travelled fome way by land, took an exact account of the fituation and courfe of the creek at the point of the fens; and it ftands delineated in the map.

Firft let it be obferved, that in this journal we have taken no notice of the latitude, this being exactly fet down in the map of this furvey.

Secondly, Let the pearl divers be perfuaded that if they do not come with a good number of people well armed and be very circumfpect, many will lofe their lives by the hands of the favages: for tho' after being baptized, they became tractable, fincere, and benevolent; yet whilft unconverted they are defigning, haughty, and cruel, and more to ftrangers than to thofe of their country with whom they are at variance. Befides being furnifhed with men and

arms,

arms, it is neceffary that they forbear exafper-
ating the Indians by any ill treatment, as robbery, bringing away their children, abufing
their wives, an injury of all others the moft
provoking; and by which, befides their natural barbarity, they are inflamed with an implacable hatred againft all ftrangers who fet
foot on their fhore. Thofe concerned in fuch
underftandings fhould fhew themfelves chriftians, and be zealous for the honour of the
Spanifh nation, on which they have brought
an indelible ftain by the moft fcandalous cowardice, particularly the laft year at San Raphael,
on an occafion which called for valour, when
the favages after treacheroufly murdering a
diver, killed another in the very fight of the
owners; and they inftead of coming to his
refcue, fled away with precipitation. This in-
fpirits them to make the like attempts on
others, and they will perpetrate them if it is
their good fortune always to meet with fuch
cowards.

In order to prevent thefe damages, and open
a way to the temporal and fpiritual reduction
of the country, a defign was formed fome years
fince to take an accurate furvey of the gulph
of California, in order find out convenient places
for garrifons, harbours, and miffions. This
could not be effected till the prefent year 1746,

when

when father Juan Antonio Balthafar, vifitor general of the miffions, fent me the father provincial's order to take a furvey of the gulph of California, fpecifying the circumftances abovementioned, in order to lay before his majefty whom God preferve, and his royal council, the opportunities which thefe coafts afford for completing the conqueft. I received the order with due obfequioufnefs, but the execution was difficult, from the great fcarcity here of every thing requifite for fuch an enterprife, the very neceffaries for the fubfiftence of the miffionaries being not acquired without great difficulty. The importance of the fervice however overcome every other confideration. The miffions having at heart this work from their zeal for the fervice of God and his majefty, contributed amidft all their ftraits, wherewith to defray the charges of canoes, feamen, provifions, and every other thing neceffary in a voyage to coafts unknown, and inhabited only by favages. They likewife added a confiderable number of chriftian Cochimies, and furnifhed them with arms and cloathing.

Captain don Bernardo Rodrigues de Rea, commandant of the royal garrifon of Loretto on this occafion, likewife, fhewed his regard for religion, and his care and activity in his majefty's fervice, exerting himfelf to provide

every

every thing with the utmoſt diſpatch, which was within his department. He procured a good canoe, appointed an eſcorte of ſoldiers, which was neceſſary for my ſafety, and of thoſe who went with me. And though his poſt as governor of the garriſon would not permit him to head the ſoldiers himſelf, he attended us far as San Carlos, the neareſt harbour to the frontiers, and the rendezvous of their canoes and ſoldiers, and where he perſonally diſpoſed every thing for the voyage, and remained there till our departure. Some days after an account came that the Gentiles had killed all of us, ſoldiers, ſeamen, and Indians, not leaving one alive, and had broke the canoes to pieces. It no ſooner reach'd the captain's ears than he prepared to go with a body of men in a canoe to the ſhore to certify himſelf of the fact, and to ſee the beſt remedy that could be applied, whilſt meaſures were taken better adapted for baffling the oppoſition, to the glory of Chriſt and the honour of his majeſty, which the devil carried on by thoſe under his influence. But the captain was perſuaded not to ſtir till he received a confirmation of this bad news, which from the Indians proneneſs to lying, and the circumſtances that the canoes would be reſolutely defended, were ſuppoſed, if not entirely, to be partly falſe.

And

And as it proved fo the captain had no occafion for putting his generous intention in execution. God and his holy mother, the patron-
nefs of thefe miffions, grant that thefe fervices
undertaken purely for their glory, the falvation of fouls, and the enlargement of his majefty's dominions, may have the defired iffue,
that we may fee this end obtained; and with
advantages which may enhance its glory and
happinefs.

A P P E N D I X IV.

A defcription of CALIFORNIA, by captain
    Woods Rogers, an Englifhman, and
    of his voyage to the South-fea in the
    year 1710.

IT is not properly afcertained whether this country be an ifland, or joined to the continent;
but we had neither time nor inclination to examine into this particular. I have heard Spaniards fay, that fome of their countrymen after
failing along the coaft of California, and as
far as 42 deg. north latitude, met with fo
many fhoals and iflands that they thought
it prudent not to go any farther. If this be
true, there is great appearance of California's
being joined to the continent a little farther to

the northward, fhoals and iflands being a general indication that fome continent is near.
But the Spaniards being already mafters of
more lands in this country than they can cultivate, their fpirit for new difcoveries is abated.
The Philippine fhips bound to Acapulco, on
their arriving in 40 degrees, fail along this
coaft, but I never heard that any one of them
ever ftood farther to the northward. In fome
old maps this country is joined to that of
Yeffo, and I am not a little inclined to think,
that this is really the cafe, but fhall not take upon
me abfolutely to affirm it; and rather, if we
will believe the Dutch, as the Hollanders took in
thefe feas a Spanifh fhip which had failed quite
round California, and confequently found it to
be an ifland. Nor is there any more certainty
with regard to its form and extent, fo that
the reader muft, for thefe particulars, have recourfe to the maps, and from thence judge
for himfelf. With regard to that part of
the country, I myfelf faw, it is full of mountains, barren, with fome fmall trees and bufhes,
bearing feveral kinds of berries. The men
whom I fent afhore in a boat to furvey the
coaft, walked near fifteen leagues to the northward, where they found great numbers of very
large trees; but with regard to the good harbours the Spaniards told us of, we could fee
nothing

nothing of them near this cape. We indeed difcerned the fmoke of fires in feveral parts, from whence we concluded the country to be pretty well peopled; though of all the parts we touched at fince our leaving England, this affords the leaft for the fubfiftence of its inhabitants. At this time of the year there is almoft conftantly a land breeze, fo that there is good anchorage all along the ftarboard fide of the bay as you enter it; but one of the beft parts is a bank, on which there are from ten to twenty fathoms water: near the rocks, however, no bottom can be found.

During our ftay here the weather was very mild and fair, and very little rain, though now and then hard gales of wind; but in the night very copious dews fell, which rendered the air very cool. We once faw near three hundred of the natives, tall, robuft, and ftrait as pine trees; but more fwarthy than any of the other Indians we faw in the South-fea, with long, lank, black hair, reaching down to their wafte. They were quite naked, except the women, who wear a kind of petticoat formed of the fibres of a certain herb, or of the fkins of animals or fowl. Thofe we faw were pretty well ftricken in years, and extremely wrinkled; the young, I fuppofe, they concealed from us, as a wife precaution not to tempt

our

our failors to ufe them ill; though I believe
they had little reafon to fear any attempt
would have been on their chaftity, our defires
being not inflammable by the beauties of California. Their pronunciation is remarkably gut-
tural, their language feemed to refemble their
features, and their behaviour appeared to us
harfh and difagreeable. I would gladly have
taken two of them with me in order to procure an account of their country, that might
be relied on; but our provifions being fhort,
I was afraid of increafing our number. Some
had bracelets, others necklaces, fome both;
made of wooden beads, pieces of fhells, red
berries, and pearls, which I fuppofe they have
not the way of piercing, they being cut all
round, and faftened with a pita thread. They
are fo fond of thefe ornaments, that they would
not accept of any of our toys, or bugle
necklaces, though I had them of different colours; but knives, and other cutting inftruments, were highly acceptable. I muft mention one thing of their honefty, namely, that
they never meddled with any thing belonging
to us, though our coopers and carpenters generally left their tools afhore.

We could not find that they had any of thofe
neceffary utenfils brought from Europe. Their
cottages are very low, and confift only of

branches

branches of trees and reeds, and, at the same
time, fo badly covered, as not to defend
them from the weather. With regard to any
thing of a garden, or cultivated land, not the
leaft veftige was to be feen. While we were
here, fifh was their whole fubfiftence; and this,
with their wretched huts, which feemed only to
be built for a time, induced us to believe that
they had no fixed dwelling, but removed hither
at this feafon, to provide themfelves with fifh.
Here we faw fifhermen without hooks or nets,
their only inftrument is a kind of wooden
fpear, with which they are furprizingly dextr-
ous at ftriking fifh, and, at the fame time excellent divers. Some of our men told me,
that they faw one of thefe Indians dive, after
piercing a fifh, and without raifing his head a-
bove the water gave it to his companion, who
was waiting in a canoe. Thofe that pleafe may
doubt of this, but I am the rather inclined to
believe it, as I myfelf have feen fome of thefe
divers, who on my throwing over board an
old knife, would feize it before it had reached
the bottom.

Their bread, if I may call it fo, is a fmall
black feed, which they grind and eat by han-
fuls. Some of our people, who ufed it to thicken
their broth, faid it had fomething of the tafte
of coffee. They have alfo a root not very

different

different from the yam, and a kind of pulfe
in a pod or fhell, and which our people com-
pared to green peas. They have alfo berries,
which, after being dried in the fire, have nearly
the fame tafte as dried kidney beans. Others,
which the natives highly value, tafte like goof-
berries; but the pulp is of an acid fweetnefs,
and in the center is a ftone. We likewife faw
a few fig trees, the fruit of which taftes like
our currants, and makes no difagreeable fauce.
Befides thefe we obferved a great variety of
plants, but we had no time for botanical curiofity.

By the animals we faw, the Californians
feem to have a particular feafon for hunting.
I obferved the inhabitants fhewed a remarkable
refpect to one perfon, whofe head was adorned
with feathers; but in all other refpects, they
feem to have every thing in common. At leaft
while they bartered fifh with us for old knives,
of which we had a plentiful ftock, we obferved that they would give them to the firft of
their countrymen, who happened to be near;
and when they had got a fufficient number,
we were at a lofs how to purchafe any more
fifh. Their predominant vice is floth, car-
ing for nothing but the prefent time. They
would gaze at our people while employed in
taking in water and wood, but never offered

to

to affift them. In fhort they feem of all the people I ever met with to have the greateft averfion to labour and fatigue. Their weapons are the bow and arrow, with which they eafily kill a bird flying. Their bows, which are about feven feet in length, are made of a white wood to which we are ftrangers, and the ftrings of their bows are of pita. Their arrows are made of reeds, pointed with a fifh bone, well fharpened: thefe are about four feet and a half long. Moft of their cutting tools are of the teeth of fea wolves. In fome of their necklaces I obferved two or three large pearls, and our Spanifh prifoners, told me that they found a great many in the gulf of California, where the miffionaries are fettled; they added, that the internal part of the country, as far as the continent of Mexico is very fertile and pleafant, abounding in horned cattle, and all kinds of provifions: when we were ftanding off to fea, fome of our people told me they had feen ftones remarkably heavy, and of a glittering appearance, as if they contained fome kind of metal; but their information was given too late, otherwife I fhould have taken fome of them on board for making experiments on them. A few of the natives, who had contracted a familiarity with us, ufed to come on board our fhips, the conftruction of which filled them

with

with admiration. They have only balzas or floats, which they guide by paddles. We gave one of them a shirt; but instead of putting it to the use intended, he tore it into several pieces and distributed them among his companions, for holding the grain they use for bread. I think they have no kitchen utensils; at least the method of dressing their fish was no other than to bury it in the sand, and make a fire upon the spot. When it was sufficiently roasted, they took it out, and eat it without any farther ceremony. Their method of procuring fire is by rubbing two dry sticks against each other; the same is used by the other Indians of America; but they constantly keep a fire in their huts. The water here is extremely good. I also saw a great quantity of sea fennel, but no uncommon birds.

The entrance of this harbour coming from the westward, is known by four white rocks, resembling those of the needles in the isle of Wight, and the two on the west side appear like sugar loaves. That nearest the land, has an arch or aperture, like a bridge, under which the water runs. In entering the harbour the rock nearest the sea must be left a cable's length on the larboard side; and as soon as you are past it, stand directly for the bottom of the bay, which is every where safe, and has from ten to twenty five

fathom,

fathom water. Here a fhip is land-locked from the north eaft to the fouth eaft; though fhould a ftrong foutherly wind fet in, a fhip would have but a very indifferent road; but this did not happen during my ftay.

APPENDIX V.

Extract of fome paffages in the voyage of commodore Anfon; with a vindication of the jefuits.

IN the laft war between the crowns of Spain and England, the latter fent in the year 1740, a fquadron into the South-fea under the command of commodore Anfon; who having doubled cape Horne, and ranged the coafts of Peru and New Spain, * fteered to the Marian iflands to wait for the Philippine galleon in her return from Acapulco. He fucceeded and found on board four millions of dollars. This rich prize he carried to China, and thence round the cape of Good Hope to Europe. Of this voyage Mr. Richard Walter, who was in the expedition, publifhed an account from the journals and papers of the faid commodore. A French tranflation of this work

* Not till he had pillaged the town of Payta and taken feveral fhips.

was

was publifhed at Amfterdam in the year 1749.

In this account mention is made of California, on occafion of the commerce to the Philippine iflands, and the courfe thither: and the
origin and ftate of its miffions are briefly touched
upon. The writer being a proteftant nothing
is to be expected from his pen, but a fatire
againft the jefuits. Nor has he taken any care
to be one of thofe few who, though proteftants
never lofe fight of candour and modefty in their
writings. It was for his intereft to pleafe the
publick of London, and he was unwilling to
lofe fo favourable an opportunity of gratifying
them with fuch a reprefentation of the jefuits,
as he thought would be moft acceptable,
though at the expence of probity and truth.
Walter's imaginary accufation of the jefuits,
would not be worth regarding, were it not for
the melancholy experience, proteftants have
publifhed nothing againft the fociety of jefuits however falfe and groundlefs, which has
not been countenanced and adopted both by the
tongues and pens of fome catholicks, who delight in venting their infults againft it; whilft
the fociety wholly attentive to fulfil thofe ends
for which its great leader has planted it in his
church, never intermeddles with any over whom
religion has not given it fome charge or fuperiority. This is the motive for delivering
my

my fentiments on the faid account, left my filence might be conftrued as a tacit acknowledgement of what Mr. Walter has advanced.

Walter employs the 10th chapter of the 2d book in defcribing the manner of carrying on the commerce betwixt the city of Manilla the capital of the ifland of Luzon and Acapulco on the coaft of Mexico: and after difcanting on the conquefts of the Philippines, the claims, contefts and compacts of the two crowns of Spain and Portugal, the grant from the pope, Magellan's voyage, the fettlements of the Spaniards, the ancient commerce with Calao, and the difficulty of the voyages in a direct courfe; he relates, that the wrong method of failing was altered by advice of a jefuit, who perfuaded the Spaniards, that in returning from the Philippine iflands they fhould fail away northward before the brizas or trade winds, till they came into the wefterly winds which generally prevail in the higher latitudes; and which would in a fhort time bring them in fight of the coaft of California. This opinion was in fome meafure right; but that it came from a jefuit is grounded only on a flying report, which may have no more truth in it than many others. He adds, that this new method has been practifed at leaft for one hundred and fixty years paft, fir Thomas Cavendifh hav-

ing in the year 1586, engaged a veffel bound
from Manilla to America. However the prefent
plan of navigation is not entirely approved of
by the Englifh admiral; and as it may be
of ufe to the Spaniards failing on thefe feas to
be acquainted with the opinion of fuch an ex-
pert and celebrated navigator as lord Anfon,
I fhall add that his writer Walter, book III.
chap. 8. fpeaking again of the route betwixt
the Philippine iflands and Acapulco, treats with
great ridicule the extraordinary precautions in
the inftructions given to the galleon at Manilla,
as rendering the voyage more tedious and fickly.
The captain is ordered not to go beyond 30
deg. northward : whereas fays he if they ftood
to the 40 or 45th, they would be affifted by
the trade winds; and thus freed from the em-
barraffments which they now labour under
from the reftriction not to make fail. In this
latitude alfo they would find the wefterly
winds much ftronger and brifker. According
to their own journals they are often five or
fix weeks in getting into the latitude of 30
degrees. Whereas in a north eafterly or northerly courfe, they would in the * fourth part
                                                    of

---

* Mr. Walter's words are as follows. " It appears
from thofe journals of theirs which I have feen, that they
are often a month or fix weeks after laying the land, before
                                                    they

of the time reach the latitude of 40 degrees, where the wefterly winds would much fooner carry them on the coaft of California.

The prefent ufual route of the galleon is to ftand to the northward, but no further than the latitude of 30 degrees, till they fall in with the wefterly winds. By the help of thefe fhe ftretches in the fame parallel along the tremendous fpace of 96 degrees of longitude from cape Spiritu Santo, till fhe finds the fea covered with a floating herb, thought to be fea wrack. This indicates that they are near California: then they fing a Te Deum; but do not make the coaft till they come into a lower latitude, by reafon of the many iflands and fhoals. They fteer away fouthward, and in their extreme precaution do not endeavour to come within fight of land, till they find themfelves near cape San Lucas; and this for afcertaining the reckoning, and receiving intelligence whether there are any enemies looking out for them. In all this immenfe tract, there is not a fingle harbour to put into. The only expedient for procuring water is from the rains

they get into the latitude of 30 degrees: whereas with a more northerly courfe it might be eafily done in lefs than a fortnight." The author it muft be obferved, relies on the French tranflation, which feems in fome inftances, to deviate fo far from Mr. Walter's words as to miftake his meaning.

which

which are generally regular betwixt the 30th and 40th degrees. This long continuance in a ship at sea produces a scurvy, which sweeps away great numbers of the people on board. But says he, were they to stand northward to the 40th or 45th degree, they would be delivered from the scurvy, the want of water and of harbours, which bring such extreme sufferings among them, only for the inconveniency of a rougher sea and harder gales. To support this opinion, Mr. Walter advances an instance, though in truth, instead of favouring his assertion, any commander of a Philippine ship who should follow his opinion, would find the great inconveniency of it. He says that a French ship in 1721, by pursuing the course which he delineates came from China to Valle de Nanderas on the coast of Mexico in less than fifty days: but he adds, that in that short space of time the scurvy made such a havock on board, that she had only five or six remaining alive. If this unfortunate ship did not, as it appears, put in any where, I am not at all surprised at that calamity, as she had stood very far to the northward. We know from experience with what violence the scurvy rages in the higher latitudes: we read of it with pity in the narratives of the voyages from our seas to the N. to Hudson's bay, Baffin's bay and others.

5

It

It appears from the late voyages of the Ruffians
to the moft northern parts of the South-fea, of
which we have given an account: it appears
from the former voyages of our countrymen;
and laftly it appears even in the furveys of the
Californian gulf, though its higheft latitude is
fhort of 33 degrees. But if that latitude of
40 or 45 afforded a harbour or fettlement
where the fhip could put in, where the fcurvy
might be ftopped in its firft ftage by the frefh
air, acids and bitter fruits and vegetables, frefh
provifions and other remedies : Laftly where a
fhip might fupply itfelf with water and provifions, the fcurvy would indeed be lefs to be
dreaded than in the prefent route from the Philippines: fo that I think that Mr. Walter, when he
was for ftrengthening his commander's opinion,
inftead of that unlucky inftance of the French
fhip might have introduced another much more
to the purpofe, univerfally known, and likewife of a French fhip Le Saint Antoine de Pa-
done commanded by monfieur Frondal who in
a voyage in the months of May, June and
July 1709, failed from China to America,
ftood northward to 45 degrees of latitude and
in the 197th degree of longitude from the
common meridian of the ifland of Ferro very
near the meridian of the Antipodes of Paris,
where the wefterly winds carried him to America.

Neverthelefs

Neverthelefs the fcurvy did not rage in his fhip
as in that other defolated fhip, which put in to
Valle de Nanderas; nor fo much as is ufually
felt in the Philippine galleon: But this was
owing to monfieur Frondal's prudence in touching on the barren and open coaft of California,
in the latitude of 31 degrees: and the confequences of this precaution, though in fuch a
wild place, enabled him profperoufly to continue his voyage. How much would the condition of the fhip have been bettered had he
met with a commodious colony, where he might
have been furnifhed with medicines, provifions
and other refrefhments.

The inference from the premifes is, that lord
Anfon's opinion concerning the courfe of the
voyage from the Philippine iflands is very juft.
But withal it is to be confidered that from putting it in practice, it is of abfolute neceffity to
have a fettlement of Spaniards or of Indians
friends to the Spaniards; or a well provided
garrifon or colony at Puerto de San Diego, or
Monte Rey, or Cabo Mendo cino, or fome
other more diftant part to be a fixed and fafe
receptacle for the Philippine galleons; as fuch
an eftablifhment is of great advantage to thefe
iflands, it may not poffibly be difficult, that
at prefent fuch a colony or garrifon may be fettled from them, under the fame meafures and
pro-

provifos. That it has been defired above a
century and a half; and was endowed by king
Philip III.

Walter adds, that the cargo of the galleon
(which tho' fettled at fix hundred thoufand dollars always exceeds that value) is at its return
fhared among the converts of Manilla, and that
the jefuits have the greateft and beft part of it.
Poffibly lord Anfon or his writer received
this information from fome interloper who had
been prifoner there, and an enemy of all the
religious orders in the Philippines; and particularly of the jefuits. Though it feems more
probable, that the writer's view in this ani-
madverfion on the religious orders was to gratify the publick at London. It is not worth
while to enter into a formal confutation of it,
all Spain, America and the Philippine iflands
being very well apprized of the manner of
carrying on this commerce; and of the regulations and ordinances which at all times have
been made concerning it. The chief part of the
cargo of the galleons belongs to the merchants
of thofe iflands; and confequently the produce
of them at their return. The religious indeed
are allowed a fmall part of its tonnage, as
otherwife how could they by way of exchange
provide themfelves with thofe American and
European goods they ftand in need of. This

portion is regulated for all without any greater diftinction or advantage to the jefuits than the others : and fo far are they from offering to tranfgrefs the ftated limits, that examples may be produced of innumerable complaints, that the religious have been defrauded even in what has been allowed them, and fettled by ordinances. Thus Walter's affertion is entirely falfe : and in America and the Philippine iflands will be matter of laughter. But there was a neceffity of afferting this under the fhelter of his lord's authority, in order to fpread a belief in England that the interefts and views which carry the jefuits and other catholick religious to the Indies, are the fame with thofe which carry the Englifh to their colonies; and that at the Philippine iflands, inftead of being catechifts and fathers of fouls, their time is taken up with lucre, as the only merchants there.

Yet it was not fufficient that the jefuits fhould be reprefented as at the head of the Manilla commerce, though they there, more than in any other part, labour under great poverty, fatigue, and oppofition; the rancour and horror with which the Englifh proteftants are filled againft the jefuits, deferved fomething more from Walter's pen. Accordingly for their farther gratification he avails himfelf of the connection

nection betwixt the Philippine iflands and California; of whofe miffions and their prefent ftate,
he for this reafon thinks, are not to be paffed
over in filence. He fays, that though from
the firft difcovery of California, fome miffionaries have vifited it from time to time; their
fervices were of no effect, till the jefuits, animated and fupported by a large donation from
the marquis de Valero, a nobleman of great
liberality and devotion, came over to this peninfula and fettled a confiderable miffion. From
what we have written it appears that Walter is
very much mifinformed concerning the fettlement of the miffions in California, tho' without
ftirring out of Europe, he might have found
a fufficient account of them in the Lettres
Edificantes, More's Hiftorical Dictionary, and
other books. The marquis de Valero when
viceroy found the miffions already eftablifhed,
and though his generofity and devotion are not
to be called in queftion; he never gave any
thing of his own to the miffions of California,
as his glorious predeceffor the duke de Linures
had done. Walter adds, that the principal
fettlement of the jefuits is at cape San Lucas,
where they have got together a confiderable
number of Indians, and been at the pains
to inftruct them in agriculture and mechanic
arts. They now make no fmall quantity of

wine

wine, the tafte of which refembles that of a middling Madeira. Here is another miftake, for
till the erection of the new garrifon in 1736,
after the murder of the venerable fathers Carranco and Tamaral, miffions were not re-eftablifhed
about cape San Lucas; and the miffions there are
very inconfiderable, with regard to the number
and character of their Indians. Their vintages
are fcarce worth mentioning: but a great deal
of wine is brought thither for exportation, as
nearly all that California produces is carried
abroad; the ufe of that liquor being juftly pro-
hibited to the Indians.

Mr. Walter is further pleafed to write, that
the jefuits are the only mafters of the Californian trade, that all their labours have no other
view than the good of the fociety; and that
the attention of the miffionaries is engaged
about the Manilla galleon; of which their
convents of the faid city are the principal pro-
prietors and adventurers. For this purpofe, he
fays, they take great care to provide all forts
of refrefhments ready for this fhip; and at
cape San Lucas, a conftant watch is kept to
look out for any of the enemy's fhips, who
may be lying in wait for the galleon in her return from the Philippine iflands; this being
the beft ftation in the world to wait for her. In
confequence of thefe meafures concerted betwixt

twixt the jesuits of Manilla and of California; the captain of the galleon is directed to fall in with the land N. of cape San Lucas, and the inhabitants on sight of the ship, are to light certain fires; and at sight of these signals the captain sends his long-boat ashore with twenty men well armed, who carry the letters from the jesuits of Manilla to their brethren of California, and bring aboard the provisions which were kept in readiness: as likewise what intelligence there may be concerning any enemies on the coast. If the captain by these advices, finds that he has nothing to apprehend, he is to proceed for cape San Lucas, thence to cape Corientes, and then coast it along for Acapulco.

Thus far mr. Walter, who deserves credit, with regard to the missionary jesuits of cape San Lucas, who take great care to provide refreshments for the Philippine galleon; and he might likewise have added, for the reception, relief, and cure of the sick. This office of charity and good policy, the jesuits alone acknowledge to be below any return; at least it is very unequal to the fervour of their desires, which must be imputed to the extreme barrenness of the country. Tho' this assistance, the look-out kept at the cape, and the order for the Philippine ship to touch there, are not owing to any measures

B b 3   taken

taken by the jefuits ; but to the wife provifions made by the kings of Spain, who, from the commencement of the Philippine trade, faw the neceffity that the fhips fhould have a fecure reception in California : and this, among others, was the capital motive for the vaft expences and powerful armaments by which they have fo often endeavoured at the reduction of this peninfula ; and for fettling colonies and garrifons, and making harbours. I fhall add, that the watch kept to look out for any enemies on the coaft, and for making the fignals to the galleon, confifts of the foldiery belonging to the new garrifon of San Lucas. This garrifon the fociety petitioned for, as a neceffary fafe-guard to its miffions ; but it was in La Paz bay, within the gulf, whither the galleon could not come, that it was erected, and not at the cape. At laft the garrifon was erected ; and very wifely the cape was the place, that it might ferve as a receptacle for the galleons. But it was erected without any folicitation of the fociety, and purely at the requeft of the Philippines, convinced of its neceffity by repeated damages, and a dear-bought experience. It was alfo erected by a viceroy, of whom, though bred up in the bofom of the company, none but a foreigner would advance that he followed the meafures calculated by-the

jefuits

jefuits purely for their advantage. Were there no other proofs of the advantages of California, and the garrifons; the actions of this very fquadron of Anfon's affords fufficient, fince California being now reduced, peopled with Spaniards, and furnifhed with garrifons, it could not fhelter itfelf there for furprifing the Philippine galleon, though the writer himfelf fays, that it is the beft ftation in the world for expecting her. Yet he chofe rather to crofs all the Southe fea as far as the ifland of Tinian; and not without great danger, as another writes, placed himfelf betwixt the Marian and Philippine iflands, in order to attack her in the ftreights of St. Bernardino.

As to the trade of California, fetting afide the diving and purchafing pearls, the manner of which I have fhewn, and likewife, that the jefuits and foldiers have no fhare in it; I frankly own that the whole commerce of the peninfula is in the hands of the jefuits. And if I fhould not own it, the thing would declare itfelf. As for what commerce it has, what Europeans can carry it on if there are no others than jefuits? But if mr. Walter envies us this commerce, I do moft earneftly defire, in return for his compliment, that the trade of England with Spain may one day, and the fooner the better, be equal to this. The

only

only commodity exported from California is
the little wine made here and there in miffions, and fold in New Spain. This is its only
product, no other commodity, merchandize,
or manufacture, can be exported hence, as it
neither has, nor is there any hopes of its
having any. On the contrary, there is fcarce
any thing for ufe or confumption but what
muft be brought from abroad: and if for
want of veffels, by bad weather or other mif-
fortunes, their fupplies are delayed, the inland
miffionaries are reduced to the nakednefs and
hunger of the Indians, and obliged to live on
roots, herbs, and wild fruits. The only fhip
which has touched at the peninfula for fome
years, was the galleon from the Philippine
iflands, as we have feen; the captain of which
in return for the refrefhments, generoufly made
a prefent to the miffionary of cape San Lucas
of fome things he had on board. This is the
whole commerce, of which the jefuits are the
fole mafters in California. Would mr. Walter
wifh that heaven would hear the prayers of him
who fhould defire to fee the whole traffic of
England enlarged to fuch an exalted pitch?

That the jefuits take all thefe fatigues upon
them only for the good of the fociety, is a
certain truth; and which I readily grant to
mr. Walter; for the fociety is not a detached
order

order only for itſelf, but relative and for the public. It is originated from God, and by him was eſtabliſhed under ſuch rules, ſuch diſcipline and government as are admired even by its greateſt enemies, purely for the ſervice of his catholic church : and that its individuals ſhould faithfully ſerve the reſpective nations of which they are ſubjects, throughout the whole extent of their inſtitutes. Therefore the good of the ſociety of jeſuits is only to anſwer thoſe ends, to labour heroically in the vineyard of their maſter, without care, without hope, without deſire, and even without acceptance of any recompence, though lawful : for it labours to be uſeful to the catholic church, and likewiſe uſeful to the temporal and ſpiritual welfare of the nations, of whom they are reſpectively a part under the rules of their profeſſion. In this ſenſe indeed, the company takes on itſelf ſuch fatigues and ſolicitudes, only for its own good; that is to ſay, for the ſalvation of the ſouls of the jeſuits, and the ſpiritual and temporal good and ſalvation of their neighbours. This is their intention : this is their view ; but this is not what the writer means, nor perhaps believes.

Laſtly, doubtleſs mr. Walter, zealous for the welfare of the Spaniſh nation, though an enemy, and acting in hoſtilities againſt it,

it, fays, that the Philippine trade is very
pernicious to Spain, as the filks from China,
and cottons from Coromandel, hinder in America the fale and exportation of the filk and
woollen manufactures of Valencia, and other
cities in Spain; and that don Jofeph Patinho
was in the year 1725, for abolifhing this trade;
but the intereft of the jefuits averted the blow.
Could I be diverted by flender confiderations,
when a great advantage to our nation is called in queftion, I fhould be filent on this head,
left it fhould be thought that my apology for
the Philippine trade proceeds from the jefuits
having, according to mr. Walter, the capital
concern in it. Poffibly he may have known
that the jefuits in treating of their miffions being reminded of it by the very fituation, might
awaken the former anxieties, or endeavours of
the Spanifh nation, for obtaining the advantages offered to it by the Eaft-India commerce,
though well regulated betwixt the feveral
branches of the nation; and by that political
fineffe was for impofing upon them by this
fear. However it be, this is too mean a motive to make any impreffion on me. Thefe are
facts know in Afia, America, and Europe; of
a nature not to be hid; and of which any one
may eafily acquire information. The bare affertion of mr. Walter will not preponderate againft
the

the fight of the whole world, and efpecially in facts of which he could be no witnefs. On the other hand, the equitable part of our nation, for whom I write, will do juftice to my candour and good intention : and though they may not agree with my fentiments, I promife myfelf that they will, at leaft, not fufpect me of having any other view than the fervice of God, and the welfare of the public.

On this account I find myfelf obliged briefly to fay, that I forbear declaring, whether on the prefent footing the trade from the Philippine iflands be pernicious to Spain or not ; but that there is no method or way whereby not only the prefent minute commerce, but even one intirely greater, may be fo modelled, as not to be pernicious either to the crown in general, whofe fubjects the inhabitants of both parts are, or in particular to Old Spain, is what I cannot believe. What thofe meafures may be, is as foreign to my province as it is above my capacity. What I know is, that in the reign of Charles V. Spain faw itfelf at the height of its profperity. The number of its towns and inhabitants, which is the bafis of the happinefs of a ftate, was much greater : not only the cities, but the fmalleft places fwarmed with people and manufactures. The products of the country were double ; and the
same

same increase was seen in the cattle. Spain carried on a trade of its own commodities and in its own ships into Italy, France, England, Flanders, and the north; had in all places Spanish merchants and factors, as may be seen in the ordinances of the consulado, or court of merchants at Burgos: likewise vast cargoes for the Indies; and these chiefly consisted of its own products and manufactures, the staple of which was Toledo, where they were laid up as in a general magazine; consequently the profits of commerce, the money, and other amazing riches of the Indies remained within the nation, without, or at least, very little of it being dissipated among strangers, by a detrimental commerce. Even then subsisted in their full vigour, the wise regulations of the catholic kings in favour of the domestic and foreign active commerce and navigation of Spain; which were in substance the same as those to which other nations owe their commerce and naval power. Such were the erecting of new docks, the encouragement of all naval arts, the appointing of rewards for ship building; procuring timber and cordage; giving privileges to those of great burthen, and stowing the cargoes with admirable order; abolishing the abuses and vexations of the customs and port fees; issuing equitable ordinances concerning

ing

ing all trades and callings within the kingdom, and causing them to be strictly observed ; removing the incumbrances of the multiplicity of jurisdictions ; securing the roads by the Santas Hermandades*; frequently rectifying the coin ; supporting, but not multiplying holidays ; suppressing tolls and duties of great vexation to the subject, and little advantage to the public ; lowering the customs and duties; and setting them particularly in books of rates drawn up with great perspicuity, to prevent all frauds and extortions ; to lay a duty of half as much more on the importation of home goods, except unwrought goods, and a few others; ordering at some ports, that on bringing in goods to the kingdom, security should be given to carry out the value in other goods of the country ; to put cities and provinces on an equal footing in commercial advantages, as near as possible ; to promote every where a plenty of the usual provisions, by regulating the prices of them ; to oblige the heads of the nation, the magistrates of cities, and the nobility of the kingdom to a steady and rigorous execution of these orders ; and many

* A brotherhood in Spain, instituted in times of great confusion to suppress robbers : and continues to this day, by which traveling is very safe, the brotherhood being spread through all Spain.

other

others relating to all political affairs: by which for many years the body of the monarchy subfisted in such power, extent, and glory, as excited the rage and jealousy of all Europe. This was the constitution of the nation in the time of Charles V. and by this it supported with honour, the great enterprizes and immense expenditures, sometimes necessary, sometimes voluntary, of that enterprising monarch. Notwithstanding this great prosperity of Spain at that time, it was then and in the subsequent years, that the repeated endeavours before-mentioned for securing a part of the East-India commerce on the side of America were made. It was not then held a detriment to the commerce of Old Spain in America, to bring hither the spices, and other goods from the islands and eastern coast of Asia; and this at a time when Spain had such a vast surplus for sale; and when its ships and large caravilas went to most parts of the world loaded with its products and manufactures. Why may not the same thing happen again: even if Spain had more goods for exportation than at present; and its own ships be loaded with them, and not those of foreigners, as is now chiefly the case? At that time the consumers in America were few, and might easily be supplied with goods from Spain. At present their

numbers

numbers are great; Spain cannot support them. At that time the manufactures and products of Spain were many; at present few; then the silver and gold came at last to the Spanish artificers and workmen; now at second-hand to foreigners: then there was no commercial rivalry in Asia, except with the Portuguese, and they were our friends, and as it were our brethren. At present all nations have assumed their parts. Nevertheless at that time the valuable commerce of the East-Indies was thought worth pursuing by such a variety of measures. And shall we be brought to think, that the Spanish nation cannot by any means restore it; that in its present state it is very pernicious, and that small as it is should be relinquished, without attention to the great opportunities of increasing it?

So mr. Walter thinks; and I believe he would be not a little pleased, could he infuse the same notions among the Spaniards. As to his own nation I observe that in his narrative, he very magnificently sets forth the advantage accruing to it from the commerce with China and the whole coast of the East Indies, and dwells on the great importance to the British crown, of supporting and increasing their settlements in those parts. On the other hand we have seen the strenuous endeavours of the
Englifh

Englifh in feeking a fhorter paffage thither from England, and the advantages which would refult from fuch a difcovery. Befides, the ardent emulation betwixt the Englifh and French Eaft India companies proves how very far thofe two nations are from thinking that their Eaft Indian trade hurts their European.

According to this, who will believe that the prodigious commerce of the Englifh in the Eaft Indies, is an extreme advantage to the crown of Great Britain, which deluges the world with goods, ftuffs and manufactures of all kinds; and at the fame time muft on the contrary be perfuaded that the annual trade of a fingle fhip from the Philippines is not only at prefent pernicious (which I proteft againft) and hurtful to the crown of Spain, becaufe the filks of China and cottons of Coromandel hinder the vent of the few filks and ftuffs made in Valencia and the other cities of Spain; but likewife that no meafures can be taken for carrying on a commerce with the Eaft Indies by the way of the Philippine iflands, that fhall not be detrimental to Old Spain. Not only England, but Holland, France, Sweden, Denmark and Pruffia, are every day pufhing their commerce in the Eaft Indies: yet the Chinefe filks and Coromandel cottons are not feen to clog the fale of their own linens and ftuffs, great quantities
both

both of the one and the other being imported
to Spain in exchange for the money we receive
from America. Portugal, which is a part of
Spain, carries on an advantageous trade to the
East Indies, but not what it might. Like Spain
it has possessions in America, where it also
has a large consumption of Asiatick goods,
which come much cheaper than those of Europe ; and is the crown of Spain the only one
which cannot follow such an example, and
take the measures pointed out to it by all the
other nations of Europe, when it has a greater
conveniency than all of them?

I am apt to think that Mr. Walter would
be very glad if the Spaniards would give over
the trade from Manilla, and abandon the
Philippine islands themselves, as without an
American and European trade, they could
not be maintained ; that in the mean time the
English should find out the so much desired
passage to the South sea, by the north of America and above California : which passage is not
universally denied, and one day may be found;
that they may fortify themselves on both sides
of this passage, and thus extend the English dominions from the north to the south of America, so as to border on our possessions. Should
English colonies and garrisons be established
along the coast of America, on the South sea

beyond cape Mendocino or lower down on California itself: his nation would then without controul reign miftrefs of this fea and its commerce, and be able to threaten by land and fea the territories of Spain; invade them on occafion from the E. W. N. and S.; hem them in and prefs them on all fides. But through the divine mercy, and the new fpirit which the wife government of the prefent moft aufpicious reign has diffufed among all ranks in the nation, it is greatly to be hoped that fuch meafures will continue to be taken on the South fea and northern parts of America as will fruftrate any defigns which may be forming by other nations, who owe their power and grandeur to our neglects.

What Walter affirms of don Jofeph Patinho, is abfolutely falfe: and I queftion whether the Englifh who have had many occafions of being acquainted with the character of that minifter, can eafily believe that in the year 1725, he was for abolifhing the trade to the Philippine iflands. About that time very warm difputes were carried on betwixt the merchants of the Philippines and thofe of New Spain, concerning the tonnage, quantity and quality of the galleon's cargo. But that this circumfpect and wife minifter, who was very far from regulating the general concerns of the crown by the contefts

of

of a few traders, fhould have thought of extinguifhing this commerce, is an affertion entirely groundlefs. But that the intereft of the fociety of jefuits averted the blow, is a downright falfity. Don Jofeph Patinho was incapable of being carried away by any influence whatfoever, fo as to do, or permit to be done, in affairs of fuch weight, what others thought fit. Likewife in all thofe mighty debates the fociety, as may be demonftrated, did not in the leaft interfere. After all, if this minifter fhould ever have entertained a thought of this nature, relating to the commerce of the Eaft Indies, the reader will be pleafed to contraft fuch a judgment, with the opinion * attributed to the fagacious cardinal Alberoni, who, a few years before, was minifter to the fame prince; and to whom the worthy Mr. Patinho chiefly owed his preferment.

* Part III. Sect. XIII.

F I N I S.

HETERICK MEMORIAL LIBRARY
979.401 V45n 1966 v.2   onuu
Venegas, Miguel / A natural and civil hist

3 5111 00110 6495

DATE DUE

WITHDRAWN FROM
OHIO NORTHERN
UNIVERSITY LIBRARY

GAYLORD			PRINTED IN U.S.A.